Fionnuala Martin

D1222210

Handbook of Emerging Fixed Income and Currency Markets

Edited by

Frank J. Fabozzi, CFA
Adjunct Professor of Finance
School of Management
Yale University

and

Alberto Franco
Senior Managing Director
Bankers Trust Company

Published by Frank J. Fabozzi Associates

ISBN: 1-883249-33-3

Table of Contents

Contributing Authors

Daniel Barkan	Bankers Trust Company
David T. Beers	Standard & Poor's
Joseph C. Bencivenga	Bankers Trust
Peter J. Carril	Bankers Trust
Marcelo Castro	U.B.S. Securities
Marie Cavanaugh	Standard & Poor's
Jonathan S. Cooper	BT Securities Corporation
Steven I. Dym	Steven I. Dym & Associates
Frank J. Fabozzi	Yale University
Alberto Franco	Bankers Trust Company
Robert S. Gay	Bankers Trust Securities
Helena Hessel	Standard & Poor's
Luis R. Luis	Scudder, Stevens & Clark
Paul G. McKeon	BT Securities Corporation
Efstathia Pilarinu	Bankers Trust Securities
Jonathan Silber	Bankers Trust Company
Alastair W. Sloan	Bankers Trust Company
Christopher Taylor	BT Securities

Preface

Emerging market assets are now accepted as a new asset class. While emerging market assets include equity and fixed income instruments, most published research has focused on equity markets. There are opportunities for return enhancement in the fixed income market that can be exploited by money managers and traders that have received little attention. *The Handbook of Emerging Fixed Income and Currency Markets* is designed to provide not only the fundamentals of the instruments and their investment characteristics, but also extensive coverage on the analytical tools and the strategies for capitalizing on the opportunities in these markets.

To be effective, a book of this nature should offer a broad perspective. The experience of a wide range of experts is more informative than that of a single expert, particularly because of the diversity of opinion on some issues. We have chosen some of the best practitioners to contribute to this book.

We wish to express our appreciation to the contributors. We are grateful to Juan Bilbao and Kelly Doherty for their support. Bankers Trust has provided continued support for this project. We thank Standard & Poor's Corporation for allowing us to adapt and publish an updated version of two of its publications describing its rating methodology (Chapters 6 and 7).

Frank J. Fabozzi
Alberto Franco

Chapter 1

Introduction

Frank J. Fabozzi, CFA
Adjunct Professor of Finance
School of Management
Yale University

Alberto Franco
Senior Managing Director
Bankers Trust Company

Emerging market assets are now an accepted asset class by institutional and retail investors. Despite this, there is no universally accepted definition of an emerging market. Moreover, there is no consensus about what countries fall into the emerging market category.

The term "emerging market" was coined in 1981 by an employee of the International Finance Corporation (a subsidiary of the World Bank).[1] In the equity area, emerging equity markets are understood to be "rapidly growing markets" or "stock markets in newly industrialized countries."[2] Most emerging market research has focused on the equity market. The focus of this book is on emerging fixed income and currency markets.

Emerging markets are undergoing a unique transformation. With the entrance of sophisticated players, these markets are being pulled in different directions — sometimes away from where the fundamentals should take them. In the fixed income market, arbitrageurs have been a dominant force in short-term yield curve realignments, often making statements through huge positions with the interest of taking the markets where "they should be." Arbitrageurs hope that by "reshaping," they can make a profit in the middle. These short-term deviations from natural market trends are the result of different market forces at work — technical versus fundamentals. It is the very essence of how all market players influence markets. It has been true for many years since the 1970s and 1980s in the so-called G7 countries and more recently in the emerging markets. How long will it take for market players to realize that fundamentals will prevail and that markets tend to trend towards their inevitable relative value? Who will benefit from these trends and how can one participate?

---

[1] Michael Keppler and Martin Lechner, *Emerging Markets: Research, Strategies and Benchmarks* (Chicago: Irwin Professional Publishing, 1997), p. 9.
[2] Ibid., p. 9.

As you read the chapters in this book, keep in mind that there are a set of macro variables that will inevitably shape these markets in the next decade. We think that economic growth will continue to be the driver for reshaping the value of these markets. The concept of leisure combined with high consumption standards as a right to be enjoyed by all, is new in human history, and even newer for emerging countries. The LDC phenomenon will intensify, generating growth and global pressure for economic development.

OVERVIEW OF THE BOOK

In Chapter 2, Luis Luis provides an investment management view of emerging fixed income and local currency markets. He sets forth the potential role of emerging markets in satisfying a broad set of investment objectives. These vehicles can be used by investors who are (1) primarily seeking high income and (2) principally seeking total return performance. Luis explains the analytical issues associated with investing in emerging fixed income securities, explaining that a fundamental approach should consider the following: sovereign risk, corporate credit, security analysis, market sensitivity, and currency risk (for local currency denominated debt). He then goes on to describe the investment process and portfolio construction.

In Chapter 3, Steven Dym reviews the universe of emerging market fixed income securities and suggests several tools for analyzing them. He then provides a general approach for integrating emerging market bonds into a global fixed income portfolio. Dym also discusses the relationships among a country's macroeconomic variables and its debt burden.

Chapters 4 and 5 take a closer look at specific sectors of the fixed income market. In Chapter 4, Marcelo Castro and Efstathia Pilarinu provide a description of the local fixed income obligations of Latin American countries (Mexico, Argentina, Brazil, Venezuela, Ecuador, and Peru). The focus is on sovereign debt. The high-yield market for emerging market corporate debt is the subject of Chapter 5. In that chapter, Joseph Bencivenga also discusses the development of the U.S. high-yield market and the types of securities issued.

Chapters 6, 7, and 8 focus on credit risk. In Chapter 6, David Beers and Marie Cavanaugh explain Standard & Poor's sovereign credit rating methodology. The quantitative and qualitative factors considered for both local currency and foreign currency debt are described. In Chapter 7 by Helena Hessel, the focus shifts to the S&P criteria for rating the transition economies of Hungary, Czech Republic, Slovak Republic, Poland, Romania, Slovenia, Russia, Kazakstan, Latvia, Lithuania, and Croatia. S&P requires a more customized approach in establishing ratings for transition economies because of their distinct political and economic legacy. In Chapter 7, Christopher Taylor discusses the unique challenges in analyzing the credit risk of emerging market corporate bonds. He sets forth the approaches to investing in corporate bonds and why he believes that investors who apply the skills gained in analyzing U.S. credits can generate significant risk-adjusted returns in this sector of the debt market of emerging markets.

Chapters 9, 10, and 11 present techniques for analyzing various sectors of the fixed income market. Relative value analysis within the emerging market Eurobond sector is explained by Peter Carril in Chapter 9. In Chapter 10, Steven Dym develops price sensitivity and other risk measures for Brady bonds. The complexities of local fixed income arbitrage are explained in Chapter 11. In that chapter, Marcelo Castro and Efstathia Pilarinu explain the arbitrage relationships between local interest rates and LIBOR, and then use three case studies to illustrate the nuances associated with local arbitrage.

A key market in any financial system is the repo market. Dealers and investors use this market for financing positions; dealers use the market for covering short positions. The repo rate is key in arbitrage strategies. The repo market is well developed in the United States. In emerging markets, the repo market began in Mexico in the early 1990s. In Chapter 12, Jonathan Cooper discusses the repo market within in emerging markets, covering the inter-dealer market, how to control risk, and the legal issues.

In Chapter 13, Robert Gay discusses the economics of retiring Brady bonds. He gives the three pre-conditions to a successful and economical buyback. At the end of the chapter, Gay lists countries that he believes are candidates for future Brady buybacks. In Chapter 14, Paul McKeon discusses the private sector's growing role in infrastructure and project financing in emerging markets. He explains the various financing sources available.

The last two chapters of the book cover emerging market currencies. In Chapter 15, Daniel Barkan and Jonathan Silber explain the exchange rate mechanisms commonly employed by central banks in countries with emerging markets: fixed exchange rates (basket mechanisms and crawling peg) and flexible exchange rate arrangements. They then explain international capital flows; specifically they discuss investor behavior and the response by central banks ("hot money" flows and intervention and sterilization).

Options on exotic currencies are the subject of Chapter 16 written by Alastair Sloan. He begins with a discussion of the limitations of option pricing models and then describes trading in exotic currency options (range bets, quattro options, bet options, barrier options, and basket options).

Chapter 2

Emerging Fixed Income and Local Currency: An Investment Management View

Luis R. Luis, Ph. D.
Managing Director
Scudder, Stevens & Clark

INTRODUCTION

Investment managers had an early and important role in the development of emerging markets fixed income as an asset class following the developing country debt crisis of the 1980s. Investment companies were created to take advantage of opportunities for excess return from investing in emerging bonds and defaulted bank loans to developing countries. Some of these initial investment vehicles were established as offshore entities, beginning in 1989, to facilitate access to the market by global retail investors who often resided in emerging countries themselves.[1] Thereafter, investment companies registered in the United States provided diversified emerging market portfolios for investors in developed countries. These dedicated funds generally aimed at providing high income with substantial potential for capital appreciation.

A second stage in the development of investment management involved the use of emerging market instruments as part of broader portfolios, often global and international bond portfolios. Emerging bonds also found their way to accounts and investment vehicles focused on U.S. bond markets. At the same time, dedicated accounts were established for institutional clients, mainly in the United States, and more recently in Europe, Japan, and other developed areas.

A third stage, evolving alongside deepening capital markets in emerging countries, is the management of local currency fixed income. The initial development of emerging fixed income was centered primarily in bonds and defaulted bank loans largely denominated in dollars and, to a lesser extent, other currencies of industrial countries. Although some use was made of instruments issued in the

---

[1] The first offshore vehicle to invest in emerging bonds is generally acknowledged to be the Sovereign High Yield Investment Company registered in Curacao, Netherlands Antilles, in 1989. This investment company was designed to invest primarily in bearer bonds issued by governments in emerging countries.

currencies of emerging markets, these were complementary rather than central to the asset class. They mostly comprised Treasury bills and other money market securities of a handful of countries, most prominently Mexico and other Latin American nations.

Investment managers face multiple challenges in seeking value while managing risk in the asset class. Value is derived from analysis of credit quality, market risk, and pricing relationships within the asset class and in relation to established bond markets. Information gaps played a major role in the early evolution of the asset class. Long lags in the availability of data, large voids in the data, and, most importantly, partial understanding of economic and political variables determining sovereign credit quality created opportunities to add value while presenting substantial risks. Value is enhanced and risk reduced in direct relation to analysis, information, and investment discipline.

As countries and other emerging issuers have strived to improve the flow and transparency of information following the 1994 Mexican peso crisis, the limiting factor is analysis of variables that determine credit quality and vulnerability to random events or shocks, not the lack of basic data and qualitative information.

As the marginal issuers in global capital markets, emerging countries are highly exposed, as may be expected, to shifting financial patterns and liquidity effects derived from core bond markets. As analysis improves and average credit quality rises, these effects are likely to diminish in size but will not be eliminated. Because relationships are not easily predictable, portfolio shifts within the asset class and in relation to other investments will characterize this market in the foreseeable future. This means that investment managers, possibly more than in other fixed income classes, are expected to design and manage portfolios in ways that take advantage of these shifts.

INVESTMENT OBJECTIVES

Investment managers view emerging markets as capable of satisfying a broad set of objectives. In general, portfolios and investment vehicles are classified into two main categories: those primarily seeking high income and those principally aiming at obtaining total return. Because price appreciation is most often a secondary objective and sometimes the primary goal, emerging markets fixed income is sometimes viewed as a "quasi-equity" asset class in contrast with traditional investment-grade fixed income investments. A third type of investor views emerging markets as primarily a means to diversify global or domestic fixed income portfolios.

Emerging market bonds are expected to provide high yield, certainly compared to investment-grade securities and even when placed against speculative grade corporate bonds. Most emerging countries are rated below investment grade. In mid-1997, emerging markets sovereign bonds had an average credit quality approximately equivalent to a BB/Ba as rated by the major agencies. Moreover, emerging bonds denominated in dollars have historically traded at wider spreads to benchmark U.S. Treasury bonds than other bonds of similar credit rating. For example, at the end of May 1997 emerging market bonds yielded approximately 417 basis points (bps) (net of collateral) and 294 bps (collateral included) over similar maturity U.S. Treasuries while similarly BB-rated U.S. high yield bonds yielded 185 bps.[2]

Spread curves for emerging market bonds in relation to U.S. Treasury bonds are upward sloping with the slope increasing in proportion to duration. This relationship holds for both normal Eurobonds and non-collateralized Brady bonds, as well as for Brady bonds which have collateralized principal and partial interest payments. In this case, market price reflects the view of the major rating agencies that collateral does not significantly improve the credit quality of the bond. This apparent paradox, captured by market pricing as well as rating agency views (even when the percentage of present value composed of high grade U.S. Treasury collateral increases as average maturity declines) provides a source of excess return for investors.

Many investment vehicles seek to generate *steady* as well as high *current* income from a portfolio of emerging bonds. Portfolios can be designed to optimize current income at the expense of other objectives such as price appreciation or stability of net asset value. As emerging market bonds comprise a wide variety of fixed- and floating-rate securities, portfolio management strategies can be found that help optimize or stabilize current income throughout the interest rate cycle. Utilization of interest rate swaps or other derivatives can contribute substantially to achieving income objectives. As an illustration, during the period of low short-term interest rates from 1992-1993, swapping floating-rate Brady cash flows to fixed rates added over 200 bps in current yield.

Investment vehicles can also be designed to generate steady *dividends* composed of current income, realized capital gains, and, depending upon accounting conventions, accretion of discount. Exhibit 1 shows the historical cumulative dividends and total return in U.S. dollars per share of the Sovereign High Yield Investment Company. The main investment objective of this fund is to provide high income with a secondary objective of capital appreciation. A steady dollar dividend has been maintained for long periods since the inception of the fund.

Investment vehicles aiming at total return are managed differently from those that primarily seek high income. Among the many differences in management and orientation, vehicles seeking total return will often consider a wider set of potential investments, particularly highly discounted bonds and loans or high spread duration bonds. Collateralized Brady bonds are also favored for strategies involving higher interest duration as the U.S. Treasury zero-coupon bonds backing the principal value of the bonds supplies additional interest duration.

---

[2] These are the approximate yields of the Emerging Markets Bond Index (EMBI) of J. P. Morgan (sovereign yield and blended yield) and of the Lehman Brothers BB index (long) of U.S. high yield bonds.

Exhibit 1: SHYIC Returns

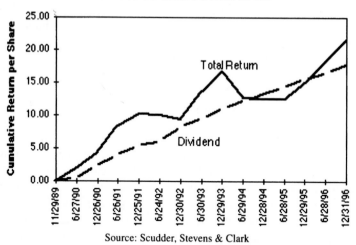

Source: Scudder, Stevens & Clark

A wide range of risk profiles is consistent with a total return orientation. Although discounts from par value — and the potential for above average price appreciation — are larger for issuers of lower credit quality, there are ample opportunities to invest in highly discounted securities of issuers with improving credit. Success in recent years in rapidly and effectively turning around countries involved in acute financial instability — Argentina, Brazil, Peru, and Poland, to name a few — provides evidence that even in cases of fragile credit quality framed in unstable macroeconomic conditions, successful turnaround can be produced within short periods of time. The record also shows that most of these major turnaround cases have led to sustained improvements in creditworthiness, breaking the cycle of stop-go progress that characterized major developing economies for most of the post-1945 years of the decade.

A number of portfolio management styles and techniques can be used to reach a total return objective. These range from long-term, research based portfolios which seek capital appreciation based on steady or improving fundamental conditions to trading-oriented vehicles which aim to take advantage of country- or issuer-specific events, U.S. bond market trends, or the global liquidity cycle. The deepening of emerging bond markets is providing increased liquidity, reducing the transaction costs of trading-oriented strategies. After the Mexican crisis at the end of 1994, a trend towards lower price volatilities lowered the cost of hedging and entering into derivative strategies which can enhance total return. Growing demand for hedging products will tend to lower transaction costs for derivatives as the markets mature.

Aggressive total return portfolios, as can be anticipated, are highly susceptible to conditions outside of the emerging markets, both of a fundamental nature and liquidity related. Brady bonds and long duration emerging Eurobonds are much more sensitive to fluctuations in the U.S. Treasury yield curve than implied by interest duration, spread duration, and other parameters that measure price sensitivity to yield or spread changes. While this sensitivity will tend to decline as discounts to par recede, markets mature, and the quality of information and analysis improves, emerging dollar bonds are likely to remain more exposed to shifts in Treasury bonds than other asset classes. Liquidity effects are another important consideration, particularly for portfolios that aim at boosting total return by employing a wide variety of trading strategies.

This pattern of sensitivity does not apply to local currency instruments, which have short duration and are segmented from global capital markets. Although the incipient development of local yield curves provides for only partial evidence, it appears that long duration bonds issued in local currencies have also reduced sensitivity to events in major global markets as compared to dollar pay issues. The segmentation of local fixed income markets from global markets results from the use of flexible exchange rates, restrictions or taxes on capital flows, and the lack of effective arbitrage between the local and international markets.

A third investment objective is asset diversification within a comprehensive investment program. It is not a distinct objective. Rather, it is achieved jointly with the other two objectives. Brady bonds and long-dated Eurobonds are sensitive to conditions in the U.S. bond market. Hence, these instruments are often not considered to provide much risk diversification for U.S. or dollar-based global bond investors. It is possible, however, to construct emerging bond portfolios which offer much greater potential for diversification by weighting more heavily emerging regions less associated with the U.S. bond market. Bonds of Asian, Central European, and Middle Eastern issuers historically have a lower correlation with the U.S. bond market than Latin American bonds. The latter account for about 80% of the mid-1997 capitalization of Brady and emerging Eurobonds.

Total return correlations of local currency markets with the U.S. and other developed country bond markets in recent years are generally not statistically different from zero at a high level of significance and as such can provide diversification advantages for U.S. and global bond investors. The substitution or addition of local currency instruments to U.S. or global portfolios can significantly reduce portfolio volatility and, sometimes, potentially increase returns. These results apply to local currency portfolios of short duration. The diversification benefits of local currencies are also enhanced because of the low correlation among the local currency markets themselves which helps explain the low volatility of local currency portfolios.

Asset diversification can be managed tactically or strategically to enhance returns during perceived favorable conditions in U.S. or global bond markets. Alternatively, diversification can be a primary defensive tool, for example by increasing the allocation to local currency investments. It too can help achieve interest duration objectives in diversified global portfolios.

ANALYTICAL ISSUES

The central principle behind a fundamental approach to emerging bond investments is that value, consistency, and risk control can be enhanced by systematic analysis. In a largely speculative asset class such as emerging markets fixed income, return optimization requires particular emphasis on risk control as the basis for portfolio construction and management. Analysis is needed as the centerpiece in gauging risks, determining relative value, and establishing potential arbitrage opportunities.

Although there are a number of ways to integrate analysis into the investment process, tilting research attention and resources towards particular aspects of the asset class, a fundamental approach, at a minimum, involves the following: sovereign risk, corporate credit, security analysis, market sensitivity, and for local currencies, currency or exchange rate risk.

Sovereign Risk

Sovereign risk encompasses several dimensions of risk. In its more general form, it measures transfer risk, sometimes denoted as *convertibility risk*. This is the probability that a government will not make foreign exchange available to meet foreign currency obligations. As such, sovereign credit quality will depend on the ability of the government to obtain foreign exchange and its willingness to maintain unimpeded flows of international capital to public and private borrowers.

The probability of default is a parameter that can be estimated either explicitly or implicitly. Ordinarily, however, the evaluation of sovereign risk involves more subtle differentiation among sovereign credits than just estimating a probability of default. Such probability tends to approach zero for periods of one year or less for investment-grade credits, but increases non-linearly as credits decline in quality below the investment-grade frontier. Nonetheless, markets are very sensitive to gradations in the perception of sovereign risk trends. Experience also indicates that markets tend to discount swiftly perceived improving trends in creditworthiness.

A key element for investment managers is the anticipation of changes in sovereign credit quality. A method to determine such changes is very useful as a guide to potential value and pricing of specific sovereign issues. This can be approached in a number of ways. The most desirable method is a thorough evaluation of macro, financial, and policy variables which will determine the government's ability and willingness to supply foreign exchange to entities operating within the country. Alternative approaches, which can be used as consistency checks, involve the use of quantitative models, indicators of creditworthiness, and check lists.

Among the key determinants of sovereign credit quality, to be assessed by thorough analysis, quantitative estimation, or other methods, are the following: the structure of the government's debt and debt service (external and internal), its international asset position, the fiscal position of the government, prospects for domestic output and demand, and a projection of dollar cash flows for the country derived from international trade and investment. The quality of economic policies in place, which can be quantified by indicators such as the status of International Monetary Fund programs, are also an important determinant. It is far more difficult to analyze and quantify institutional and political stability. Nonetheless, it is apparent that both markets and rating agencies devote considerable importance to this element which often helps to explain discrepancies in rating from that implied by more objective criteria.

Econometric analysis suggests that the structure of external debt is the central element involved in ratings of emerging markets by the major agencies. That this is the case should not be a surprise. After all, the probability of continuing to service external obligations will vary inversely with the burden of the debt. This is also the most readily quantifiable indicator of creditworthiness. It can be represented in simple form by the ratio of external debt to exports of goods and services. Other alternative ratios are also calculated, for example, the ratio of external debt to GDP. Likewise debt service ratios are often used to measure the current burden of servicing external debt.

Statistical analysis of sovereign debt ratings of the two major rating agencies, Moody's and Standard and Poor's, suggests that a small set of debt and economic indicators fits well the variation of ratings from a sample of 23 of the most important emerging countries. The results of two regressions, shown in Exhibit 2, indicate that the ratio of external debt to total exports, the ratio of total interest payments to exports, the trend growth of real GDP (average of the last three years) and the level of inflation for the last year account for 82% of the variance of Moody's ratings and 75% of the variance of ratings from Standard and Poor's. These results do not imply that the rating process used by the agencies is based solely or even primarily on these commonly used indicators. The standard errors of 0.39 rating and 0.53 rating, respectively, indicate that these equations are approximations of the process. Likewise, having 11 of 23 ratings split between the two agencies point out the important judgmental elements involved in the rating process. A statistical difference between the agencies appears to be that Standard and Poor's assigns somewhat greater weight to macroeconomic stability and growth than does Moody's as can be seen in the larger coefficients for trend growth and inflation in the regressions.

*Exhibit 2: Determinants of Sovereign Credit Ratings**

	Constant	Debt/Exports	Interest/Exports	Trend Growth	CPI Inflation		
Moody's	4.58	0.008	−0.027	−0.072	0.0084	R2 = 0.82	
(t ratio)	19.2	2.85	−0.58	−2.88	2.2	s.e.= 0.39	
Standard & Poor's	4.51	0.009	−0.049	−0.077	0.016	R2 = 0.75	
(t ratio)	13.95	2.33	−0.79	−2.29	3.13	s.e. = 0.53	

* Estimated from data in the Institute of International Finance, *Near Term Prospects for Emerging Market Economies* (Washington, D.C., April 1997). Ratings are those in effect as of June 1, 1997. For purposes of estimation, ratings were converted to a numerical equivalent where BBB/Baa is equal to 5.00 and BB/Ba equals 6.00 and so forth.

An evaluation of the mix of economic policies used by the government to attain financial and price stability and to help foster investment, growth, and financial deepening is essential in determining whether a country is on its way to achieving sustainable economic growth. Largely because of the diffusion of policy know-how and evidence that market-led policies instill confidence on investors and consumers, the quality of policies followed by developing countries has improved greatly in the 15 years since the debt crisis of 1982, the debacle which deeply set back development prospects for many middle-income countries. The lesson of the 1990s is that markets are rapid to acknowledge the benefits of stabilization based on a sound fiscal, monetary, and deregulatory policy mix. Likewise, selling state assets can rapidly provide signals to markets of a change in direction and an increase in the potential for solid fiscal policies.

A checklist can be a useful device to gauge the quality of the institutional and political environment in a country. The checklist may include factors such as the likelihood of a smooth transition of power, the stability of governing coalitions, and the chances for continuity of policies. Absent high political instability, which can lead to sharp reversal of policies, shifting coalition governments, and other nonviolent signs of political change are not necessarily a huge negative in the evaluation of credit quality. It is when policies are affected negatively by either peaceful or violent political change that potential for a major reversal in credit trends exists.

Corporate Credit

Debt securities of emerging country corporations provide a means to enhance returns in emerging debt, high yield, or other fixed income portfolios. Credit research is essential in determining proper valuation and the identification of investment opportunities. Corporate credits can also be a source of diversification as a complement or an alternative to sovereign credits. On the other hand, corporate credits can be very sensitive to movements in sovereign credit quality in the country of corporate residence. It follows that corporate credits do not always provide much diversification to emerging debt portfolios.

Evaluation of corporate risk in emerging markets presents formidable challenges. Rapidly evolving operating environments, accounting and legal systems, and rapid shifts in financial variables compound uncertainty in assessing credit risk for corporations. Management quality is arguably even more of a determining variable in developing countries than in industrial ones. Because of these factors, financial outcomes for emerging country companies are often subject to greater error than is the case in developed economies.

The operating environment for companies in developing countries is deeply affected, almost by definition, by rapid structural change arising out of institutional development, liberalization of markets, the creation and transformation of regulatory systems, and the opening to competition from foreign companies. It is also characterized by greater cyclical variation in demand and output than in developed countries.

Accounting standards are shifting rapidly in many emerging countries and are converging gradually to U.S. GAAP. Some countries such as Chile and Argentina now use accounting standards which are close to those of the United States and other developed countries. The issuance of American Depository Receipts and international bonds by many emerging country corporations also forces these companies to restate their financial statements in harmony with either U.S. or commonly accepted international standards. Privatization is another force pressing for updating accounting standards as widening interest in state companies by potential strategic or portfolio investors requires a thorough restatement of financial data. The pace of change is strongest among many larger Latin American and East Asian companies which are now accessing the international capital market. Central European, South Asian, and African companies lag in these efforts.

There is a debate regarding the relative evaluation of corporate and sovereign credits. Traditionally, the sovereign ceiling, or the credit rating given to the government, has set a limit on the rating of corporations residing and largely operating in that country. In some cases, however, market prices signaled that investors viewed corporations as a better credit. For example, some Argentine corporate credits traded for substantial periods of time with spreads through sovereign bonds of comparable duration or maturity. Recently some credit agencies, among them Standard and Poor's and Fitch, have indicated conditions under which corporate credits could be subject to a higher hard currency credit rating than the sovereign.[3]

Historical price behavior gives some support to the view that corporate bonds may be more susceptible to systemic shocks than sovereign bonds. A shock is an unexpected shift in a financial or real variable that substantially alters the probabilities given by investors and consumers to normal economic outcomes. A sudden devaluation of the currency or a large drop in the price of a key commodity, such as copper for Chile or oil for Nigeria, can generate shocks. After the devaluation of the Mexican peso in December 1994, spreads of Eurobonds issued by Mexican and other Latin American companies widened significantly over comparable maturity sovereigns. In this case, the currency devaluation in one of the most prominent emerging debtors provided a systemic shock to the market which deeply hit corporate credits. A systemic shock affects a set of international investors and markets as opposed to a country-specific shock which disrupts only investors in a given country and its securities.

Banks and other financial companies in emerging countries are especially sensitive to the stress generated by structural change and to the dislocations provided by shocks. The combination of rapid credit growth, often prevalent in

---

[3] This refers mainly to "dollarized economies" where there is little or no difference between credit quality measured in local currency or in dollars. The limiting case of a dollarized economy is one where the dollar is legal and sole legal tender, such as Panama. Countries with a currency pegged to the dollar through a "currency board" system or other mechanism that maintains full backing of the monetary base by dollar reserves or equivalent assets can be considered dollarized. For a company operating in a fully dollarized economy, transfer risk approaches zero.

emerging economies during price stabilization and deregulation of the financial sector, and inadequate risk management and other controls at lending institutions, leads to a deterioration of loan portfolios. Shocks can exacerbate the situation by causing rapid downward shifts in economic activity or an increase in key prices and interest rates. Banking difficulties are common throughout the developing world and, paradoxically, in the more rapidly developing countries. Analyzing financial credits is one of the most challenging aspects of corporate credit evaluation in emerging markets.

Bonds issued by companies facing steady demand through the economic cycle and capable of reacting rapidly to shocks offer less risk and at times present opportunities for yield and yield-compression significantly over the sovereign. This is the case of some electric utilities and companies in the food processing sector. Transformation of energy pricing and regulation in emerging countries to systems based on fuel and capacity costs or, alternatively, on marginal cost pricing, such as in Argentina and Chile, are reducing uncertainty in evaluating company cash flows while increasing the likelihood that adequate interest coverage ratios can be maintained.

Investing in debt securities of all but the largest listed companies in emerging markets requires specialized credit work and wide access to local data and company management. Locally traded debt securities as well as private placements offer ample opportunities for excess return. However, this is a market segment which remains terra incognita for most investors located outside of the domestic market. The comments above regarding credit analysis, which pertain largely to the better capitalized corporations, are even more applicable to this much larger set of companies where the problems of risk evaluation are compounded by local operating environments, regulatory questions, and limitations of data and institutional understanding.

Security Analysis

Sovereign and corporate credit analysis provide essential inputs for security evaluation, country selection, and portfolio management. Additional evaluation is necessary to proceed with security selection in the investment process. Much like other debt securities, emerging bonds can be analyzed in terms of parameters determining yield and return, price sensitivity, and properties of the yield curve. The analytical issues are similar to those encountered in the evaluation of other debt securities. Analytical questions of special relevance for emerging market bonds concern collateral and unusual coupon structures in many Brady bonds, the abundance of floating-rate issues, and embedded options.

Collateral associated with Brady bonds requires calculation of stripped yields and spreads or, as alternatively called, sovereign yields and spreads, apart from the usual yield-to-maturity calculations. A stripped yield is derived from the cash flows net of collateral. This is straightforward when only the principal is collateralized, typically by a matching U.S. Treasury zero. It becomes more complex as two, or sometimes three, coupons are also collateralized. Such coupon collateralization can be evaluated by using alternative methodologies which incorporate the probability of default per coupon period.

Spread duration measures the sensitivity of price to changes in sovereign yield, as contrasted to ordinary yield-to-maturity (YTM) or "blended yield." This calculation is necessary for all Brady bonds except fixed-rate, non-collateralized bullets, where ordinary YTM calculations produce identical results. Spread duration is a central parameter in Brady bond evaluation and portfolio construction and management. It provides a measure of the sensitivity of total return of Brady bonds to changes in sovereign spreads over comparable U.S. Treasury bonds or other base yields.

Floating-rate bonds of intermediate and long-maturities were issued by the 15 countries that completed Brady debt restructurings in the 1989-1996 period.[4] Floating-rate syndicated loans of several countries, among them Russia and Morocco, trade actively in international markets. Several countries issued floating-rate Bradys and Eurobonds of varying maturities as part of their financing programs. These floaters have low or negative modified interest duration. Because of the discounts on most of these floating-rate bonds, interest duration provides a weak measure of the sensitivity of these bonds to shifts in the U.S. Treasury curve as well as to the sensitivity of the bonds to shifts in credit spreads. It is therefore essential to evaluate sovereign spread duration for these floaters as part of relative value, total return, and other portfolio summary statistics.

Call options to the issuer are embedded in most Brady bonds and in some sovereign Eurobonds. Corporate bonds are also issued in callable form. As long as call options on Brady bonds were deeply out-of-the-money, their value was safely ignored by investors. Brady bonds traded at deep discounts immediately after their issuance upon exchange of restructured loans. As Brady prices approach levels where the call options offer significant value, option-adjusted-spread (OAS) calculations become necessary as a means of establishing precise valuation, helping portfolio construction, and trading. OAS evaluation methodologies for Brady bonds are not yet standard and tend to produce substantial differences. This partly follows from Brady bonds' complex structures with one or two types of collateral and discrete coupon patterns. Furthermore, the probability distribution of Brady prices appears to differ appreciably from the lognormal distribution utilized widely to price options.

Market Sensitivity

Emerging market bond prices show, as a rule, high sensitivity to random events and to the impact of changes in international markets. For example, emerging bonds show more responsiveness to shifts in the U.S. yield curve than indicated by intrinsic measures of price sensitivity such as interest and spread duration. That this is so should not be a big surprise. Partly, it can be explained by the prevailing discount in most emerging bonds or other measures of risk premium.

---

[4] These countries are Albania, Argentina, Brazil, Bulgaria, Costa Rica, Dominican Republic, Ecuador, Jordan, Mexico, Panama, Peru, The Philippines, Poland, Uruguay, and Venezuela.

Exhibit 3: Sensitivity to Changes in U.S. Yield Curve
(December 1990 to April 1996)

	Sensitivity	Interest Duration (years)
EMBI	−11.9	5.4
Fixed Rate Bonds	−15.0	10.7
Floaters	−8.7	0.4

Source: Calculated from J.P. Morgan's Emerging Markets Bond Index.

Brady bonds are highly sensitive to conditions in U.S. markets. Sensitivity of the Emerging Markets Bond Index of J.P. Morgan, which is composed mostly of Brady bonds, to changes in the U.S. yield curve in the period December 1990 to March 1996 is −11.9. This means that a change in U.S. rates on average produces a percentage change about −12 times larger in the EMBI index. This was calculated by regression of the EMBI on a U.S. yield curve (3 months to 30 years) weighted to produce interest duration equal to that of the EMBI plus a variable for emerging market shocks (such as the Real Plan in Brazil and the Mexican peso shock of December 1994).

Fixed-rate Bradys show a sensitivity of −15 compared, for example, to interest duration of 10.7 years. The data also show clearly that Brady floating-rate bonds are also very sensitive to shifts in U.S. interest rates. While the interest duration of floating Bradys (April 1996) is only 0.4 years, they show a statistical sensitivity of −8.7. Markets overshoot when U.S. rates fall as credit risk is perceived to decrease. Conversely, markets react negatively to rising interest rates partly because credit risk is negatively impacted. Vanishing liquidity, in turn, compounds these effects. This applies to both fixed- and floating-rate Bradys. Consequently, in periods of weakness in U.S. markets, Brady bonds will tend to overreact. Market sensitivity of Brady bonds to the U.S. yield curve may be presumed to fall as discounts recede.

There is an additional explanation for the sensitivity to the U.S. market. Emerging countries are the marginal issuers in international debt markets and they — and the holders of their debt securities — will be among the first to be affected or benefited by changing patterns of international capital flows. As risk is perceived to decrease, either because of changes in fundamental trend or improved information and analysis, sensitivity may tend to decline.

Can market sensitivity be measured in any systematic and reliable way? Usual calculations, including those implied by the capital asset pricing model, such as betas, or other statistical relationships, similar to those in Exhibit 3, are typically not very stable. Likewise, there are reservations about usual measures of variability, such as the standard deviation, since total return of individual emerging debt securities may show deviations from normality.

The heightened volatility of emerging debt securities appears to be related to the size of the risk premium. It may also be argued that often this risk premium may be larger than is implied by the excess volatility of emerging debt securities. While this is debatable, the risk premium is a potential source of excess returns and arbitrage opportunities.

Options on emerging bonds suggest as well that there is a premium paid for excess volatility, apart from premia caused by other factors such as liquidity and shortcomings in option modeling. Implied volatilities exceeded actual volatilities for the main Brady bonds in the two years to mid-June 1997. This is probably derived from a period of declining long-term volatility in the market. Nonetheless, the additional risk premia has probably hindered the use of hedging strategies.

Currency or Exchange Rate Risk

Investment in emerging debt securities issued and payable in local currencies presents separate analytical issues in addition to the topics covered above. The central issue presented by these local currency investments is the evaluation of currency risk. This is the risk of devaluation of the currency in terms of dollars. In most instances, devaluation risk could be narrowed further as the risk of a real devaluation of the exchange rate, or a devaluation in excess of the inflation differential with the United States. Measuring the risk of real devaluation enables comparisons among currencies of exchange rate risk.

Investing in local currency securities can provide excess returns over those of securities of similar duration in developed markets. Part of this return arises from prevailing local yields which in real terms are higher than required by underlying credit and currency risks. This could be the result of the need to maintain high positive real interest rates during financial stabilization and disinflation or derived from rigid expectations of policy or market behavior.

Evaluating the probability of a real devaluation enables the quantification and cross country comparison of currency risk. In most emerging countries, this requires the evaluation of the exchange rate regime and the policy rule followed. Most emerging currencies are managed according to preset rules, i.e., by pegging to the dollar or a basket of hard currencies, by keeping the currency within limits of a peg, or following a crawling peg. Quantification of the expected devaluation then involves evaluation of the policy rule and the ability of the central bank to follow it. Since most emerging currencies are managed against some central peg, as a rule they are more predictable and less volatile than developed currencies. In the 12 months to the end of May 1997, for example, the exchange rates of the deutsche mark and yen to the dollar were more volatile than the rates against the U.S. dollar of 15 of the more widely traded emerging currencies.

INVESTMENT PROCESS AND PORTFOLIO CONSTRUCTION

Portfolio construction and management are designed to reach the investment objectives within the risk tolerance indicated in the investment guidelines or prospectus. Alternative approaches to portfolio construction are determined by the investment process established to manage the portfolio. The investment process integrates all the elements needed to achieve investment objectives.

Investment Process

Emerging debt securities are generally in the lower segment of the credit quality spectrum. Investing in emerging debt consequently requires an especially rigorous process of country, security, and asset allocation as a means to control risk and provide for consistency of returns. It also requires comprehensive knowledge of trading conditions to provide for efficient timing of entry, exit, and hedging decisions.

While conceivably a variety of investment processes may produce superior and consistent performance, all of them require close integration of research and analysis on the one hand, and portfolio management and trading on the other. Likewise, a variety of investment styles will produce a number of investment processes, for example, very active, arbitrage-oriented portfolios or longer-term, value-oriented approaches.

Independent of the characteristics of the investment process, analytical support for the process involves a top-down component, centered on fundamental sovereign, sector, and market analysis and a bottom-up component that incorporates security, corporate, or sub-national analysis. This is then integrated with the timing decision, which requires a sharp understanding of trading conditions for specific securities.

Some investment processes emphasize security selection and the bottom-up aspect of the process. This may be akin to traditional corporate high yield investments. However, in emerging markets, companies operate within a wide variety of macroeconomic and institutional environments. So it is not easy to succeed with a pure bottom-up approach to the investment process, and a foundation of macro analysis is required to provide for differentiation across countries and interpretation of national and global events. Inasmuch as emerging markets become more integrated into the international economy through lifting of barriers to trade and capital, national operating conditions could become somewhat less important. The central premise in a bottom-up approach is security valuation.

A second type of process emphasizes the top-down component and the identification of potential gains from credit improvement or pricing divergence derived from analysis of fundamental country and macro trends. Just as the first approach requires integration with macro analysis, the top-down orientation must involve security analysis as an essential input in the determination of value. This said, since the majority of emerging countries are issuers of a few or even only one liquid security, country and security analysis often converge to the establishment of relative value in terms of individual securities.

In practice, disciplined investment processes involve both a top-down and a bottom-up component. The differentiation comes from the relative importance of each approach and the time dimension of investment decisions. Trading-oriented approaches may emphasize flow analysis, event appraisal, and global market effects, for instance, as the force driving investment decisions. These approaches can be viewed as complementary where they make most sense in managing global emerging market portfolios. For specialized portfolios, they can be considered stand-alone processes, for example, in managing country funds, where the investment process will largely be driven by security analysis.

Portfolio Construction

Construction of emerging market portfolios follows the same principles as other fixed income portfolios. Conceptually, this involves estimating, over the investment horizon, total return and its components for each security in the investable universe as well as estimation of risk characteristics. Research inputs are necessary in the estimation of total return. Risk characteristics could formally be projected from historical data on price and spread movements or from appropriate matrices of correlation coefficients. In practice, however, experience quickly teaches that such calculations have wide confidence intervals and are not stable enough to be interpreted without a great amount of care and sophistication. Quantitative analysis of risk and return and the use of optimization techniques can provide a rough and useful guide to the return and risk parameters for a portfolio.

One approach to portfolio construction involves having core and trading positions within the portfolio. Core positions will be driven by fundamental value to be realized within an intermediate investment horizon, say, three to six months, which in the dynamics of emerging countries can contain a sizable number of fundamental events. Core positions are adjusted as fundamental views change. They are changed in response to price action to realize price targets or implement a stop loss. Positions can also be altered as risk patterns change, for example, because of major deviations in volatility or security correlations. Nonetheless, the idea behind the core is that it should represent long-term views of credit direction, value, and relationship to the U.S. and other more developed bond markets.

Maintaining a core position requires much portfolio discipline and reliable inputs from analysis and research. By reason of the rapid change in emerging nations and the young stage of their financial institutions, governance, and markets, investors are continuously exposed to a substantial flow of information denoting the evidence of change and the resistance to and costs of change. Inevitably, this will be mixed news, often suggesting signals of some impending catastrophe. Exposed to this information flow and accompanying events, it helps to understand why turnover ratios in emerging debt portfolios are high.

A good example of the virtues of having core portfolios is provided by the massive correction and spectacular recovery that followed the devaluation of the Mexican peso in December 1994. The veritable collapse of the Brady bond market after the devaluation was followed with a sharp turnaround. Liquidity effects, including deleverage, rather than any sharp deterioration of fundamentals explained the market reaction, as well as the rapid recovery of prices. Sustaining core positions through this massive upheaval was no mean task, but it paid in terms of ultimately benefiting with the rapid recovery in prices. This would have required strong conviction derived from competent analysis. Instead, most investors tried timing the turning points in such rapid recovery, and a few succeeded.

Trading positions aim to take advantage of mispricing, event anticipation, and other elements which can give rise to temporary deviations from fundamental value. To be effective and to maintain overall control of risk, trading positions should be separate from the core. Of course, in a limiting case, the entire portfolio can be viewed as a collection of trades, subject to constant adjustment. This may work well, but strict accounting of trading and hedging costs must be made to ascertain the merits of the strategy.

Buy-and-hold portfolios are the other limiting case, when there is no adjustment of positions other than resulting from a change in core views. This could be derived from long-term fundamental views, or, in another limiting case, because the portfolio may be entirely passive, tracking a given benchmark. The latter are not used very widely, and it is not difficult to show that emerging market benchmarks are unlikely to be optimal from return or risk characteristics. Buy-and-hold portfolios may have limited room for flexibility when they are designed to match, directly or synthetically, certain desired characteristics such as maturity, duration, or current income. Specific purpose investment structures composed of emerging debt securities often fit well in the portfolios of insurance companies, banks, and other financial institutions.

Ordinarily, portfolio adjustments are made continuously as a result of changes in pricing or trading opportunities, and, less frequently, following the appreciation of shifts in fundamental value. Adjustments are also made when the portfolio profile no longer is within desired characteristics of spread and interest duration, currency exposure, or risk.

In a smoothly working investment process, initiative for portfolio changes may come from traders and portfolio managers, who are close to the price action, or from analysts who gauge credit or macro trends. In cases when fundamental variables drive adjustments, analysts can become involved in the process, even as origination may come from the portfolio management team. In practice, rapid events challenge the portfolio management process, as communication lags, for example, can lead to incomplete integration of the investment process and decisions which do not fully use the potential of the investment management team.

Failure to perform consistently up to expectations is usually the consequence of a failure in appraisal of fundamentals and not of errors in market timing. Of course, gauging the probability and impact of powerful positive or negative events adds value. It does and can provide for a large measure of success in managing emerging debt portfolios. Market and event related decisions, such as the timing of Brady buyback announcements, which have been made by several of the most prominent issuers of Brady bonds (Mexico, Argentina and Brazil), can be gauged by analysis of government finances and cash flows but equally require a keen understanding of capital market conditions.

One of the crucial aspects of managing emerging portfolios is the need to appraise the impact upon emerging borrowers of variables outside the investable universe, that is, financial and economic changes and expectations in advanced countries. This calls for an investment process integrated closely with fundamental and market analysis of U.S. and international bond markets. The flow of causality is almost exclusively from developed to emerging markets. Defensive or hedging strategies as well as strategies to take advantage of patterns in benchmark markets are a key part of the portfolio management process.

CONTROLLING RISK

Risk management is an essential ingredient in emerging markets fixed income. Risk management can be viewed in several ways, depending on the dimension of risk. In emerging markets, limiting credit risk, sovereign and corporate, is a central aim of the investment process and of portfolio management.

Risk control also involves mitigating market risk. This often involves reducing price or total return volatility. Investors will have widely differing levels of tolerance for volatility, depending on their ultimate aim. For an equity investor who views emerging debt as an equity alternative, maintaining low or moderate portfolio volatility may not be important or even highly desirable. On the other hand, a fixed income investor who aims at seeking excess return over U.S. bonds but maintaining volatility within some upper bound of the U.S. bond market will want to have a different portfolio profile than an equity-oriented investor.

Risk could also be viewed asymmetrically, for example, reducing downside risk. This can also be approached in a number of ways. The selected strategy to reduce downside risk will vary with the prospectus or guideline restrictions. At one end, it may require capping downside price movement by purchasing put options. Or, it may involve selling call options, matching assets and liabilities, or simply lowering interest duration. The cost of reducing downside risk will be gauged in the context of overall investment objectives and may not always be by itself a determining variable.

Another potential area for risk control would be to reduce the risk of underperformance versus a established benchmark or appropriate index. This can be thought of as aiming to keep tracking error within bounds from a benchmark. Tracking error is the standard deviation of the difference in performance (usually total return) between a portfolio and the benchmark. A portfolio guideline or constraint may be to maintain tracking error within ±2% of total return for a given benchmark or reference index. Since emerging market portfolios can have high volatility, there could be a sizable cost in potential return for keeping tracking error low, for example, at less than 1%. Limiting tracking error is probably best viewed as an exercise in performance management rather than risk management as it merely focuses on a narrow aspect of the risk dimension.

Comprehensive risk management can also be viewed from a value-at-risk perspective. This would involve ascertaining the potential loss resulting at a given level of confidence from a change in some variable. It could measure, for instance, the impact of a change in the price of the 10-year U.S. Treasury note on emerging Eurobonds in the portfolio at a 95% level of confidence.

Managing Credit Risk

Management of credit risk requires making sound judgments on sovereign and corporate credits. Fiduciary responsibilities usually require that investment managers make independent evaluation of credit risk and do not rely on the judgment of credit rating agencies, brokers, or other intermediaries. Credit agency ratings are an important guide to credit quality and have great bearing on security pricing and price movements. In many cases, investment guidelines impose a constraint based on agency credit ratings. This means that agency ratings have to be taken as a central reference point for investment managers, who, nonetheless, will have to form their own opinions regarding the quality of the credit.

Managing sovereign risk requires continuing assessment of factors that may imply or signal a deterioration of risk. Such monitoring can be done by research analysts or even by portfolio managers. Dependence on market information, made available by third parties such as banks, brokers, consultants, and the press does not relieve investment managers of their responsibilities versus clients.

The following steps are recommended as part of a continuing credit review process: (1) weekly, or at least monthly, review of all credits in a portfolio; (2) assessment of the impact on capacity to service debt of major changes in operating capability, government policies, external factors, or other exogenous changes; (3) analysis of interrelations among credits focusing on material impact that changes in one credit may have on other credits; (4) mitigation of elements that can lower the probability of serious impact upon the credit; and, (5) use of a value-at-risk or similar approach to quantify overall sensitivity to changes in key variables.

While quantitative techniques and management systems will enhance capabilities, management of credit risk involves a continuing assessment of fundamental variables that affect valuation. A review of technical, flow, or statistical associations that may affect market prices is very useful but not the central aspect. That is, managing credit risk involves making fundamental judgments about intrinsic risk that can potentially be expressed in fundamental value.

Managing Market Risk

Investors in emerging debt usually concern themselves with two types of market risk — volatility and pricing risk. The first is associated with variation of total return or prices as measured by traditional statistical measures such as the standard deviation or the standard error of estimate. In this section we will direct our comments mainly to the management of volatility and not to pricing risk.

Pricing risk is often a consequence of the lack of liquidity in issues with thin secondary markets. While a concern in portfolios that seek value and diversification by investing in minor sovereign and, especially, corporate issues, pricing risk is generally low in all the major Brady bonds and large sovereign issues. One obvious way to reduce pricing risk is to confine investments to major liquid issues.

Emerging debt is usually viewed as one of the most volatile fixed income asset classes. This is generally the case for long duration emerging bonds, particularly Brady bonds and long Eurobonds. On the other hand, as discussed in the next section, portfolios of local currency investments exhibit low volatility when properly diversified.

In the two years since the Mexican peso crisis, the volatility of Bradys and liquid Eurobonds declined steadily as indicated in Exhibit 4. By June 1997, the volatility of the Emerging Brady Bond Index Plus produced by J.P. Morgan (EMBI+), the most widely used benchmark, reached a little over 8% (26 week annualized volatility) from levels of around 25% at the beginning of 1995. Lower volatility is reflected in pricing of options on Brady bonds.

Investors assign variable degrees of importance to volatility. For some investors it is of secondary importance in the context of attaining investment objectives and no restrictions are desired to limit volatility beneath a given threshold. For others high volatility may be undesirable or must be kept within bounds to match liabilities, complement other assets, or to keep within a range of the benchmark.

The following approaches to managing volatility can be used in emerging debt portfolios: portfolio diversification, asset allocation, and sell disciplines. Option strategies are a fourth alternative, which can be used tactically or as an integral part of core portfolios.

Portfolio Diversification

One of the virtues of portfolio diversification is that it can dampen market risk as well as provide a mechanism for managing other types of risk (sovereign, credit, currency, event) over a set of securities. The capability of diversification to dampen market risk is a function of the interaction of price and return among emerging debt securities and with securities in other asset classes.

Exhibit 4: EMBI+ Volatility

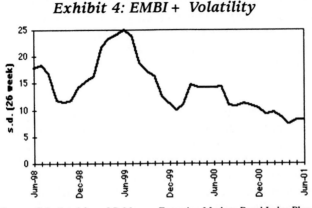

Source: Calculated from J.P. Morgan Emerging Markets Bond Index Plus.

Correlations and other statistical measures of association show that Brady bonds and Eurobonds are closely correlated. In addition, as mentioned before, volatility is not necessarily dampened in close proportion to the bonds' duration and other intrinsic properties. This means than when considering portfolios consisting mainly of Bradys and Eurobonds, there is only reduced scope for limiting low volatility by diversification within this asset class.

Other alternatives, such as strategies which imply use of options and other derivatives, can reduce volatility but their cost is generally high. This limits derivatives-based techniques to tactical and trading strategies, where they can add the most value. Ordinarily they do not provide an efficient approach to capping downside risk to the entire portfolio. As a comprehensive approach, extensive use of put options, covered calls, and other protective techniques is too costly for all but the most defensive strategies. Derivatives have an important role, when allowed by investment guidelines, in tactical positioning of portfolios or as a means of attaining implicit leverage. The growth of emerging debt derivatives trading in over-the-counter markets and in exchanges offers smooth execution and much more efficient pricing than was possible in the early stages of the evolution of the asset class.

One possible diversification strategy, blending Bradys and emerging Eurobonds on one side and local currency emerging debt on the other can often provide desirable risk-return characteristics and a substantial reduction in portfolio volatility.

Asset Allocation

Brady bonds and emerging market Eurobonds have lower correlation with other fixed income and equity securities than among themselves, providing for the possibility of constructing portfolios that will meet a wide range of desired objectives. The correlation matrix in Exhibit 5 illustrates correlations for 1993-1997 among the main emerging market debt indices — the EMBI and EMBI+ — and other fixed income and equity indices. In particular, it shows that whereas the EMBI+ and EMBI have moderate correlation with the U.S. bond and equity markets (Lehman G/C and S&P 500), correlation with global bonds (G. Govt) is essentially not statistically different from zero. This suggests that emerging bonds can be a useful complement to global and international bond portfolios. It implies also that adding global bonds to emerging market portfolios could be an efficient strategy in terms of risk-return trade-off for many investors who do not wish to have full exposure to emerging market risk.

Sell Disciplines

Emerging markets debt management requires strict sell disciplines in portfolios and trading strategies. There are several reasons for this emphasis on sell disciplines. Emerging countries are in the process of solidifying policies, institutions, and regulations aiming at providing a constructive environment for long-term investments and market development. But, unfortunately, setbacks and failures occur frequently, sometimes in difficult to predict conditions. This calls for continuing evaluation of positions and the taking of swift action to reduce, alter, or eliminate positions from the portfolio.

Exhibit 5: Emerging Markets Correlation Matrix
(Monthly data — December 1993 to March 1997)

Index*	Annualized Volatility	EMBI+	EMBI	ELMI	ELMI-EW	S&P 500	Lehm G/C	G. Govt.	MS EAFE
EMBI+	17.81	1							
EMBI	17.75	0.98	1						
ELMI	7.62	0.54	0.50	1					
ELMI-EW	3.74	0.42	0.34	0.82	1				
S&P 500	10.22	0.48	0.52	0.13	0.07	1			
Lehm G/C	4.89	0.45	0.47	0.02	0.07	0.60	1		
G. Govt.	5.14	0.03	-0.01	0.04	0.32	0.27	0.52	1	
MS EAFE	10.85	0.20	0.20	0.15	0.05	0.45	0.12	0.36	1

Source: Calculated on the basis of index data from J.P.Morgan, Lehman Brothers, and Morgan Stanley Capital International.

*Indices are as follows:
    EMBI+: J.P. Morgan Emerging Market Bond Index Plus
    EMBI: J.P. Morgan Emerging Market Bond Index
    ELMI: J.P. Morgan Emerging Local Markets Index
    ELMI - EW: Adjusted Equal-Weighted ELMI
    S&P 500: Standard and Poor's 500 Stock Index
    Lehm G/C: Lehman Brothers Government/Corporate Index
    G. Govt: J.P. Morgan Global Government Index
    MS EAFE: Morgan Stanley Capital International, Europe, Australia and the Far East Index

The high sensitivity of emerging bonds to conditions in global fixed income markets also calls for strict sell disciplines as a defensive posture when faced with potential setbacks in the U.S. bond market or, for many Asian issuers, in Japanese money or bond markets. Alternative management techniques can be used to complement sell disciplines such as careful management of interest and spread duration. As explained above, however, duration strategies do not always work well in emerging debt securities.

Trading-oriented investment processes likewise need to be based firmly on precise sell disciplines. This is, of course, critical in leveraged portfolios or those which employ short positions. Even in portfolios where leverage on short positions are not allowed by prospectus or investment guidelines, tactical positions must be controlled and gains taken or losses curtailed as price action surpasses set limits.

Derivatives can substitute for sell actions and can frequently be a superior alternative. As pricing efficiency increases, options can be employed at lower cost to cushion portfolios from adverse price movements. The fall in price volatility in Brady and Eurobonds in the two years to mid-1997 supports arguments that volatility is priced reasonably low compared to the historical trend in the market. The contrary argument is that implied volatilities remain higher than historical volatilities for most Brady bonds as of mid-1997.

LOCAL CURRENCY MARKETS

Local currency markets are the fastest growing component of the emerging debt asset class, driven by the explosive development of capital markets in developing nations. Three factors argue for an even more rapid development of liquid markets for local debt securities: (1) the deregulation of local capital markets; (2) the revolution in pension and savings systems in developing countries; and, (3) the swift advances in price and financial stability by nearly all large emerging nations.

Local debt markets are now the largest part of the emerging debt asset class. Money markets instruments and local bonds in 75 emerging countries by the end of 1996 exceeded $850 billion, according to estimates derived from International Monetary Fund, World Bank, and national data. By contrast, the market value of Brady bonds and other Eurobonds issued in international markets by governments and corporations in the same countries is estimated at $230 billion. Some $370 billion of local markets securities are located in Asia, $250 billion in Latin America, $90 billion in Africa south of the Sahara, and the rest in Central and Eastern Europe and the Middle East. These numbers exclude many government and corporate bond issues and commercial paper of lesser liquidity.

The bulk of liquid local assets are money market instruments, mainly government securities. Commercial paper is usually placed privately. A handful of countries have developed liquid bond markets, most importantly Argentina, South Africa, and, to a lesser extent, Chile and the Czech Republic. Government bills and notes are traded extensively in most countries, mainly in the interbank market but also in other active secondary markets. Clearing and custody are often sophisticated with book entry at the central bank or other central depository a common practice.

Local instruments are rarely traded offshore in direct form. However, liquid forward markets for local currencies are rapidly developing in major emerging countries and others that do not have strict capital controls. Offshore markets are also found in lesser currencies. By mid-1997, forwards and offshore notes were available in some 30 emerging currencies, most with reasonable liquidity. Banks are also active in designing offshore structures to capture the properties of local money market instruments when trading may be hindered by local operational practices such as lack of proper custody or certain types of exchange controls. These services are gradually becoming more competitive as international banks set up operations in new countries and local banks begin to enter the business through their offshore subsidiaries.

Exhibit 6 provides a sample of monthly money market returns in dollar terms comprising the ten emerging countries in J.P. Morgan's Emerging Local Markets Index (ELMI). The exhibit shows an average correlation of 0.11 from inception of the index in December 1993 to October 1996. Most coefficients in the exhibit are not statistically significant or negative among pairs of countries. Even among countries in some regions, the correlations are low. For example, the average correlation among the four Southeast Asian countries in the matrix is only 0.09.

Exhibit 6: Local Currency Correlation Matrix
(Monthly data — December 1993 to October 1996)

	Argen	Czech	Indon	Malay	Mexico	Philip	Poland	S.Afri	Thaild	Turkey
Argentina	1									
Czech Republic	−0.279	1								
Indonesia	0.200	−0.260	1							
Malaysia	0.239	0.240	−0.032	1						
Mexico	0.218	−0.219	0.384	0.145	1					
Philippines	0.218	−0.119	0.135	0.191	0.196	1				
Poland	0.098	0.564	0.030	0.183	−0.216	−0.086	1			
South Africa	−0.161	0.208	0.160	−0.204	−0.178	0.019	0.346	1		
Thailand	0.026	0.637	−0.046	0.375	0.106	−0.089	0.583	0.019	1	
Turkey	0.239	0.134	0.183	0.198	0.084	0.152	0.049	−0.023	0.154	1

* Based on portfolio of 90-day money market securities at market exchange rates.
Source: SS&C on the basis of data from J.P. Morgan.

Low correlations could well increase over time as currencies within a region may move together given an external shock or a change in external variables. Likewise, a successful speculative attack on one currency may well encourage speculators and investors to attack a neighboring currency or pull out massively from the currency. Recent evidence suggests that there may be links between attacks on currencies in separate regions, such as pressure on the Philippine peso following the Mexican peso 1994 devaluation and spillover effects from the Thai baht to neighboring currencies and the Czech koruny. Increased cooperation in Southeast Asia and other regions to share foreign assets and reserves should help reduce systemic currency risks. In effect, the Mexican peso devaluation of December 1994 had little impact on other Latin American currencies. Its impact was largely concentrated on bond and equity markets. Only Argentina experienced a sustained increase in money market rates resulting from the Mexico crisis.

As shown in Exhibit 5, the Emerging Markets Correlation Matrix in the previous section, ELMI had a correlation of 0.02 with the U.S. bond market as expressed by the Lehman Brothers Government/Corporate Index. The correlation with J.P. Morgan's Global Government Index was 0.04 and 0.15 with the EAFE index of Morgan Stanley Capital International. The correlation with the Emerging Markets Bond Index of J.P. Morgan was 0.50, reflecting the ELMI's nearly 25% average weight in Mexican pesos in most of the sample period of December 1993 to March 1997.

Greater diversification can reduce the volatility of local currency investments. This is shown by the use of an equally-weighted ELMI index or ELMI-EW, which could be considered as a potential alternative benchmark. This involves giving a 10% weight to each of the ten components of the standard J.P. Morgan index. Calculations were performed using a monthly sample for the period from the end of 1993 to March 31, 1997. As can be expected, this significantly improves the performance of the index in terms of portfolio volatility and lowers the correlation with the EMBI and EMBI+ index. Annualized monthly volatility of total return of the ELMI benchmark during the period was 7.62% as against 3.74% for the ELMI-EW. Correlation of the ELMI-EW with the EMBI was 0.34 compared with 0.50 for the ELMI. Comparisons with the EMBI+ are 0.54 and 0.42.

Aggressive investors may want to look at high yielding local currency investments such as those provided by countries in earlier stages of stabilization and reform than other emerging countries. In these cases also, diversification of local currency portfolios will help lower volatility as interest rates and currencies are determined principally by domestic factors and events.

The next stage in the development of local currency markets is the formation of full yield curves. In nearly all emerging countries, bonds with an average life longer than two years issued by governments and corporations are held to maturity by local banks, insurance companies, pension funds, and wealthy individuals. Thus there is no liquid secondary market. In some countries, there is limited liquidity of corporate and municipal bonds which can trade at the main security exchanges. Only in Argentina and South Africa is there extensive secondary trading of sovereign and corporate bonds issued in Argentine pesos and rands with ample participation by local and foreign investors. With the improvement in credit quality and the growth of financial savings in many emerging countries, issuance in local currency is likely to be transformed in coming years. Corporate and municipal issuers look at the local securities markets as a largely untapped and natural source of financing which could provide an alternative to bank financing as a source of long-term funds.

Chapter 3

Integrating Emerging Market Bonds into a Global Portfolio

Steven I. Dym, Ph.D.
President
Steven I. Dym & Associates

INTRODUCTION

The middle years of the 1990s witnessed a change in the attitudes of institutional investors towards bonds of developing countries. What once would not be considered part of "traditional" portfolios has now become an important ingredient in them. However, because of the newness of these instruments, the tools available to portfolio managers and analysts are just catching up to the need. The purpose of this chapter is to present a number of useful tools for analyzing emerging market bonds and a general approach for integrating them into a global fixed income portfolio.

HISTORICAL MEASURES OF RETURN AND RISK

In this section, some historical measures of return and risk for emerging market bonds are presented. These statistics show why this asset class has become so popular. The next section summarizes the different types of emerging market fixed income assets. Then tools for analysis are presented, followed by the new "budget math" applicable to developing countries. Throughout these sections, the corresponding measures for bonds of industrialized countries are provided for comparison. The final section goes through the dynamics of decision making the investment manager must navigate in order to successfully integrate emerging market bonds in the portfolio.

Due to their significant risk of default, developing country bonds carry a high credit risk premium. This is particularly evident in their U.S. dollar-denominated issues. In principle, the risk of default should be relevant to any sovereign entity. But a government's theoretical ability to tax (and in some cases to require the central bank to purchase its debt) means that its ability to repay its *own* currency-denominated debt is not at risk — instead, the value of its currency is at risk. But servicing *foreign* currency-denominated debt requires the ability to convert its own currency into foreign exchange, something which may not always be possible for governments of relatively small, developing economies. This is why the rate of return requires a default risk premium. It is this variable which produces the distinct asset class, and raises the expected return from emerging market debt securities relative to industrialized countries. Its absence from portfolios limited to industrialized country bonds means that adding emerging market debt must improve the portfolio's risk-return trade-off and expand the "efficient frontier."

During some years spreads of developing country over U.S. Treasury bonds went well into double digits, at times over 20%! While such situations are not the norm, they are also not rare, occurring, for example, when one country is experiencing major macro-economic difficulties — such as Mexico in late 1994 and through 1995 — and resulting investor nervousness spilling over into almost all other emerging markets. The bonds' high yields, their wide risk premiums and substantial movements have produced very attractive rates of return for this asset class, accompanied, of course, by outsized volatility. Exhibit 1 displays the rates of return for one type of emerging market bonds — Brady bonds — since their inception, along with those for government bonds of the United States and of industrialized countries. Clearly, Brady bonds compare very favorably with the other issues. They well outperformed Treasury bonds over the 1990-1997 period, due to their hefty risk premium on top of Treasuries and the general narrowing of credit spreads over that time. The spread narrowing, in turn, reflected improved credit fundamentals of the Brady bond countries as a group, as well as increasing investor acceptance of the securities. Of course, this narrowing was not smooth, which shows up in the comparative volatilities of the two asset classes, as shown in Exhibit 2. Brady bonds also compare favorably with non-dollar government bonds (and with the World Government Bond Index, a market weighted average of U.S. and non-U.S. industrialized country bonds). Currency movements impart a great deal of volatility to non-dollar bonds. While this element of risk is absent in Brady bonds, their volatility is still greater, but, as Exhibit 2 shows, they offered a superior return over the period.

Exhibit 1: Annualized (Non-Compounded) Monthly Rates of Return
May 1990 (Inception of Brady Index) to
April 1997 (Salomon Brothers' Monthly ROR Data)

	Percentage
U.S.	8.533
Non-U.S.	10.917
WGBI	9.678
Brady	19.760

Exhibit 2: Standard Deviation of Monthly Rates of Return
May 1990 (Inception of Brady Index) to
April 1997 (Salomon Brothers' Monthly ROR Data)

	Percentage
U.S.	1.261
Non-U.S.	2.566
WGBI	1.752
Brady	4.063

Exhibit 3: Correlation Coefficients
May 1990 - April 1997

	U.S. Treasuries	World Gov't Bond Index	Non-Dollar WGBI	Brady Index
U.S. Treasuries	1.000	0.603	0.390	0.400
World Gov't Bond Index	0.603	1.000	0.966	0.025
Non-Dollar WGBI	0.390	0.966	1.000	−0.090
Brady Bond Index	0.400	0.025	−0.090	1.000

Is this comparison of emerging market bonds to those of industrialized countries valid? From one perspective it is. They are all government issues and, therefore, should carry the lowest yield among issuers in their respective countries. (On this, see the next section.) From a different perspective, though, the comparison may be inappropriate. Brady and most developing country Eurobonds are dollar denominated. Hence, they are not "government bonds" with respect to the currency in which they are denominated. Their substantial risk of default imposes a high risk premium on the bonds, much like high-yield corporate issues which must offer a yield in excess of that of the government bonds of the currency country. For this reason, a number of institutional investors — especially those who accessed the developing country bond market relatively early in its development — consider them a high-yield issue, belonging in the same class, so to speak, as high-yield corporate bonds. In fact, as spreads on high-yield corporates contracted during the 1990s, many investors looked to Brady bonds and other emerging market bonds as high-yield alternatives.

There is much to be said for this line of reasoning. Indeed, the sovereign risk analysis described in a later section is in many ways similar to that performed for corporate bonds. Yet there are good reasons to consider developing country bonds in a global government bond portfolio. When all is said and done, we are analyzing countries. The currency risk, the current account deficit, the ability to service debt from tax revenue, the inflation factor are all *macro*-economic concerns. Hence, many of the tools used to analyze bonds issued by foreign industrialized countries, properly amended, are useful for these bonds. Furthermore, a number of emerging market countries have graduated, or are expected to graduate, from developing to developed status. Finally, emerging market bonds "fit" into a global portfolio because they have low to negative correlation with non-dollar developed country bonds, as Exhibit 3 shows. This is an attractive attribute in an increasingly interrelated global financial market. Perhaps more surprising is that, despite their dollar denomination, Brady bonds have had a relatively low correlation with U.S. Treasury issues.

In short, developing country bonds present an excellent diversification tool, allowing an expansion of a global portfolio's "efficient frontier." This combination of high yield, potentially high rates of return, macro-economic/country choice, and diversification benefits points to emerging market bonds as an important ingredient to a well-rounded global portfolio.

EMERGING MARKET FIXED INCOME SECURITIES

There are four segments to the emerging debt market: bank loans, Eurobonds, local issues and Brady bonds.

A Brief History

Institutional investor interest in emerging market debt securities predates the creation of Brady bonds, although the Brady Plan and its resulting bonds certainly were the catalysts for their acceptance into the more traditional institutional portfolios. Low savings rates had forced many developing countries to look abroad for financing development and other projects intended to raise domestic living standards.

Capital was provided by official sources, such as governments and international agencies, and by commercial banks. The latter largely took the form of U.S. dollar-denominated loans, and were tied to a floating interest rate, usually LIBOR. When short-term interest rates surged during the early 1980s, debt service became very difficult. Coupled with the second "oil price shock" (most developing nations are petroleum importers) and recessions in industrialized countries which reduced their imports from the developing world, a number of debtor nations defaulted on their borrowings (the preferred term then was "moratorium").

The idea spread to more countries, until a veritable "LDC (less developed countries) debt crisis" was created. During the early stages of the crisis, the responses of bank lenders was similar to those applied to corporate defaults, that is, trying to work out the problem through maturity extensions, new money, and other traditional means. However, over time the situation deteriorated, affecting the creditworthiness of the banks themselves. Many major U.S. and some foreign commercial banks wrote off much of the value of these loans, and attempted to sell the remainder. Inter-bank trading of these loans therefore constituted the original primary market for distressed LDC debt. But since banks as a whole were trying to dispense of their remaining loans, prices remained depressed for a long time. Debt-equity swaps were successful to some extent, but their potential was limited. A number of non-bank investors entered the market at this time. However, these were typically speculators, as most of the loans were non-performing.

Bank Loans

The market for developing country loans still exists today, but primary trading activity has shifted to the Bradys and Eurobonds. Some of the original loans, though, are performing — Morocco, for example, has continually serviced its obligations. Those that are non-performing are sold with or without past due interest. Bank loans are offered to investors as assignments or by way of participations. The advent of the Brady Plan has created a new type of loan trading strategy — purchasing a non-performing loan in anticipation of it becoming "Bradied."

Eurobonds

Developing countries have issued (and defaulted) on their foreign bonds for at least 100 years. In the modern era, these countries' Eurobonds have had an excellent credit record, having been serviced even during the years of the bank LDC loan crisis and subsequent defaults. This may explain why yields on developing country Eurobonds are significantly lower than the same country's Brady issues.

Other possible reasons include the relatively small size of these obligations compared to bank debt and their resulting Brady issues), so that defaulting on them is much less economical, and the perceived need of having at least one unblemished market to access when necessary. But a more fundamental reason may be the nature of bonds relative to loans. The latter involve a small and relatively homogeneous group of creditors. A default leads to negotiations in which the health of the country is a concern to the creditors, since they likely wish to maintain a good relationship with the debtor, who may well provide more business in the future. Bondholders, by contrast, are a large, diverse group who, in the event of default, wish to recoup as much as possible *now* and have less to gain by working to preserve the long-run health of the debtor. In this respect, Brady bonds are more like Eurobonds, and deserve a narrower yield spread than loans.

Eurobonds are sold by the sovereign countries directly, by various government agencies as well as by state-run and large private corporate entities. The Eurobond market is the source of "new money" bond issues (as opposed to the Bradys which primarily repackage "old money.") Included in this category are Yankee bonds (developing country bonds issued in the U.S.) and the more recent global bonds (issued simultaneously in a number of world markets).

Local Issues

A number of developing countries have well-functioning and relatively liquid domestic debt markets. Because of historically high and variable inflation rates, these securities tend to be limited to money market maturities and, if longer in term, are denominated in dollars. U.S. and other foreign investors have increased their interest in and allocation to these assets in recent years (notwithstanding a net withdrawal of funds during the period surrounding the Mexican devaluation), becoming more comfortable with the credit as well as the currency risk inherent in them. Because of the currency factor, these bonds contain another layer of complexity, as will be explained later.

Brady Bonds

In the midst of the developing country debt crisis of the 1980s, various attempts were made at resolution, each ending in failure. Simply extending new loans did not go over well with the creditor banks, as they had tried that in the early years of the crises with counterproductive results. And the increased supply of loans only depressed prices further. International lending agencies also resisted providing new funds, as borrower countries did not meet mandated targets. The Brady Plan differed from previous approaches in a number of respects. It addressed the

underlying fundamental economic problems of the debtor countries (such as pro-
tected markets and controlled prices), which had generally not been done before.

With respect to the bank loans, the plan's innovation was to focus on
enhancing the value of *existing* loans rather than extension of new money. In some
cases the original loan amount was discounted. In others, the coupon was set at
below market rates. By effectively decreasing the supply of loans, these features
raised the value of the loans in the secondary market. By lowering the debt burden
of the borrowers, the risk premium was reduced, adding to the loan's value. And by
transforming the loans into bonds, their appeal to investors was enhanced.

Finally, for some of the bonds, U.S. Treasury zero-coupon securities
were purchased to serve as collateral for the principal payment. The result of all
this was the creation of a new market, that of Brady bonds. Most of the bonds are
U.S. dollar denominated, and a host of different payment features exist: fixed- and
floating-rate (and hybrids); partially collateralized and un-collateralized; bullet
and amortizing bonds. Brady bonds now command the lion's share of emerging
markets debt trading volume.

TOOLS OF ANALYSIS

Begin with a U.S. Treasury bond, of arbitrary maturity. Assume the bond is purchased on its coupon date and the investor has a 1-year horizon, which avoids
accrued interest calculations on both the purchase and sale dates, as well as reinvestment rates for the coupon payments. (The 1-year horizon assumption is
relaxed later, where the complications of reinvestment in the presence of potential
default is dealt with.) For simplicity, assume the full coupon is paid annually. Let

P = current price of bond
C = coupon
P^* = expected sale price of bond
ROR = expected rate of return

Then

$$P = \frac{C + P^*}{1 + ROR} \tag{1}$$

Solving for the expected rate of return,

$$ROR = C/P + (P^* - P)/P \tag{2}$$

The bond's rate of return equals its current yield plus any capital gain or
loss. We can use the familiar duration approximation to write:

$$ROR = cy - Dur \cdot \Delta y \tag{3}$$

where cy is the bond's current yield, y its yield to maturity, Dur its (modified)
duration and Δ denotes change.

Dollar-Denominated Brady or Eurobonds

How do equations (1) through (3) change for dollar-denominated emerging market bonds? Because there is no foreign-exchange risk, the structure of equations (1) and (2) are the same. Obviously, the current yield is higher, as the bond contains a hefty risk premium for possible default. In addition, the final term of equation (3) must explicitly incorporate the possible change in the risk premium and its effect on the bond's price on the horizon date. For this, we will use the following notation:

$$t \quad = \text{ yield of corresponding maturity Treasury bond}$$
$$r \quad = \text{ credit risk spread of emerging market bond}$$
$$Dur_t \; = \text{ Duration with respect to Treasury yield change}$$
$$Dur_r \; = \text{ Duration with respect to credit spread change}$$

Then equation (3) is modified to:

$$ROR = cy - Dur_t \cdot \Delta t - Dur_r \cdot \Delta r \qquad (4)$$

A change in Treasury yields will affect the bond's price, as will a shift in the risk premium the market applies to the bond. The two duration measures are not necessarily the same. If it is a fixed rate bond, then only if the bond is uncollateralized will the durations be equal. They will obviously differ if it is a floating-rate issue, but here, too, the measures depend on the existence of collateral.[1]

Clearly, understanding the determinants of the risk premium is crucial. The greater the risk of default, the higher the risk premium. What determines the market's assessment of a country's default risk? This is the central idea of sovereign risk, analysis of which is briefly summarized in the next subsection.

Sovereign Risk

Many measures, too numerous to mention, are relevant to assessing expected default for a developing economy.[2] An efficient approach is to compartmentalize these measures into three categories: structural, solvency and serviceability. In addition to making the analysis more manageable by removing redundancies, this categorization produces a "term structure" of expected default rates, akin to the well-known notion of term structure of interest rates.

Structural Factors

Measures classified as structural factors describe the long-term fundamental health of the country. These measures include economic variables such as reliance on a particular commodity for export earnings and the inflation experience of the country, welfare indicators such as per-capita GNP, and social/economic measures such as income distribution. More subjective factors are the perceived integrity of the country and its integration into the world economy. Structural variables are gener-

---

[1] For the actual durations, see Chapter 10.

[2] For a discussion of the approach by Standard & Poor's sovereign ratings, see Chapters 6 and 7.

ally not directly linked to default. But countries with poor such fundamentals are likely to develop economic problems that do bring on default. Further, given two countries with similar other variables, the one with the inferior structural measures will likely have a lower tolerance to adverse economic shocks and default earlier.

Solvency Factors

Compared to the longer-term structural variables, the solvency class contains intermediate-term measures of a country's health. (A loose analogy to an industrialized country's yield curve would be to put business cycle variables into the intermediate class and savings rate and productivity measures into the long term class.) In particular, solvency variables should reflect the country's ability, over time, to meet its central government debt obligations. Both internal and external debt are included, but debt denominated in foreign currency must be distinguished from own currency borrowing. In either case, we will see that a crucial element is whether the country's economy is growing at a rate in excess of the real cost of its borrowing.

Serviceability Factors

Serviceability factors are of short-term, if not immediate, concern. They reflect the country's foreign exchange reserve position relative to its obligations Despite good or improving fundamentals and strong solvency measures, a developing country may be forced into a liquidity type crisis if its reserves are deficient or likely to become so when a foreign debt payment is due.

The importance of these sovereign risk measures lies in the link between them and the probability of the country defaulting on its obligations. A deterioration in any of the factors raises the likelihood of default. Should a default occur, the investor's rate of return falls precipitously, with the precise ROR depending on the recovery value of the bonds. The appendix to this chapter presents a methodology for estimating expected rate of return over a long-term horizon for various recovery and reinvestment rates, as well as different default probabilities. Our concern here is with the effect of an increase in the likelihood of default on the bond's value, even if a default does not actually occur. In equation (4), this raises the value of the risk premium, r, reducing the rate of return according to the bond's credit spread duration. For example, suppose the outlook for inflation in a developing country worsens, although it is not yet reflected in current price trends, and the currency is little affected. Since this is a structural factor, it impacts the risk premium on the country's longer-term bonds more than its shorter maturity issues. On the other hand, a temporary decline in foreign exchange reserves will have a greater effect on shorter-term bonds, reducing their rates of return more than for longer-term securities.[3]

---

[3] This analysis relates default probability movements to changes in the credit risk premium, then the latter to its effect on the bond's price, hence its rate of return. In S. Dym, "Identifying and Measuring the Risks of Developing Country Bonds," *Journal of Portfolio Management* (Winter 1994), a methodology to go directly from implied default rates to bond price changes is presented.

Local Currency Issues

An investment in the local currency obligations of developing countries brings another variable into the analysis: foreign exchange rate movements. Here, equation (1) must be amended as follows:

$$P/e = \frac{(C + P^*)/(e^*)}{1 + ROR} \tag{5}$$

where e is the spot exchange rate of the local currency for one U.S. dollar, and e^* is its expected rate at the end of the 1-year holding period. The investment's rate of return then includes an additional term:

$$ROR = (C/P) + (P^* - P)/P - (e^* - e)/e \tag{6}$$

Exchange rate movements can profoundly affect rates of return. Looked at this way, there is nothing special about currency risk for emerging market bonds. But, in fact, there is.

Market participants need little reminding that developing country currencies can quickly lose much of their value. This type of risk — which we can call "wipe-out" risk — is essentially absent in industrialized countries' currencies. During stable periods, this risk is low, and a developing country's currency can behave and react to the fundamental variables in a manner qualitatively similar to that of an industrialized country. But when debt ratios, as modeled in a later section, rise to unsustainable levels, or a special event occurs — such as runaway inflation, a loan default, renouncement of a currency peg, or a coup — the wipe-out risk parameter takes over, overpowering any of the other fundamental variables until confidence is restored (or, in the extreme, a new currency regime is imposed).

Let w be the probability of this occurring by the end of the horizon. Then equation (6) needs to be modified to

$$P/e = \frac{(1 - w) \cdot (C + P^*)/e^*}{1 + ROR} \tag{7}$$

Examine equation (7) from the perspective of a *required ROR*. Notice what this does to the currency's *spot* value, e. Given an expectation for P^*, a higher wipe-out risk, w, must lower P/e, in order to generate the required *ROR*. P will fall, too, but the less developed the economy, the more likely is the risk to be translated into currency depreciation.

Responses to Shocks

Using the above analysis, it is easy to see that the effects of various economic shocks on developing country bonds may differ from their effects on industrialized country issues. Exhibit 4 summarizes a few examples. Notice how, for example, economic growth affects Brady and Eurobonds differently from domestic bonds of a developed country. The textbook response of greater economic activity is higher interest rates, as liquidity becomes tighter (unless offset by the central bank). But in the case of developing countries, because the country's economic condition is reflected in the credit spread, the yield on its dollar-denominated bonds actually falls, as the improving economic conditions reduce the probability of default.

In the next section we develop a more rigorous framework for analyzing the relationships between the various economic variables in Exhibit 4 and sovereign risk measures.

THE NEW BUDGET MATH

Budget math is not new. The relationships among a country's macro-economic variables and its debt burden are important for industrialized as well as developing countries. Indeed, recent years have witnessed a renewed interest in these calculations even for developed nations since they are a crucial element in considering a country's entry into the European Monetary Union. Therefore, we start the analysis by developing the budget math relevant to any country. Then we introduce a new variable — foreign debt — of paramount concern to developing countries, and show how this affects the analysis.

Review of "Standard" Budget Math

Some new notation is necessary. Let:

d = ratio of stock of government debt to *nominal* GDP
b = share of operational budget deficit in GDP
r = real interest rate on domestic government debt
g = real growth rate of economy

Exhibit 4: Responses of Securities to Various Economic Shocks

Economic shock	Industrialized country bond	Dollar-denominated Brady or Eurobond	Local currency emerging market bond
Faster growth	Yield rises; stronger currency unless inflation accelerates	Sovereign risk decreases as solvency improves; hence credit spread on borrowings narrows	Yield rises; currency strengthens
Higher inflation	Yield increases, currency *may* depreciate unless central bank tightens	Sovereign risk increases, hence credit spread widens	Yield increases currency depreciates
Global capital tightening	Yield rises, but degree depends on the country's global sensitivity	Underlying U.S. rate rises, credit spread increases as well as debt service costs rise	Same as dollar denominated bond
Trade deficit worsening	Yield may fall due to decline in economic activity; currency surely depreciates	Sovereign risk increases, raising credit spread	Yield increases; currency falls for both sovereign risk and trade reasons

Recognizing that the level of debt increases with the budget deficit plus the interest on outstanding debt, it is easily shown that:[4]

$$\Delta d = b + d \cdot (r - g) \tag{8}$$

Investors and international agencies worry if the d ratio is rising, as it implies instability — a solvency factor in our breakdown of sovereign risk. Thus, if r is greater than g, this suggests that in order to prevent d from rising, b should be negative (a budget surplus), or at least declining. Conversely, if g is greater than r, this means b can be positive, but with an upper limit. Of course, government spending can influence g. During a recession, for example, an increase in b may raise g, but d will be reduced only if the resulting impact on real interest rates is not larger than the increase in growth.

Highlighting Foreign Debt

When a government funds a substantial portion of its deficit abroad, as is the case with most developing countries that have large capital development needs together with low savings rates, its foreign debt must be explicitly recognized. Let:

d_f = ratio of dollar denominated government debt, valued in domestic currency, to GDP

r_f = real interest on U.S. debt

If we allow the dynamics of the currency to follow purchasing power parity, then we find:

$$\Delta d = b + d \cdot (r - g) + d_f \cdot (r_f - r) \tag{9}$$

Notice that r_f includes the risk premium paid by the country to foreign lenders. Increasing growth is still the best way to reduce the overall debt/GDP ratio. But if $r_f < r$, then accessing foreign markets reduces the ratio as well. However, increasing the foreign debt share to take advantage of this interest rate differential increases the country's exposure to foreign lenders, tending to raise the risk premium included in r_f. The next section relates foreign borrowing to the current account deficit.

Current Account Deficit and Foreign Debt Dynamics

Foreign borrowing is an important element in a government's overall debt/GDP ratio, as shown above, and hence a solvency factor in the country's sovereign risk. In addition, the foreign debt to GDP ratio is a serviceability factor. Whereas the previous section was concerned with *government* debt in both domestic and foreign form, here we examine the *total* stock of *foreign* debt. A deficit on the coun-

---

[4] The development of this relationship, as well as the two that follow in this section, is provided in S. Dym, "Budget Arithmetic for Developed and Developing Countries," unpublished paper.

try's foreign account increases its foreign indebtedness. If c is the ratio of the current account deficit to GDP, then it can be shown that:

$$\Delta d_f = c + d_f \cdot (r_f - g) \tag{10}$$

Higher growth can offset a rising current account deficit, as long as the country's foreign borrowing rate does not exceed the growth rate.

    We now have a basic understanding of sovereign risk. A change in this risk affects the bond's risk premium, in turn impacting its price via spread duration as shown above. A change in U.S. Treasury yields affects the bond's price via its Treasury duration. But it will also affect sovereign risk through its influence on the country's foreign debt service. The next section pulls all this together by looking at dynamic decision making for a truly global portfolio.

TRULY GLOBAL PORTFOLIO MANAGEMENT

A truly global fixed income portfolio — from a dollar-based investor's perspective — consists of U.S., foreign industrialized, and developing country debt instruments. With the tools above, the portfolio manager can make analytically sound global portfolio allocation decisions. A few examples are provided below.

Increase in U.S. Interest Rates

Suppose a portfolio manager expects an increase in U.S. interest rates more than implied by the yield curve. Obviously, this calls for a reduced exposure to U.S. bonds. Deciding which foreign industrialized countries to shift the portfolio's exposure to depends on the degree the foreign country's interest rates responds to the U.S. move, and on the effect of the new yield differential on the foreign currency, requiring a country by country analysis. Dollar-denominated emerging market bonds will, as a group, likely underperform (ignoring the foreign exchange effect on developed country bonds), as the higher U.S. rate is directly reflected in the bonds. But their risk spreads will likely widen as well, since debt service costs will rise. The degree of this effect depends on the foreign debt/GDP ratio, as developed above, and the maturity structure of this debt. Developing countries' own currency denominated bonds should be hurt as well, for the same reason as the foreign developed country bonds, plus this sovereign risk effect.

Global Capital Tightening

As summarized in Exhibit 4, a tightening of global capital will raise interest rates in industrialized countries, with the individual country effects dependent on the degree of global sensitivity present in the country's domestic capital markets.[5]

---

[5] Estimates for these global sensitivities can be found in S. Dym, "Global and Local Risk Components of Foreign Bonds," *Financial Analysts Journal* (March-April 1992).

U.S. rates will rise as well, according to its sensitivity, bringing developing country bonds down along with it. Here, though, it is not clear that Brady and Eurobonds will underperform industrialized country bonds, since in this case the latter are directly affected by the global shock, while the former's effect is via U.S. rates, plus a deterioration in their credit, depending on the country's reliance on foreign borrowing.

Flight to Quality

Clearly a movement by investors to higher quality issuers will force a major widening of developing country credit spreads. While these countries will suffer most, there will be some spillover to a handful of weaker developed nations. U.S. bonds will be affected the least; indeed, they may rally as global funds enter the country as a haven. This will help the Bradys and Eurobonds, given their dollar denomination. However, the net effect will be negative, as the risk spread widening will dominate the beneficial effect of the U.S. bond rally.

APPENDIX

RATE OF RETURN FORMULAE WITH VARYING DEFAULT AND RECOVERY RATES

An individual bond will either default or not. Hence the default rates discussed here are to be considered either in an expected value sense, or as a percentage of the portfolio of bonds that default. We will use the following notation in addition to those used in the text for rate of return:

$$def = \text{default rate}$$
$$R = \text{reinvestment rate}$$
$$Recov = \text{recovery rate in event of default}$$
$$h = \text{investor's horizon date}$$

Then the expected values of each period's cash flows are:

Event	Period 1	Probability	Period I	Probability	Horizon	Probability
pay	$C(1+R)^{h-1}$	$1-def$	$C(1+R)^{h-i}$	$(1-def)^i$	$C+P*$	$(1-def)^h$
default	$Recov(1+R)^{h-1}$	def	$Recov(1+R)^{h-i}$	$(1-def)^{i-1}def$	$Recov$	$(1-def)^{h-1}def$

Summing all the expected cash flows, we have the total expected proceeds on the horizon date:

$$\text{Proceeds} = (1-def)^h \cdot P* + [(1-def) \cdot C + def \cdot Recov]$$
$$\cdot [(1+R)^h - (1-def)^h]/(R+def)$$

Then, we calculate:

$$P = \frac{\text{Proceeds}}{(1 + ROR)^h}$$

The text distinguished among three general types of sovereign risk — serviceability, solvency, and structural, and suggested that they correspond to a term structure of default risk. The investor's horizon, h, may span all three of these periods, just two of them, or only one. Here we will deal with the most general case, that is, a horizon spanning all three periods. The near period lasts from today until year a, the intermediate period from year a to b, and the far period from b to h. Assume the associated default probabilities are def_1, def_2, and def_3. Further, allow the reinvestment and recovery rates to vary as well, with R_1, R_2, and R_3, and $Recov_1$, $Recov_2$, and $Recov_3$. Define the following functions:

$$F(def, Recov, R) = [C \cdot (1 - def) + Recov \cdot def] \cdot (1 + R)^h$$

$$G(def, R, s, t) = \left[\left(\frac{1 - def}{1 + R}\right)^s - \left(\frac{1 - def}{1 + R}\right)^t\right] / (R + def)$$

where s and t will take on the values 0, a, b,　or h.

Then the bond's total expected proceeds on the horizon date are:

$$\begin{aligned}
\text{Proceeds} = {} & F(def_1, Recov_1, R_1) \cdot G(def_1, R_1, 0, a) \\
& + F(def_2, Recov_2, R_2) \cdot G(def_2, R_2, a, b) \\
& + F(def_3, Recov^3, R_3) \cdot G(def_3, R_3, b, h) \\
& + (1 - def_1)^a \cdot (1 - def_2)^{b-a} \cdot (1 - def_3)^{h-b} \cdot Pe
\end{aligned}$$

For collateralized bonds, we need two more terms:

r = U.S. Treasury zero coupon spot rate relevant to the remaining maturity, m, of the collateral

f = Recovery value of bond on top of collateral value, taken as fraction of difference between face value and recovery value

Assume a flat Treasury spot curve, as well as a constant value for f along the three periods. Recognizing that

$$Recov_i = \frac{100}{(1 + r_i)^{m - i}}$$

and defining

$$H(def, f, r, R) = 100 \cdot def \cdot (1 - f) \cdot (1 + R)^h / (1 + r)^{m-1}$$

$$j(def, r, R, s, t) = \left(\left[\frac{(1-def)\cdot(1+r)}{1+R}\right]^s - \left[\frac{(1-def)\cdot(1+r)}{1+R}\right]^t\right) / \left(\frac{1+R}{1+r} - (1-def)\right)$$

$$K(def, f, R) = [C \cdot (1 - def) + f \cdot 100 \cdot def] \cdot (1 + R)^h$$

we find

$$
\begin{aligned}
\text{Proceeds} = {} & H(def_1, f_1, R_1, r_1) \cdot J(def_1, r_1, R_1, 0, a) \\
& + H(def_2, f_2, R_2, r_2) \cdot J(def_2, r_2, R_2, a, b) \\
& + H(def_3, f_3, R_3, r_3) \cdot J(def_3, r_3, R_3, b, h) \\
& + K(def_1, f_1, R_1) \cdot G(def_1, R_1, 0, a) \\
& + K(def_2, f_2, R_2) \cdot G(def_2, R_2, a, b) \\
& + K(def_3, f_3, R_3) \cdot G(def_3, R_3, b, h) \\
& + (1 - def_1)^a \cdot (1 - def_2)^{b-a} \cdot (1 - def_3)^{h-b \cdot Pe}
\end{aligned}
$$

and continue as above to calculate ROR.

Chapter 4

Local Fixed Income Instruments in Latin America

Marcelo Castro
Vice President
U.B.S. Securities

Efstathia Pilarinu, Ph.D.
Vice President
Bankers Trust Securities

INTRODUCTION

In this chapter we provide a description of the local fixed income securities available in some Latin American countries. The countries covered are the "big four" (Mexico, Argentina, Brazil, and Venezuela), Ecuador, and Peru. Our focus is on sovereign debt as it is the most developed sector in all countries. We discuss the types of instruments, the nature of the foreign exchange markets, and tax and custody issues.

MEXICO

The Mexican government issues a variety of fixed income instruments. *Cetes* and *Bondes* are peso denominated instruments, *Tesobonos* are dollar indexed and *Ajustabonos* are inflation indexed. Exhibit 1 summarizes the characteristics of these securities. Furthermore, there is an active repo market (reverse repurchase agreement) for these securities.

The peso exposure in these securities can be hedged through currency forward contracts called *Coberturas*. The Cobertura is financially equivalent to a currency forward, with the peculiarity that it locks into the spot peso rate instead the forward rate. Unlike a conventional forward, there is an initial cash outlay. At the onset of the Cobertura contract, the buyer pays a premium in pesos for each dollar covered, to have the right and the obligation to buy dollars and sell pesos at the "free official exchange rate," as calculated by the Bolsa Mexicana de Valores on the starting date. Coberturas are denominated in dollars, but are redeemed in pesos at the free official spot exchange rate prevailing two business days prior to liquidation of the contract. Local participants usually quote Coberturas up to a maturity of 1 year.

Exhibit 1: Description of Mexican Government Securities

Name	Tenor	Characteristics	Redemption	Placement
Cetes (Certificados de Tesoreria)	14 days - 2 years	Zero coupon bond	Bullet	Weekly auctions
Bondes (Bono de Desarrollo del Gobierno Federal)	1 - 2 years	Monthly pay/reset based on the maximum of 28 day Cetes rate and Pagares rate	Bullet	Extraordinary auctions
Tesobonos	28 days - 180 days	Peso denominated U.S. dollar-linked, zero coupon bond	Bullet	Extraordinary auctions
Ajustabonos (Bono Ajustable del Gobierno Federal)	3 - 5 years	Quarterly fixed coupon applied to the inflation adjusted face value	Inflation-adjusted	Extraordinary auctions

Source: Bankers Trust

Bankers acceptances are discount money market instruments issued by local banks for terms between 7 and 182 days. Bank promissory notes (*Pagares con rendimiento liquidable al vencimiento*) are notes issued by banks for terms between 1 day and 12 months with fixed interest rates. Corporations also issue commercial papers (*papel comercial*) for terms up to 91 days, at a discount.

There are no restrictions for foreign investors to invest in local fixed income government securities. Bank instruments are subject to a 15% withholding tax on the yield. This tax also applies to gains on Cobertura contracts, whose losses may not be used to offset other tax liabilities.

ARGENTINA

The Republic of Argentina issues *Letras de Tesoro* (LETEs) usually on a monthly basis. LETEs are discount securities denominated either in dollars or in Argentina pesos with tenors ranging from 3 months to 1 year. The Republic has also issued tranches of 1-year U.S. dollar coupon securities called *BONTEs*. There is also an active secondary market of other local bonds (see Exhibit 2) that were issued in order to restructure internal debt. For example, the "Pre" bonds were issued to restructure debt to pensioners.

The Argentina peso has been fixed to one U.S. dollar per peso under the convertibility plan implemented on April 19, 1991. However, there exists an over-the-counter Argentinean peso forward market which allows investors to either hedge convertibility risk or take a view on the sustainability of the convertibility system.

There are no restrictions for foreign investors to invest in local fixed income markets. Loans or instruments made to or issued by the Argentinean government are exempt from taxation.

Exhibit 2: Description of Argentina Government Securities

Name	Maturity	Characteristics	Redemption
BIC V	May 1, 2001	Peso denominated, pays weighted avg. cost of funds plus 0.9% per month premium	117 monthly payments of 0.85% starting Aug.1, 1991; final payment of 0.55% at maturity
BOTE 2	Sep. 1, 1997	USD denominated, pays 3-month LIBOR, quarterly	16 quarterly payments of 6% starting Sep 1, 1993; final payment of 4% at maturity
BOTE 10	Apr. 1, 2000	USD denominated, pays 3-month LIBOR, quarterly	29 monthly payments of 3.3% starting Jan 1, 1993; final payment of 4.3% at maturity
PRE 1	Apr. 1, 2001	Peso denominated, pays daily weighted avg. savings rate, monthly	47 monthly payments of 2.08% starting May 1, 1997; final payment of 2.24% at maturity
PRE 2	Apr. 1, 2001	USD denominated, pays 30-day LIBOR, monthly	47 monthly payments of 2.08% starting May 1, 1997; final payment of 2.24% at maturity
PRE 3	Sep. 1, 2002	Peso denominated, pays daily weighted avg. savings rate, monthly	47 monthly payments of 2.08% starting Oct 1, 1998; final payment of 2.24% at maturity
PRE 4	Sep. 1, 2002	USD denominated, pays 30-day LIBOR, monthly	47 monthly payments of 2.08% starting Oct 1, 1998; final payment of 2.24% at maturity
Bonex 87	Sep. 1, 1997	USD denominated, pays 6-month LIBOR, semiannually	8 annual payments of 12.5% starting Sep 7, 1990
Bonex 89	Dec.28, 1999	USD denominated, pays 6-month LIBOR, semiannually	8 annual payments of 12.5% starting Dec 28, 1992
PRO 1	Apr. 1, 2007	Peso denominated, pays daily weighted avg. savings rate, monthly	119 monthly payments of 2.08% starting Oct 1, 1998; final payment of 2.24% at maturity
PRO 2	Apr. 1, 2007	USD denominated, pays 30-day LIBOR, monthly	119 monthly payments of 2.08% starting Oct 1, 1998; final payment of 2.24% at maturity

BRAZIL

Brazil has undoubtedly the largest and most mature local fixed income market amongst the Latin American countries. Size, variety of issuers, variety of instruments, availability of hedging instruments, and electronic trading are all present in Brazilian local markets. The sole disadvantage are the capital controls that are imposed to foreigners. Exhibit 3 describes the characteristics of Central Bank securities and Exhibit 4 covers securities issued by the Treasury.

Privatization bonds have minimum maturity of 4 years, and maximum maturity of 30 years, usually originated from debt restructurings. Each bond has different cash flows. Some of them were issued by other government agencies aside from the Treasury, like OFND (National Development Fund Obligations), and CEF Mortgage Notes. Some are traded with a reasonable frequency, such as

Siderbrás debentures, SIBR910815, TDAEs, and SUNA950915. Others are quite illiquid, such as *Interbrás* debt, SUPR940901 and AGRO950816. To date, all the privatization securities have been issued with the face value adjusted either for inflation, currency depreciation, or the TR rate.[1] All securities are accepted (at face value plus accrued interest) as a means of payment in auctions to privatize government assets (privatization auctions). However, at each auction the government sets the percentage of the company price that may be paid with bonds. There is a wide range of Brazilian privatization securities. A detailed description of these securities and strategies involving them are beyond the scope of this chapter.

Exhibit 3: Description of Brazilian Securities Issued by the Central Bank

Name	Period	Characteristics	Redemption	Placement
BBC (Bônus do Banco Central)	28 days and longer	Zero coupon bond	Bullet	Weekly auctions
LBC (Letra do Banco Central)	6 - 30 months	Floaters off the average daily repo rate on government securities	Face value plus accrued interest	Extraordinary auctions
NBC-E (Nota do Banco Central)	3 - 18 months	Pays 6% per annum semi-annually	Face value linked to the R$/USD exchange rate	Extraordinary auctions

Exhibit 4: Description of Brazilian Securities Issued by the Treasury

Name	Period	Characteristics	Redemption	Placement
LTN (Letra do Tesouro Nacional)	28 days - 1 year	Zero coupon bond	Bullet	Monthly auctions
LFT (Letra Financeira do Tesouro)	6 - 30 months	Floaters off the average daily repo rate on government securities	Face plus accrued interest	Extraordinary auctions
NTN-B (Nota do Tesouro Nacional)	12 months or longer	6% p.a. on the adjusted face value	Inflation adjusted face value	Extraordinary auctions
NTN-C (Nota do Tesouro Nacional)	12 months or longer	6% p.a. semiannually on the adjusted face value	Inflation adjusted face value	Extraordinary auctions
NTN-D (Nota do Tesouro Nacional)	3 months - 24 months	6% p. a. semiannually	Face value is linked to the R$/USD exchange rate	Monthly auctions
NTN-H (Notas do Tesouro Nacional)	90 days - 1 year	Zero coupon bond	Face value is adjusted to the change of TR[*]	Monthly auctions

* The TR (i.e., reference rate) is an average of 30-day bank deposit rates, minus a spread that is determined by the Central Bank.

---

[1] The TR (i.e., reference rate) is an average of 30-day bank deposit rates, minus a spread that is determined by the Central Bank.

Both banks and corporations issue fixed income securities in Brazil. The main instrument of banks are CDBs (bank certificates). About 90% of the CDBs is fixed-rate paper, but they can also issue TR-linked or floating-rate paper. Corporations issue commercial paper and debentures. The former is usually a short-term instrument, whereas the latter bear characteristics of longer-term debt obligations. Debentures are particularly complex instruments. They often present interest rate optionality (e.g. paying the higher of inflation plus 12% and TR+15%), and many of them are convertible into the issuer's common stock. Credit aspects may vary since some may be junior debt and others may offer real assets or receivables as collateral. Finally, debentures may have call clauses, resetting features, redemption options allowed by the security holder, or additional remuneration linked to the performance of the company.

The *Bolsa de Mercadorias e Futuros* (BM&F) offers a wide range of hedge instruments. Some are extremely liquid, whereas others are barely traded. Yet, one can eventually find a few local participants that may quote the least liquid ones. The main BM&F contracts are listed in Exhibit 5. In addition to the BM&F, swaps can also be registered at the Cetip (see below).

Custody and Settlement Issues

Virtually all Brazilian bonds are traded through electronic systems. There are two main clearinghouses: the *Selic* (Special Clearance and Custody Service) and the *Cetip* (Center for Custody and Financial Settlement of Securities). The Selic handles all transactions related to the securities issued by the Treasury or the Central Bank (see Exhibits 3 and 4). Some bonds issued by states are also handled by the Selic, which controls foreign exchange transactions and bank reserves, as well. The Cetip handles all private sector securities, some state bonds, along with the privatization securities. Securities transactions are settled on the same day upon delivery, thus eliminating the credit risk of the counterparty.

Foreign Exchange Markets

Brazil has a dual exchange rate market. The *commercial rate* is reserved for imports and exports, foreign currency investments in Brazil, foreign currency loans to Brazilian residents, and certain other transactions involving remittances abroad that are subject to prior approval from the Brazilian monetary authorities. The *tourism exchange* market was developed initially for the tourism industry and was later expanded to allow certain other transactions where payment in foreign currency (both to and from Brazil) qualify for exchange on this market.

The key distinction between these markets is that, while both operate at floating rates freely negotiated between the parties, the commercial exchange market is restricted to transactions that require prior approval from the Brazilian monetary authorities, and the tourism exchange market is open to transactions that do not require prior approval from the Brazilian monetary authorities.[2]

---

[2] Free transcription of a legal opinion on the dual exchange rate market from Pinheiro Neto Advogados, a Brazilian local counsel.

Exhibit 5: Description of Brazilian BM&F Contracts

Contract	Description	Negotiation	Liquidity
Interest rates futures	Theoretical zero coupon bond maturing the 1st day of each month	Exchange traded	USD 5 on notional volume for the first 5 contracts
R$ futures	Forecast of the R$ at the end of each month	Exchange traded	USD 5 bn notional volume for the first 5 contracts
R$ Tourist rate futures	Forecast of the R$ tourist rate at the end of each month	Exchange traded	Little liquidity
USD interest rate futures	Forecast of the USD local interest, between the trade date and the 1st day of each month	Exchange traded	Little liquidity
Interest rate swaps	Fixed vs. floating local interest rate, net settlement in R$ at maturity	Over-the-counter, registered in the BM&F	Approximately USD 100 mm/day on 1 year swaps. More liquid on shorter tenors
Currency swaps	USD fixed rate vs. R$ floating rate, net settlement in R$ at maturity	Over-the-counter, registered in the BM&F	Approximately USD 100 mm/day on 1 year swaps. More liquid on shorter tenors
R$ Tourist rate swaps	USD fixed rate (as quoted in the tourist market) vs. R$ floating rate, net settlement in R$ at maturity	Over-the-counter, registered in the BM&F	Little liquidity
Options on interest futures	European options on interest futures, maturing on the first day of each month.	Exchange traded	Little liquidity
Options on R$/USD rate	European options on the R$ at the end of each month	Exchange traded	Call options trade approximately USD 40 mm/day on 3 months maturity
Options on R$/USD tourist rate	European options on the R$, as quoted in the tourist market, at the end of each month	Exchange traded	Little liquidity
Flex options	counterparties establish the characteristics of the option	Over-the-counter, registered in the BM&F	Little liquidity

Regulations for Foreign Investors

The Central Bank established several accounts restricting the access of foreign investors to local fixed income securities. Some of the accounts were structured as mutual funds. However, foreign investors are allowed to have discretionary control over the fund portfolio, as well as to be its sole shareholder.

Investments in local fixed income entail upfront taxes, income taxes, and portfolio restrictions. Such regulations have substantially changed, but regulators tend to observe two precepts: (1) barriers on the way in, not on the way out; and (2) although the local instruments are basically liquid and short term, the investment decision must bear a long term perspective. As of the first quarter of 1997, the funds that the Central Bank used to restrict capital flows are as follows:

Fixed Income Fund: This is an upfront tax (IOF) that has ranged from 3% to 9% on the initial investment. A 15% income tax is due on the earnings of each security, as expressed in local currency. The fund is allowed to purchase all types of fixed income securities,[3] as well as to trade derivatives.

Privatization Fund: IOF has ranged from 0% to 5% on the initial investment. A 15% income tax is due on the earnings of each security, as expressed in local currency. This fund can only purchase privatization securities.

Annex IV: IOF has ranged from 0% to 1%. Foreign investors can only purchase stocks and convertible debentures, issued after November 1, 1996. The latter are also subject to a 15% income tax. All foreign exchange transactions on the three accounts above are performed in the commercial exchange market.

CC5 account: IOF had been inapplicable until August 1995, when it was set 7%. A 15% income tax is due on the earnings of each security, as expressed in local currency. There are no portfolio restrictions. Foreign exchange transactions in the CC5 account must be executed in the tourist exchange market.

VENEZUELA

Subsequent to the establishment of a floating exchange rate system on the Venezuelan currency (Bolivar) on April 22, 1996, the Venezuelan Central Bank started issuing *Títulos de Estabilización Monetaria* (TEMs) as a tool for monetary policy. TEMs are coupon-bearing certificates denominated in Bolivars with maturities ranging from 27 days to 1 year. The coupon is paid at maturity and it is subject to a withholding tax (on the coupon only) which varies depending on whether the holder of the security is a local or a foreign entity.[4]

TEMs are auctioned weekly (every Wednesday) and the auction size has ranged from 50 billion to 200 billion Bolivars. TEMs are physical certificates and although settlement is two days, the issuance of the certificates has been consistently delayed by the Central Bank. The Central Bank also places paper based its on daily liquidity needs. These TEMs have been zero-coupon securities with tenors shorter than 90 days.

There is a possibility that TEMs, as a tool for monetary policy, may be phased out. The Ministry of Finance is expected to start issuing Treasury bills (which may replace the Central Bank instruments) as the debt settlement between the Central Bank and the government gets completed. (The expected date is the end of March 1997.)

---

[3] There are some portfolio restrictions regarding the concentration of the portfolio on some private sector securities.

[4] Based on regulations effective as of March 1997, the tax withheld for local entities is 4.95% and for foreigners it is 34%.

Foreign Exchange: Bolivar

The official fixed exchange rate was at 290 Bolivars per U.S. dollar prior to setting it to 500 Bolivars per U.S. dollar on April 22, 1996[5] and allowing it to float. The exchange rate appreciation during the first year of the free floating rate system (from April 22, 1996 to December 31, 1996) was 10% on an annualized basis.

On July 1, 1996 the Venezuelan government announced a band system whereby the Bolivar would be allowed to float within a band with a central tendency of 1.5% per month (starting from a level of 472 Bolivars) and a width of plus or minus 7.5%. The Central Bank does intervene frequently in the foreign exchange market in order to maintain a stable foreign exchange rate. Due to the significant amount of revenues from the government-owned oil industry, the Central Bank has been a major player in the foreign exchange market. On January 2, 1997 the Central Bank announced a change in the band system with a flatter slope of 1.32% per month and a starting level of 470 Bolivars.

ECUADOR

The Central Bank of Ecuador holds weekly auctions of zero-coupon Sucre denominated bonds called *Bonos de Estabilizacion Monetaria* (BEMs). The auctions are held at the Bolsa de Valores. Tenors for this paper range from 90 days to 1 year. BEMs are sold at a discount. The Ministry of Finance also issues Sucre-denominated zero coupon bonds called *Certificates of the Treasury* (CETEs). The tenors are up to 1 year, but the auctions are not regular.

The Ministry of Finance issues dollar bonds and Sucre-denominated but dollar indexed bonds to finance various projects. These bonds are called *Bonos del Estado*. For example, the Ecuadorian Ministry of Finance issued approximately $230 million face of dollar-denominated zero-coupon 1-year Bonos del Estado from March to July 1996. On October 1996, dollar-denominated coupon bearing Bonos del Estado with an average life of 2 years were issued. Finally, from April to July 1996, the Ministry also issued approximately $70 million (face) of 1-year zero-coupon Sucre-denominated but dollar indexed Bonos del Estado.

BEMs, CETEs, and Bonos del Estados all settle locally and the physical certificates require a local custodian. The auctions are conducted as follows. An average yield is calculated based upon all submitted bids above a minimum price. All bids below the average yield are filled at the average yield and all those above the average are filled at the bid level, up to the amount offered.

There is no tax withheld or any capital gains tax in Ecuador.

Foreign Exchange: Sucre

Ecuador has had a free floating exchange rate system. A band system was introduced on August 12, 1996 immediately after the inauguration of the government

---

[5] This exchange rate was set from the implicit Brady bond rate on the close of April 18, 1996.

of Abdala Bucaram. The band system had a central tendency with a slope of 18.5% per annum and a width of plus or minus 5%. The Central Bank intervened regularly to maintain a relatively stable currency within an interband region. On March 3, 1997 the new government of Alarcon changed the slope of the band to 21% per annum and shifted the center of the band from 3,663 to 3,800 Sucres. The government also announced that it will not maintain an interband system, but will intervene through regular bid, ask, and spread auctions in the foreign exchange market among market participants.

PERU

The only sovereign debt in Peru is the Central Bank Certificates of Deposit (CDs) denominated in New Soles. Tenors range from 4 to 12 weeks. The CDs are issued at par, and yields are quoted based on effective yield rather than nominal.[6] Dutch auctions are held twice a week (every Tuesday and Thursday). However, it is not unusual for the Central Bank to offer no CDs as part of managing liquidity in the financial system. The CDs are in book entry form and there is a one day settlement.

According to Peruvian legislation the tax treatment for foreign and local investors is exactly the same. There is no capital gains tax as long as the trade is done through the exchange.

Foreign Exchange: New Soles

The New Soles is a free floating currency. However, the Central Bank closely monitors the exchange rate through open market operations. The old currency was the Inti which was set to be equal to 1,000 (old) soles on February 1985. On July 1991 exchange controls were eliminated and the New Soles were introduced. It completely replaced the Inti and its value was set equal to one million Intis.

---

[6] For example, a 28-day CD trading at a 15% yield, has a price of $[(1 + 0.15)^{-(28/360)}] = 98.91\%$ instead of a price of $[1 + 0.15(28/360)] = 98.84\%$.

Chapter 5

Guide to the U.S. High-Yield Market for Corporate Emerging Market Issuers and Investors

Joseph C. Bencivenga
Managing Director
Bankers Trust

INTRODUCTION

For non-U.S. corporate issuers traditional sources of funding have been equity capital and restrictive senior bank debt. Medium- and long-term (7-10 years) subordinate debt has not been available. While a fledgling effort is underway in Europe, the only "liquid" market for this type of capital is the U.S. high-yield market. Non-U.S. corporate issuers can now benefit from the expanded investor universe. This market provides corporate issuers from Latin America, South East Asia, Eastern Europe, and other regions access to long-term, much less restrictive capital. Exhibit 1 shows selected emerging market corporate issuance in 1996.

The U.S. high-yield market developed as an extension of the investment-grade market. From both the U.S. high-yield market and the sovereign emerging market, demand for non-U.S. corporate issuers developed. U.S. high-yield investors began by investing in Brady bonds and sovereign loans in the 1980s. In the 1990s, fueled by historically low interest rates and dizzying equity valuations in the United States, traditional high-yield investors have broaden their portfolios to include non-U.S. corporates. Many U.S. high-yield mutual fund prospectuses now permit allocations of up to 20% of total assets in non-U.S. securities.

Interest in emerging market corporates was also aided by the availability of benchmarks. These comparable securities or loans help gauge appropriate risk versus return parameters. Once the appropriate benchmarks have been established, investment can more easily follow. With the growth in the emerging market over the last 10 years, many emerging market sovereign and corporate benchmarks now exist. Exhibit 2 shows several recent Latin American benchmark issues and a U.S. high-yield counterpart.

Exhibit 1: Selected Emerging Market Corporate Issuers in 1996

Pricing Date	Issuer	Country	Ratings	Size	Maturity	Issue Spread	Coupon (%)
16-Dec-96	TV Filme	Brazil	B2/B	140mm	15-Dec-04	+656	12.875
4-Dec-96	Banco Noroeste	Brazil	NA	50mm	17-Dec-04	+360	9.50
4-Dec-96	BCN	Brazil	NA	125mm	11-Dec-04	+375	9.50
27-Nov-96	Banco Itau via Cayman Branch	Cayman Isl.	NA	100mm	4-Dec-97	+130	7.00
26-Nov-96	YPF	Argentina	B1/BB–	300mm	18-Dec-01	+209	8.75
25-Nov-96	Banco America do Sul	Brazil	NA	55mm	3-Dec-99	+350	9.25
18-Nov-96	Petrobras Distribuidora SA	Brazil	NA	150mm	28-Nov-97	+200	7.50
8-Oct-96	Pemex	Mexico	BB/Ba2	300mm	29-Oct-99	+175	7.75
26-Sep-96	Acesita	Brazil	NR	150mm	15-Oct-04	+472	11.125
18-Sep-96	Comtel Brasileira	Brazil	NR	310mm	26-Sep-04	+395	10.75
9-Aug-96	IWC (Intlwireless)	Various EM	NR	100mm	15-Aug-01	+775	zero
22-Jul-96	Central Puerto	Argentina	NR	100mm	1-Aug-01	+414	10.72
15-Jul-96	Cemex	Mexico	B1/BB	300mm	15-Jul-00	+425	10.75
15-Jul-96	Cemex	Mexico	B1/BB	300mm	15-Jul-06	+587	12.75
1-Jul-96	Elevadores Atlas	Brazil	NR	75mm	11-Jul-04	+460	11.00
28-Jun-96	Bahia Sul	Brazil	NA	100mm	10-Jul-04	+417	10.625
18-Jun-96	Reliance	India	Baa3/BB+	100mm	24-Jun-16	+325	10.375
17-Jun-96	Reliance	India	Baa3/BB+	100mm	24-Jun-26	+245	9.375
29-May-96	Cibinong Int'l Finance	Indonesia	NR	150mm	5-Jun-03	+150	Float
15-May-96	Lojas Americanas	Brazil	NA	150mm	4-Jun-04	+450	11.000
9-May-96	Banco Bozano	Brazil	NA	75mm	23-May-04	+395	10.375
9-May-96	Ayala	Supra	NA	110mm	30-Nov-01	+173	8.125
26-Mar-96	Banco Rio De La Plata	Argentina	NA	200mm	27-Dec-96	NA	Zero
25-Mar-96	Banco De Galicia	Argentina	B1/BB–	200mm	15-Apr-99	+370	FRN
12-Mar-96	PT Matahari	Indonesia	BB	150mm	15-Mar-01	+520	11.250
5-Mar-96	Banco Safra S.A.	Brazil	B1/NR	100mm	26-Mar-04	+337	9.00
26-Feb-96	Telmex	Mexico	NR/Baa1	280mm	26-Mar-97	NA	L+62.5
30-Jan-96	Banco do Boston S.A.	Brazil	NA	110mm	2-Feb-04	+412	9.125

Source: Bankers Trust

Exhibit 2: Relative Value
Argentine Corporate Eurobond Issues

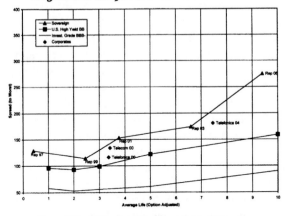

Brazilian Corporate Eurobond Issues

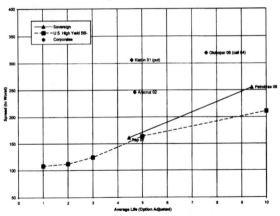

Mexican Corporate Eurobond Issues

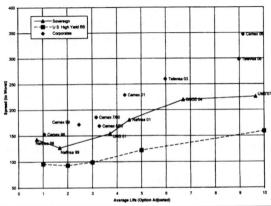

OVERVIEW OF THE U.S. HIGH-YIELD MARKET

High-yield bonds are corporate bonds rated below investment grade by either Moody's (below Baa3) or Standard & Poor's (below BBB-). Unrated securities are deemed to be high-yield if their spread over the comparable Treasury bond is substantially higher than that of its investment grade counterparts.

Markets for higher yielding instruments have existed in the United States since the 1890s when high-yield preferreds (yielding 400 basis points over governments at the time) were used to finance the expansion of the county's railroad system. The first high-yield corporate bonds were not new issues but were created from existing investment-grade bonds after the crash of 1929 and the following depression. The late 1960s and early 1970s set the stage for the modern high-yield bond market's growth as companies suffering from weak economic conditions and the increasing cost of floating-rate bank debt sought alternative financing. At the same time U.S. equity investors were looking for ways to improve their foundering returns.

New issue high-yield bonds emerged in the United States in the late 1970s. In the 1980s, the high-yield bond market gained prominence for its ability to supply large amounts of capital for both mid-sized company growth and large leveraged acquisitions. This period of unprecedented access to capital came to a close in 1990 due to the combination of a difficult regulatory environment, high historic debt levels, a recessionary environment, and negative press regarding the demise of Drexel Burnham.

The high-yield market has grown to approximately $300 billion in size. In the 1990s, the high-yield market has become an accepted and important source of capital. The single biggest change in the high-yield market since the 1980s has been the investors. The market has benefited greatly from broadening and maturing of its investor base. Investment by traditional investment-grade and equity buyers that now regularly purchase new issues is bolstered by the combination of low interest rates and rocketing equity markets. Exhibit 3 shows the change in ownership in the high-yield bonds from 1987 to 1997.

Traditional high-yield investors focus on industries they know best from a credit perspective and have positive investment success. Exhibit 4 shows the percentage of new issues by industries in 1995 and 1996. These areas are where high-yield portfolio managers and analysts have spent most of their time in 1995 and 1996. It is clear that while the U.S. high-yield market has financed many industries, the telecommunications and media sector has been by far the largest in recent years.

ADVANTAGES TO NON-U.S. CORPORATE ISSUERS

Traditional sources of corporate funding, equity capital, and senior bank debt are important but lack many vital attributes required for rapidly growing, medium- or large-size companies. The U.S. high-yield bond market provides a far more flexible source of capital. Through the U.S. high-yield bond market, these companies could obtain (1) medium- (5 year) and long-term (7-10 years) maturities; (2) less restrictive covenants; (3) access to U.S. dollar debt; (4) wide range of use of proceeds; (5) greater visibility in global capital markets; (6) increased institutional ownership; and, (7) an alternative to limited, highly unpredictable local equity and bank markets.

Exhibit 3: Ownership of High-Yield Bonds, 1987 and 1997

	1987	1997
Non-Investment Grade Mutual Funds	30%	47%
Insurance Companies	30	9
Money Managers/Pension Funds	15	23
Investment Grade and Equity Mutual Funds	NA	16
Foreign Investors	5	NA
Savings & Loans	8	NA
Retail	5	1
Corporations	3	NA
Securities Dealers	1	1
Hedge and Distressed Funds	NA	2
Other (including CBOs)	3	1
Total	100%	100%

Source: Bankers Trust and Joseph C. Bencivenga, "The High Yield Bond Market," Chapter 15 in Frank J. Fabozzi (ed.), *The Handbook of Fixed Income Securities: Fourth Edition* (Irwin Professional Publishing, New York, 1995).

Exhibit 4: Percentage of New Issues by Industry
1995

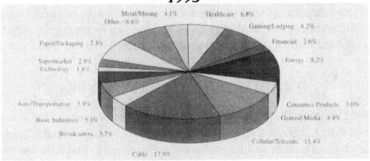

1996

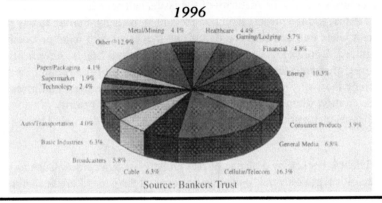

Source: Bankers Trust

High-yield debt is primarily (but not always) subordinated capital, with covenants that are generally less stringent than those included in bank debt, but often have more protection for investors than traditional investment-grade bonds. While the cost of subordinated debt is more costly than senior debt, subordinated debt often generates senior debt capacity and provides longer term capital, giving issuers the flexibility to grow.

An issuer in the U.S. high-yield bond market generates incremental interest by both debt analysts and equity buyers due to the visibility created by the road show process and ensuing debt offering. Often, debt buyers at large institutions encourage their equity colleagues to analyze a company's stock when they are recommending a purchase of that issuer's bonds.

Access to the U.S. high-yield bond market gives the company an alternative to local bank or equity markets. This enables the issuer to achieve both the most stable long-term capital structure and a low blended cost of capital. Due to the highly developed nature of the U.S. high-yield bond market, issuers enjoy a wide range of financing options. For example, bonds may be issued to finance mergers and acquisitions or provide a financial sponsor a way of taking out a dividend.

Because subordinated debt generally has the fewest restrictive covenants (while still providing protection for bondholders), it is the layer of debt in the capital structure closest to equity. To the advantage of the issuer, however, subordinated debt does not give away equity upside potential, but rather provides investors with a fixed rate of return in the form of interest payments or interest accretion. Subordinated debentures tend to be much less volatile than the underlying equity (in a public company) because of their senior position in the capital structure, but as with all fixed income instruments, prices are related to interest rate fluctuations.

TRADITIONAL SECURITY TYPES

High-yield securities have been issued in many different forms, from secured debt to high-yielding preferred stock. All corporate bonds share certain features. The promise of bond issuers and the rights of investors are set forth in the indenture. The indenture specifies the maturity of the issue, call schedule, coupon or dividend rate and dates, and the principal amount of due at maturity. Failure to pay principal or interest when due constitutes a default by the issuer, and legal proceedings can be instituted. Bondholders, as creditors in the United States, have a prior legal claim over preferred and common stockholders to a firm's income and assets. Bankruptcy laws vary widely from country to county so issuers and investor alike must use caution when analyzing non-U.S. securities. The priority of various traditional classes of securities differs, according to the terms discussed below.

Secured Debt

Secured debt is backed by a pledge of real property or other assets (such as stocks or other securities) as collateral to the investor beyond the general credit standing of the issuer. A typical example is a first-mortgage lien on the issuer's properties, which gives secured debt holders the right to liquidate those assets to satisfy unpaid claims.

Senior Debt

Senior debt is not secured by a pledge of real property or other assets, but does have first priority over the claims of other unsecured general creditors. Indentures for senior debt typically carry provisions limiting the total amount of the issuer's senior debt, as well as a negative pledge clause which provides that the debt will rank equally with any additional senior debt issued in the future. Issuers also may be restricted in their ability to pay dividends, repurchase stock, and may be required to maintain certain financial ratios and tests.

Senior Subordinated and Subordinated Debt

Senior subordinated and subordinated debt have a residual claim on the firm's income and assets, after the claims of secured and unsecured senior debt holders. Subordinated debt ranks after senior subordinated creditors in the capital structure. Indentures for these instruments normally specify that there can be no new ranking of debt between the senior and senior subordinated and the senior subordinated and the subordinated levels ("anti-layering") in order to preserve the priority of the various classes. The claims of junior subordinated debt come after the claims of all other subordinated debt.

Convertible Debt

Convertible debt provides investors the option to convert into a specified number of common shares of the issuing firm. Conversion terms are defined in the indenture. Investors can convert at any time during the life of the bond. However, convertibles are generally converted into common shares when the following two conditions apply: (1) common share price exceeds the conversion (or exercise price); and, (2) the issuer redeems the bonds, thereby forcing investors to choose between the redemption price and the conversion value. If the share price exceeds the conversion price, the investor will choose to convert. Convertible debt is mainly subordinated, placing it at the lowest priority in the capital structure. A company can issue a convertible into equity of a different company whose equity it owns.

Preferred Stock

Preferred stock is a hybrid security which can be viewed as debt or equity, depending on the specific terms. Preferred stock with mandatory redemption provisions will be viewed more as a debt instrument while perpetual straight preferred stock is closer to equity. Generally, preferred stock has priority only over the common shareholders. Preferred stock may be callable like its debt counterpart. Dividends are usually fixed, although they may increase at a specific rate; the dividend may also be cumulative. In the United States, preferred dividends are not tax deductible.

At the company's option, usually after a fixed period of time, exchangeable preferred stock can be exchanged into debt of the issuing firm, with similar terms. Convertible preferred stock can be exchanged for a specific amount of common stock in the issuing firm after a minimum time period.

HIGH-YIELD INNOVATIONS

Over time, new features have been introduced to high-yield securities which allow issuers greater flexibility in managing change. Some securities, such as increasing-rate notes (terms now normally found in bridge loans) originated to facilitate leveraged buyouts, whereas payment-in-kind and discount bonds were devised to provide issuers with additional flexibility to manage cash flow. Below is a summary of three common types of securities currently used by both U.S. and non-U.S. companies which tap the high-yield market.

Increasing-Rate Notes (Bridge Loans)

The increasing-rate note form of capital is mainly issued to provide bridge financing for leveraged buyouts and acquisitions. Created as senior loans and not securities, bridge loans have coupons which normally float over LIBOR and increase quarterly, at predetermined rates, usually 25 to 50 basis points. The final rate is normally capped and does not increase indefinitely. Typically, the increasing interest rate provides issuers with an incentive to refinance the bridge loan with more permanent bank debt or a bond. In some cases, warrants to acquire common stock are attached to the loan and take a predetermined amount of shares at specified future dates, if the loan remains outstanding.

Discount Bonds

Typically discount bonds can be either non-cash pay for life (e.g., a zero-coupon bond) or interest can accrete, like a zero-coupon bond, during the first three to five years, after which the bond pays a cash coupon generally equal to the accretion rate. Because the interest accretes, these bonds are issued at a discounted price calculated by using the stated coupon rate in effect the day the bond becomes cash pay. These securities help the issuer manage cash flow by minimizing cash interest payments during the accretion period. Discount bonds will generally trade cheaper (i.e., higher yields) than cash pay securities of equal seniority.

Pay-in-Kind Bonds and Preferreds

At the issuer's option, payment-in-kind and preferreds (PIKs) pay interest in either cash or in additional securities for one to five years. PIKs like discount bonds help the issuer manage cash flow by minimizing cash interest payments during the PIK period. Most often, PIKs will be deeply subordinated and most senior lenders view them as quasi-equity. Most PIK preferreds are exchangeable into PIK debentures, with similar terms, at the company's option. Calculating the true yield on a PIK security requires a modified discounted cash flow analysis if the security is trading at a discount or premium, because the realizable value of the additional payments is equal to the current market value of the underlying issue, not par. As a group, PIK bonds trade flat (i.e., without accrued interest). The price of a PIK is expected to reflect an amount representing accreted interest or dividends since the last payment. It is this and other market factors which sometimes cause PIKs to trade at even higher yields than discount securities of equal seniority.

DISCLOSURE REQUIREMENTS FOR ISSUERS

Most issues currently sold to high-yield investors are sold under SEC Rule 144a with registration rights. Therefore registration requirements must be met. First time non-U.S. issuers are typically unprepared for the disclosure requirements demanded by U.S. investors. These typically include, three to five years of audited historical financial statements prepared in accordance with U.S. generally accepted accounting principles (GAAP), a Management Discussion and Analysis section in the financials, and other disclosures. Financial statements must be sent to investors on a quarterly basis and audited financials sent at least annually. Investors also expect issuers to hold quarterly conference calls with board members to discuss earnings and demand a direct dialog with senior management. To a lesser degree, the U.S. investor will purchase 144a securities without registration rights. This route is often preferred by non-U.S. issuers because it requires the least amount of management time and it is less costly. In this case, the issuer can use existing local accounting and will not be subject to other SEC requirements. As the U.S. investor places a high value on liquidity, and is limited by charter as to the percentage of unregistered securities held, issues of this type tend to have higher coupons.

CONCLUSION

The U.S. high-yield investor is better able to analyze credit issues than political issues. However, ever since the Mexican peso crisis and the subsequent "Tequila Effect," high-yield analyst and portfolio managers have spent a great deal of time exploring the political side of investing outside the United States. This effort has spawned many investor trips and conferences on these foreign issuers as high-yield investors attempt to educate themselves. However, there remains significant challenges to overcome. In the meantime, the convergence of the U.S. high-yield market and the corporate emerging market is leading to increased cross-market, cross-border opportunities for both issuers and investors.

Chapter 6

Sovereign Credit Ratings: A Primer

David T. Beers
Managing Director
Sovereign Ratings Group
Standard & Poor's

Marie Cavanaugh
Director
Sovereign Ratings Group
Standard & Poor's

INTRODUCTION

Standard & Poor's sovereign credit ratings — which now cover local and foreign currency debt issued by governments in 69 countries and territories (see Exhibit 1) — are an assessment of each government's capacity and willingness to repay debt according to its terms. The agency's appraisal of the sovereign's overall creditworthiness is both quantitative and qualitative. The quantitative aspects of the analysis incorporate a number of measures of economic and financial performance as outlined below. The analysis is qualitative because of the importance of political and policy developments in the analytical process, and because Standard & Poor's ratings indicate future debt service capacity.

The agency divides the analytical framework into eight categories so that all important factors contributing to sovereign default are considered in turn (see Exhibit 2). Each category relates to two key aspects of credit risk — economic risk and political risk. Economic risk addresses the government's ability to repay its obligations on time and is a function of both quantitative and qualitative factors. Political risk addresses the sovereign's willingness to repay debt.

Willingness to pay is a qualitative issue distinguishing sovereigns from most other types of issuers. Partly because creditors have only limited legal redress, a government can default on some or all of its obligations for political reasons, even when it possesses the financial capacity for timely debt service. In

---

This chapter is adapted from an article with the same title that appeared in the April 16, 1997 issue of Standard & Poor's *CreditWeek*.

practice, of course, political and economic risks are related. A government that is unwilling to repay debt usually is pursuing economic policies that weaken its ability to do so. Willingness to pay, therefore, encompasses the range of economic and political factors influencing government policy.

Exhibit 1: Standard & Poor's Sovereign Long-Term Credit Ratings
Ratings are as of April 10, 1997

Issuer	Local Currency	Foreign Currency	Issuer	Local Currency	Foreign Currency
Austria	AAA	AAA	Indonesia	A+	BBB
France	AAA	AAA	Latvia	A−	BBB
Germany	AAA	AAA	China	N.R.	BBB
Japan	AAA	AAA	Qatar	N.R.	BBB
Liechtenstein	AAA	AAA			
Luxembourg	AAA	AAA	Colombia	A+	BBB−
Netherlands	AAA	AAA	Slovak Rep.	A	BBB−
Norway	AAA	AAA	Tunisia	A	BBB−
Singapore	AAA	AAA	Croatia	A−	BBB−
Switzerland	AAA	AAA	Egypt	A−	BBB−
United Kingdom	AAA	AAA	Greece	A−	BBB−
United States	AAA	AAA	Hungary	A−	BBB−
			Poland	A−	BBB−
Belgium	AAA	AA+	Oman	N.R.	BBB−
Canada	AAA	AA+			
Denmark	AAA	AA+	Philippines	A−	BB+
New Zealand	AAA	AA+	India	BBB+	BB+
Sweden	AAA	AA+	South Africa	BBB+	BB+
Taiwan	N.R.	AA+	Trinidad & Tobago	BBB+	BB+
Australia	AAA	AA	Uruguay	BBB	BB+
Finland	AAA	AA	Panama	BB+	BB+
Ireland	AAA	AA			
Italy	AAA	AA	El Salvador	BBB+	BB
Spain	AAA	AA	Mexico	BBB+	BB
Bermuda	N.R.	AA	Argentina	BBB−	BB
Portugal	AAA	AA−			
Cyprus	AA+	AA−	Jordan	BBB-	BB−
Korea	N.R.	AA−	Paraguay	BBB-	BB−
			Romania	BBB-	BB−
Iceland	AA+	A+	Kazakstan	BB+	BB−
Malaysia	AA+	A+	Brazil	BB+	BB−
Malta	AA+	A+	Lebanon	BB	BB−
Slovenia	AA	A	Russia	N.R.	BB−
Thailand	AA	A			
Hong Kong	A+	A	Dominican Republic	N.R.	B+
Czech Republic	N.R.	A	Pakistan	N.R.	B+
Chile	AA	A−	Turkey	N.R.	B
Israel	AA−	A−	Venezuela	N.R.	B

N.R.— Not rated.

Exhibit 2: Sovereign Ratings Methodology Profile

Political Risk
- Form of government and adaptability of political institutions
- Extent of popular participation
- Orderliness of leadership succession
- Degree of consensus on economic policy objectives
- Integration in global trade and financial system
- Internal and external security risks

Income and Economic Structure
- Living standards, income, and wealth distribution
- Market, non-market economy
- Resource endowments, degree of diversification

Economic Growth Prospects
- Size, composition of savings, and investment
- Rate, pattern of economic growth

Fiscal Flexibility
- General government operating and total budget balances
- Tax competitiveness and tax-raising flexibility
- Spending pressures

Public Debt Burden
- General government financial assets
- Public debt and interest burden
- Currency composition, structure of public debt
- Pension liabilities
- Contingent liabilities

Price Stability
- Trends in price inflation
- Rates of money and credit growth
- Exchange rate policy
- Degree of central bank autonomy

Balance of Payments Flexibility
- Impact on external accounts of fiscal and monetary policies
- Structure of the current account
- Composition of capital flows

External Debt and Liquidity
- Size and currency composition of public external debt
- Importance of banks and other public and private entities as contingent liabilities of the sovereign
- Maturity structure and debt service burden
- Debt service track record
- Level, composition of reserves and other public external assets

As part of the committee process Standard & Poor's uses to assign credit ratings, each government is ranked on a scale of one (representing the highest score) to five (the lowest) for each analytical category in relation to the universe of rated and unrated sovereigns. There is, however, no exact formula combining the scores to determine ratings. The analytical variables are interrelated, and the emphasis can change when, for example, differentiating the degree of credit risk between a sovereign's local and foreign currency debt.

Because the default frequency of sovereign local currency debt differs significantly from foreign currency debt, both types of debt are analyzed. The same political, social, and economic factors affect the government's ability and willingness to honor local and foreign currency debt, though in varying degrees. A sovereign government's ability and willingness to service local currency debt is supported by its taxing power and control of the domestic financial system, which gives it potentially unlimited access to local currency resources.

To service foreign currency debt, however, the sovereign also must secure foreign exchange, usually by purchasing it in the currency markets. This can be a binding constraint, as reflected in the higher frequency of foreign than local currency debt default.[1] The primary focus of Standard & Poor's local currency credit analysis is on the fiscal, monetary, and inflation outcomes of government policies that support or erode incentives for timely debt service. Standard & Poor's places more weight on the interaction between fiscal and monetary policies and the balance of payments, the impact of these policies on the growth of public external debt, and the degree of each country's integration in the global financial system, when assessing a sovereign's capacity and willingness to honor foreign currency debt.

LOCAL CURRENCY DEBT RATING FACTORS

Key economic and political risks Standard & Poor's considers when rating sovereign debt include:

- the stability of political institutions and degree of popular participation in the political process,
- income and economic structure,
- fiscal policy and budgetary flexibility,
- monetary policy and inflation pressures, and
- public debt burden and debt service track record.

These factors, more than any others, directly affect the ability and willingness of governments to ensure timely local currency debt service. Further, because fiscal and monetary policies ultimately influence a country's external balance sheet, they also affect the ability and willingness of governments to service foreign currency debt.

The stability and perceived legitimacy of a country's form of government are important considerations because they set the parameters for economic policy-making, including how quickly policy errors are identified and corrected. France's 'AAA' credit standing, for instance, in part reflects a democratic political framework that makes policy-making transparent and the response by government to policy errors predictable over time. Russia's political institutions, by contrast, constrain its 'BB–' foreign currency rating; the future evolution of economic policy clearly is less predictable.

A country's economic structure comes into play since the decentralized decision-making of a market economy, with legally enforceable property rights, is generally less prone to policy error, and more respectful of the interests of creditors, than one where the state dominates. If market reforms succeed in the transition economies of Central and Eastern Europe, the credit standing of their sovereigns could converge over time with those of Western Europe, North America, and Asia-Pacific, where market economies are well-entrenched.[2]

---

[1] See David T. Beers and Rashique Rahman, "Sovereign Defaults Decline Again in 1995," *CreditWeek* (June 12, 1996).

[2] See Chapter 6.

A government in a country with a growing standard of living, and income distributions regarded as broadly equitable, can more readily support high public debt levels, and withstand unexpected economic and political shocks, than can a government with a poor or stagnant economy. Yet a sovereign with a recent history of default generally must manage with lower levels of leverage to rebuild credibility than one that has maintained an unblemished debt record. The U.K., rated 'AAA', has a track record of honoring its obligations extending over centuries punctuated by war and financial distress. Argentina's ('BBB–' local currency and 'BB' foreign currency) ratings still reflect the legacy of many years of economic mismanagement, including default. Its credit standing, while improving, is not as strong as the U.K.'s even though the Argentine government now has less debt in relation to national income.

These factors, in turn, influence the conduct of fiscal and monetary policies, and their impact on future changes in the public debt burden. When evaluating fiscal policy, Standard & Poor's focuses on three interrelated issues:

- the purpose of public sector borrowing,
- its impact on the growth of public debt, and
- its implications for inflation.

Deficit financing can be an appropriate policy tool for any government. Public sector infrastructure projects, for example, are prudently financed by borrowing when they generate revenues — either directly or through enhanced tax collection — sufficient to cover future debt service. Malaysia ('AA+' local currency and 'A+' foreign currency) has transformed itself into a prosperous, manufacturing- and service-based economy over the past 35 years partly by astute investment in its public infrastructure.

More typically, governments borrow to finance combinations of consumption and investment that raise public debt. Still, analysis of public finance factors is complicated by the fact that the taxing and monetary powers unique to sovereigns permit them to manage widely varying debt levels over time. Depending on their political support, policy-makers can raise taxes to meet their obligations. But a growing tax burden can adversely affect the economy's growth prospects. Moreover, public opinion often favors the lowest possible tax burden — so much so that proposals to raise tax rates occasionally drive governments from office. Efforts to cut spending can be stymied by powerful interests that benefit from government programs. Absent a political consensus favoring conservative fiscal principles, sovereigns thus sometimes succumb to the temptation to print money owing to their monopoly over the currency and their control of the banking system.

INFLATION AND PUBLIC DEBT

Significant monetization of budget deficits fuels price inflation, which can undermine popular support for governments. As a result, policy-makers usually respond with measures to contain it. If they do not, and price increases accelerate, serious economic damage and an erosion of public trust in political institutions can result. Such conditions are fertile ground for a sovereign default. For these reasons, Standard & Poor's regards the rate of inflation as the single most important leading indicator of sovereign local currency credit trends. Inflation benchmarks, and their relationship to different local currency rating categories, are shown in Exhibit 3.

In evaluating price pressures in each country, Standard & Poor's considers their behavior in past economic cycles. The analysis is based in part on the level and maturity structure of the general government debt burden — total borrowings of central, regional, and local governments in relation to GDP — together with the likely extent of future borrowing. Off-balance-sheet, public sector pensions, and contingent liability items — such as banks and other enterprises — are scrutinized for their possible contribution to inflation. Related indicators include rates of money and credit expansion. Taking all these factors into account, Standard & Poor's makes a conservative assessment of average inflation over the next cycle.

In addition, Standard & Poor's looks at institutional factors affecting inflation. For instance, an autonomous central bank with a public mandate to ensure price stability can be a strong check on fiscal imbalances; less so a central bank tied closely to the government. Among industrial countries, 'AAA' rated Germany and the U.S. provide excellent examples of central banks where strong traditions of independence have evolved over the years. Similar examples among developing countries include the central banks of Chile ('AA' local currency and 'A–' foreign currency) and Israel ('AA–' local currency and 'A–' foreign currency). On the other hand, Mexico's credit standing ('BBB+' local currency and 'BB' foreign currency) does not particularly benefit from the Banco de Mexico's formal autonomy, given the federal government's continued influence over the institution.

The depth and breadth of a country's capital markets also can act as an important discipline. The sovereign has fewer incentives to default on local currency obligations when they are held by a broad cross-section of investors, rather than concentrated in the hands of local banks. For this reason, the establishment of mandatory, privately funded pension funds in a number of countries — such as Chile and Argentina — help bolster their credit standings by creating an influential new class of bondholders. The experience of many OECD countries suggests that even when public debt reaches high levels, creditworthiness can be sustained over long periods when policy-makers are responsive to constituencies with vested interests in safeguarding the value of money.

Exhibit 3: Sovereigns: Inflation Ranges

Local Currency Rating Category	Annual Inflation (%)
BB	25-100
BBB	10-50
A	7-25
AA	4-15
AAA	0-10

FOREIGN CURRENCY DEBT RATING FACTORS

The same economic and political factors that affect a sovereign's local currency credit standing also impact its ability and willingness to honor foreign currency debt — often to a greater degree because of the binding constraints the balance of payments can impose. As a result, Standard & Poor's analysis of foreign currency debt focuses on how government economic policies influence trends in the level of public external debt over time.

In addition, from a political risk perspective, the extent of each country's integration in the global trade and financial systems must be considered. A high degree of integration in the world economy generally gives the government strong incentives to meet its external obligations because of the correspondingly high political, as well as economic, costs of default.

Liberia (not rated), in default on its foreign currency bank loans since 1981, has struggled almost continuously in recent years with civil insurrection and the breakdown of effective administration — its political and economic links with the outside world are at a low ebb. 'AAA' rated Luxembourg, by contrast, is a small country highly integrated with Europe and the rest of the world. As a result, it has very strong incentives to play by the international financial rules of the game. All sovereigns fall somewhere between these two extremes in terms of their integration in the global economy.

At the same time, relations with neighboring countries must be examined with an eye for potential security risks. National security is a concern to the extent that military threats can place significant burdens on fiscal policy, reduce the flow of potential investment, and put the balance of payments under stress. As Iraq's invasion of Kuwait in 1990 demonstrated, the very existence of the sovereign itself can sometimes come into question. Lebanon ('BB' local currency and 'BB–' foreign currency) and Qatar ('BBB' foreign currency) are two examples of sovereigns whose credit standings are constrained by their vulnerable geopolitical positions.

BALANCE OF PAYMENTS FLEXIBILITY

Standard & Poor's balance of payments analysis focuses on the impact of economic policy on the external sector, as well as its structural characteristics. In the short run, the ability of policy-makers to manage financial pressures from abroad partly depends on the structure of merchandise trade, services, and transfers, and the like. Yet balance of payments pressures do not appear spontaneously, or reach large magnitudes, for structural reasons alone. In most cases, they can be traced back to flawed economic policies. Standard & Poor's approach reflects the premise that macro- and microeconomic policies discussed earlier affect balance of payments behavior.

For this reason, the size of a country's current account deficit, even when very large, may not by itself be an important rating consideration. The tendency for some countries to run current account surpluses, and others current account deficits, is well-documented historically. It is the product of many factors, not all of them negative, and not all related to government policies. 'AAA' rated Singapore ran very large current account deficits for much of its modern history, ones readily financed because they were not the by-product of fiscal mismanagement. However, as Mexico's debt servicing crisis in 1995 well illustrated, current account deficits are a concern when government policies result in a public external debt structure vulnerable to sudden changes in investor sentiment.

EXTERNAL FINANCIAL POSITION

Consequently, Standard & Poor's examines each sovereign's external balance sheet (assets and liabilities vis-à-vis nonresidents) alongside its analysis of balance of payments flows. The main focus is on trends in the public external debt position, the magnitude of contingent liabilities of the government, and the adequacy of foreign exchange reserves to service the country's external obligations. To complete the picture, Standard & Poor's calculates an international investment position. This is the broadest measure of a country's external financial position. It adds the value of the private sector's debt and equity liabilities to the public sector's external indebtedness denominated in local and foreign currencies.

Four important variables are:

• net public external debt,
• net external debt of financial institutions,
• net external debt of the nonbank private sector, and
• total debt service.

Public sector external debt includes nonresident holdings of the direct and guaranteed debt of the central government, obligations of regional and local governments, and the nonguaranteed debt of other public sector entities. Net public external debt equals total public sector debt minus public sector financial assets, including central bank reserves. Debt of subnational levels of government are analyzed, and consolidated with those of the national government, if legal and political circumstances expose the sovereign to internal and external financial risks from this source.

To evaluate the magnitude of public sector debt, Standard & Poor's compares it with annual flows of exports of goods and services (together with net public and private transfers where they are positive). For the 69 sovereigns with public ratings in April 1997, the median net public sector external debt-to-export ratio is 53%. Sovereigns with roughly this degree of leverage currently include New Zealand ('AAA' local currency and 'AA+' foreign currency), Israel, and Hungary ('A–' local currency and 'BBB–' foreign currency).

Other sectors' external debt also are measured in this way. Financial institutions' net debt equals their total external liabilities minus total external assets. Net debt of the nonfinancial private sector equals its external debt minus deposits and nonequity investments abroad. Debt of the private sector is examined because, in some circumstances, it can become a liability of the state.

Problems in the financial sector, in particular, can impair the sovereign's credit standing when there are official rescues of failing banks. Finland ('AAA' local currency and 'AA' foreign currency) and Sweden ('AAA' local currency and 'AA+' foreign currency) are sovereigns whose foreign currency ratings were downgraded earlier this decade partly because of the impact on their external debt of their rescuing banks. Currently, Hungary's banks weigh on the sovereign's credit standing — asset quality is weak and, in a worst-case scenario, may need to be offset by official financial support. By contrast, New Zealand's banking sector has little adverse impact on the sovereign's credit standing. Asset quality is generally sound and, importantly, the system's largest institutions are owned by creditworthy foreign banks.

Sovereign external debt also is evaluated in terms of its maturity profile, currency composition, and sensitivity to changing interest rates. Along with new borrowings, these factors influence the size of future interest and amortization payments. Debt service — including interest, scheduled amortization of long-term debt, and outstanding short-term debt — therefore is compared to projected exports. Debt contracted on concessionary terms to some extent can offset a high public debt burden. Russia, for instance, has high public debt of around 122% of exports in 1997. Yet, favorable terms on restructured foreign currency debt previously in default mean that its debt service ratio is relatively low at 22% of exports.

INTERNATIONAL LIQUIDITY

Central bank reserves are another external indicator, but one whose importance varies across the ratings spectrum. Reserves usually act as a financial buffer for the government during periods of balance of payments stress. They include foreign currency and gold holdings, with gold valued at market prices. Reserve adequacy is measured in relation to imports, as well as projected current account deficits and total debt service. Whether a given level of reserves is adequate is judged in relation to the government's financial and exchange rate policies and, consequently, the vulnerability of reserves to changes in trade and capital flows.

The U.S. maintains very low reserves, but can do so because the U.S. dollar generally has been floating against other major currencies since 1971. The dollar's unique status as the key currency financing global trade and investment also reduces the need for gold and foreign exchange. Most other high investment-grade sovereigns with floating currencies and little foreign currency debt require relatively modest reserves.

At lower rating levels, though, international liquidity is more critical when, as is often the case, most government debt is denominated in foreign currencies. Public finance setbacks and other economic or political shocks consequently can impair financial market access. Most Latin American sovereigns fall into this category, and many of them maintain above-average reserves as a result. Lebanon, which maintains reserves equal to nearly a year's worth of imports, is something of a special case. The economy's highly dollarized nature is closely related to the country's vulnerable geopolitical position, and this creates the need for an especially large financial cushion to maintain investor confidence.

LOCAL AND FOREIGN CURRENCY RATING DISTINCTIONS

Any divergence between a sovereign's local and foreign currency ratings reflects the distinctive credit risks of each type of debt. For example, long-standing political stability, and fiscal and monetary policies resulting in relatively low inflation, are characteristics of sovereign issuers of 'AAA' rated local currency debt. The manageable public sector external debt burdens of these issuers, and their high degree of international economic integration, in turn, result in foreign currency credit ratings at the upper end of the investment-grade spectrum.

Differences between local and foreign currency credit ratings can widen further down the ratings scale. Such sovereigns typically fall into one of two categories. The first category includes sovereigns that have long records of timely service on both local currency and foreign currency debt. Inflationary pressures are moderate, public finances are relatively sound, but foreign currency indebtedness may be relatively high or likely to become so over time. Sovereigns in the second category also have unblemished local currency debt servicing track records, but relatively recent histories of foreign currency default. The local currency and foreign currency debt ratings assigned to them often balance substantial improvements in inflation and public finances with the risks inherent to still-heavy foreign currency debt burdens.

At the lower end of the rating scale, however, such rating differences tend to narrow. Some sovereigns in this category have emerged from local and/or foreign currency debt default quite recently, and still carry the risk of policy reversals that can result in renewed default. Other sovereigns in this category may not have defaulted, but face high inflation and other forms of social and political stress that carry a material risk of local currency default after payment of foreign currency debt can no longer be assured.

Canada ('AAA' local currency and 'AA+' foreign currency) is a good example of a government shouldering general government debt burden on the order of 100% of GDP — well above the OECD country average — but where the political commitment to low or moderate rates of inflation seems well entrenched. Conversely, when public finances are weak and inflation is left unchecked, the stage can be set for an accelerating spiral that leads to default. Government-inspired indexation of debt and other contracts to price inflation often abets the process, as in the defaults of Brazil ('BB+' local currency and 'BB−' foreign currency) earlier this decade. But not all countries that have experimented with indexation suffer hyperinflation and default. Chile and Colombia ('A+' local currency and 'BBB−' foreign currency) are sovereigns with long records of timely local currency debt service. Conservative fiscal policies have bolstered their general credit standing in recent years by helping to unwind inflation and contain the external debt burden.

Ratings of EU states joining the European Monetary Union (EMU) present a special case. Governments entering the EMU, scheduled to be launched in 1999, will cede monetary and exchange rate responsibilities to the new European Central Bank. As a result, Standard & Poor's expects to rate each government's Euro and foreign currency debt the same going forward. Fiscal analysis, important in the past, will be the main criterion for differentiating credit quality of sovereigns inside the EMU.[3]

SOVEREIGN RATING CHANGES

Until relatively recently, the sovereign sector was an exclusive club of the world's most creditworthy governments. In 1981, Standard & Poor's rated debt of just 14 sovereigns — all at the 'AAA' level. Rating downgrades were relatively rare over the remainder of that decade and when they occurred, usually they were modest. Today, the rated sovereign sector is far larger and more heterogeneous. The 69 sovereigns Standard & Poor's monitors carry ratings between 'AAA' and 'B.' Given this range of credit quality, rating changes occur more frequently.

Current economic and financial indicators alone do not determine ratings. Sovereign ratings measure future debt service capacity, and the future, of course, is uncertain. As a result, Standard & Poor's sovereign rating committees consider reasonable "worst-case" scenarios over a three- to five-year time horizon to gain a better understanding of future downside risks. The government's medium-term financial program, when available, is scrutinized alongside independent forecasts. The agency then looks at the interaction between public finances, external debt, and other variables, such as real export growth and changes in overseas interest rates.

Rating changes occur when new information significantly alters Standard & Poor's view of likely future developments. (Analysts generally meet with government officials at least once annually, but the timing of on-site meetings itself is not a factor determining when Standard & Poor's raises or lowers ratings.) For example, New Zealand's foreign currency rating was upgraded to 'AA+' from 'AA' in January 1996 in light of the substantial budget surpluses projected for the remainder of the decade. The Philippines' local and foreign currency ratings were upgraded to 'A−' and 'BB+', respectively, in February 1997, reflecting declining fiscal deficits, stronger exports, and improving inflation prospects. By contrast, Turkey's 'B+' foreign

---

[3] See David T. Beers, "Stronger-Rated Sovereigns Will Lead the Way Into EMU," *CreditWeek* (November 13, 1996).

currency rating was placed on CreditWatch with negative implications in July 1996, and downgraded to 'B' the following December — these actions resulted from the government's inability to stem rising fiscal and external debt service pressures.

As these examples illustrate, the impact of public finances on external debt usually is a key factor driving changes in foreign currency credit ratings. Similarly, significant changes in the inflation outlook figure in local currency rating changes. However, the implications of rating changes can vary across the credit spectrum. Fiscal pressures were behind the loss of New Zealand's 'AAA' foreign currency rating in 1983, and subsequent downgrades to 'AA−' through 1991. Still, the erosion in its credit quality was neither sudden nor very great. This reflects an important characteristic of most high investment-grade sovereigns, namely their ability to correct financial imbalances, and even to bounce back in credit terms over time.

Turkey, however, may tell a somewhat different story. Its credit standing has fallen sharply since it was first assigned a 'BBB' foreign currency rating in May 1992. There still are few signs that a political consensus is forming that will spur policy makers to tackle the country's fiscal problems decisively. Often in such cases, one or more financial crises may be required to break the political impasse and ward off default.

SOVEREIGN RATINGS AND CORPORATE CREDIT RISK

Sovereign credit risk is always a key consideration in the assessment of the credit standing of banks and corporates. Sovereign risk comes into play because the unique, wide-ranging powers and resources of each national government affect the financial and operating environments of entities under its jurisdiction. Past experience has shown time and again that defaults by otherwise creditworthy borrowers can stem directly from a sovereign default.

In the case of foreign currency debt, the sovereign has first claim on available foreign exchange, and it controls the ability of any resident to obtain funds to repay creditors. To service debt denominated in local currency, the sovereign can exercise its powers to tax, to control the domestic financial system, and even to issue local currency in potentially unlimited amounts. Given these considerations, the credit ratings of non-sovereign borrowers most often are at, or below, the ratings of the relevant sovereign. When obligations of issuers are rated higher than the sovereign's, this reflects their stand-alone credit characteristics and other factors mitigating sovereign credit risk.[4]

---

[4] See William Chambers, "Understanding Sovereign Risk," *CreditWeek* (January 1, 1997).

Chapter 7

Rating the Transition Economies

Helena Hessel
Director
Sovereign Ratings Group
Standard & Poor's

INTRODUCTION

The 26 former Communist countries now have several years of transition experience. The process began in the Central and East European countries in 1989-1991 and in the Baltics and the Commonwealth of Independent States (CIS) in 1992. The dramatic reforms that have been implemented in some of these countries created new economic institutions and infrastructure which, in turn, have laid the foundations for pluralistic, democratic societies and functioning market economies.

The more successful transition countries are increasingly entering the international capital markets. Standard & Poor's currently rates 11 of these countries, and the ratings of several others are expected in the near future. Reflecting the diverse initial economic and political conditions, as well as differences in the pace and nature of the reforms, Standard & Poor's foreign currency ratings vary markedly among the transition economies, ranging from relatively high investment-grade ratings of 'A' for the Czech Republic and Slovenia to speculative-grade ratings of 'BB−' for Romania, the Russian Federation, and Kazakstan (see Exhibit 1).

ASSESSING CREDIT RISK IN TRANSITION ECONOMIES

Standard & Poor's criteria for rating transition economies follow the general sovereign rating methodology described in Chapter 6. The distinct political and economic legacy of these economies, however, calls for a somewhat tailored approach. Credit analysis of transition economies puts particular emphasis on four issues.

This chapter is adapted from an article with the same title that appeared in the February 19, 1997 issue of Standard & Poor's *CreditWeek*.

Exhibit 1: Transition Economies: Rated Sovereigns

Country	Ratings FC	LC	First Rated — First FC Rating
Hungary	BBB–	A–	February 1992 — BB+ Positive
Czech Republic	A	N.R.	July 1993 — BBB Positive
Slovak Republic	BBB–	A	November 1994 — BB– Stable
Poland	BBB–	A–	June 1995 — BB Positive
Romania	BB–	BBB–	February 1996 — BB– Stable
Slovenia	A	AA	May 1996 — A Stable
Russia	BB–	N.R.	October 1996 — BB– Stable
Kazakstan	BB–	BB+	November 1996 — BB– Stable
Latvia	BBB	A–	January 1997 — BBB Stable
Croatia	BBB–	A–	January 1997 — BBB– Stable
Lithuania	BBB–	BBB+	June 1997 — BBB– Stable

FC = Foreign currency; LC = Local currency; N.R. = not rated

1. *Progress on the creation of a democratic political system.* This encompasses the effectiveness and robustness of democratic political institutions; the transparency and cohesiveness of the political decision-making process; and the political commitment to economic reform and the ability to implement it.

2. *Progress on achieving financial stability and economic growth.* This includes the effectiveness of fiscal/monetary and exchange policies in maintaining low inflation and interest rates and a stable convertible exchange rate.

3. *Progress on transition from a planned to a market economy.* The following factors are of particular interest:

   • *The role of the private sector in the economy.* To examine this, Standard & Poor's looks at progress in privatization of the existing state sector; private enterprise start-ups; the extent of enterprise restructuring; the effectiveness of corporate governance, and the evolution of general social attitudes toward tax and payment discipline.

   • *Liberalization of economic activity.* This comprises price liberalization; opening up to and easing entry for new domestic and foreign enterprises; and opening up to and easing foreign trade and foreign investment activity.

   • *Soundness of the financial sector.* This includes the development of the banking sector and its regulatory framework; progress on financial intermediation; and the development of securities markets and nonbank financial institutions.

   • *Development of market institutions.* This includes development of effective institutional and legal infrastructure, as well as implementation of practices conducive to the functioning of markets, including property rights legislation, bankruptcy laws, contractual laws, collateral laws, etc.

4. *Reorientation of trade from East to West.* This is shown in the pattern of growth and the composition of exports and imports and their sustainability over time; participation and/or association in international economic and trade organizations; the role of foreign direct investment as a source of finance, management, and technology transfer, and improved corporate governance.

MAJOR CREDIT CHALLENGES

The credit challenges facing transition countries are numerous and, often, not easily discernible. First, although political liberalization and a democratic institutional framework have come quickly in most of these countries, other essential political reform elements require more time. Creating and sustaining a democratic process, allowing democratic values to mature, and modernizing administrative and legal infrastructure are critical for sustained economic and political stability, especially when vast political liberalization is combined with enormous equity shifts.

Second, liberalization of economic activity in the transition economies must be accompanied by tough stabilization policies. Sound fiscal and monetary stabilization efforts, which have been critical in controlling inflation in many of these countries, are important determinants of credit quality. The experience of transition economies indicates that the faster inflation is contained, the sooner growth recovers. In addition, popular support for government policies has often come as a result of monetary stability rather than from any inherent confidence in liberalized market activities (Russia is perhaps the best example).

Third, although privatization is necessary for the transition to a market system, it is by no means sufficient for meaningful restructuring of enterprises that antedate the reforms. The ability of newly privatized industries to withstand competitive pressures in unprotected markets, which is indicative of such restructuring, still remains difficult to assess in many countries of the region.

Effective operational and portfolio restructuring of enterprises requires not only time, but also significant resources, and obtaining these resources may necessitate a shift of corporate power in many privatized enterprises away from "insiders." Changes in corporate governance structures, however, are necessarily political in nature and invariably involve development of formal institutional arrangements, such as capital markets, regulatory agencies, effective judiciary, etc.

Fourth, the transition to a market economy must also be accompanied by the transformation of the public sector and its role in the economy. Extensive fiscal decentralization now under way in many transition countries is the key dimension of this transformation. Public sector spending in all transition economies has had to be significantly reduced, and the new local governments have created institutional capacities assuring their fiscal accountability.

In most transition economies, social and support programs — pensions systems in particular — continue to consume a very large share of government budgets. The need to rationalize these programs is commonly recognized; yet, this is not only challenging economically but also potentially explosive politically, and even the earliest reformers have postponed most of the painful decisions.

Fifth, the financial sector remains a problem area throughout the transition economies, and tends to constrain many ratings. Large bank failures are occurring in the 'A' rated Czech Republic as well as in 'BB–' rated Russia and 'BBB' rated Latvia. In most of these countries, macroeconomic shocks, lack of experience in credit appraisal, mushrooming of smaller new banks, and inadequate banking supervision have resulted in large stocks of nonperforming loans. Bankruptcies in the banking sector can seriously undermine public confidence, and how countries handle the banking sector has a direct impact on the amount of their public debt and, thus, on their sovereign credit quality.

Finally, the evolution of institutional, legal, and regulatory environments is markedly different across various countries, and Standard & Poor's ratings reflect these differences. Even among the most advanced and highly rated countries, weaknesses persist in critical areas, such as property rights (especially with respect to tenancy), contract enforcement, bankruptcy and liquidation procedures, the depth of capital markets, securities regulation, and competition policies. Capital markets lack liquidity and tend therefore to be volatile.

Even though the transition economies have undergone unprecedented changes over the past seven or so years, many formidable tasks remain. However, the systemic changes that have taken place largely seem irreversible in all countries rated by Standard & Poor's. The political comeback of parties descendent from former Communist elite, which has occurred in a number of countries (Poland and Hungary, for example), has not materially undermined the general direction of the ongoing transformation (although it might have slowed down some reforms, particularly privatization of large state enterprises, in individual countries). This is not to say, however, that some temporary and/or partial reversals, such as reintroduction of some price or exchange controls, trade restrictions or similar measures, can be completely ruled out in some distress situations. Indeed, among rated countries, Romania constrained currency convertibility in 1996, while unrated Bulgaria reintroduced some price controls.

INVESTMENT-GRADE COUNTRIES

The eight countries rated investment grade by Standard & Poor's have reached what the European Bank for Reconstruction and Development (EBRD) calls "advanced stages of transition." (Estonia is the other country so classified, but is not yet rated by Standard & Poor's.) In all of these countries, political democracy is well-established, as demonstrated by orderly parliamentary and presidential elections and orderly changes of government when needed. By and large, a solid policy consensus has been reached on major aspects of transition.

Still, "political risk" differs significantly among these countries. Croatia's and Slovakia's ratings are most constrained by political factors. In Croatia, further stabilization of the geopolitical situation — consolidating the peace with Yugoslavia and supporting lasting peace in Bosnia — is required to improve credit quality. Also, the country's record of creating and sustaining a more open and pluralistic society has been relatively short and untested by key elections.

Slovakia's progress in transforming itself into an open democratic political system has been more painful and questionable than that of most other countries in the group. Indeed, Slovakia provides a good example of a situation in which the democratic values and culture of the governing elite lag the establishment of democratic infrastructure. As a result, Slovakia's attractiveness to foreign investors suffers.

By contrast, the Czech's Republic's political scene has been the most cohesive, stable, and conducive to financial stability and reforms among the transition economies, even if it has recently showed signs of strain which led to attacks on its currency.

ECONOMIC REFORM AND PRIVATIZATION

In all seven investment grade-rated countries, prices are free (except for utilities, transport, and housing), and foreign trade is mostly liberalized. Small-scale enterprises have been fully privatized. Privatization of large enterprises, however, shows pronounced differences among the rated countries. In Croatia, Slovenia, Latvia, and Poland, large-scale privatization has lagged other reforms. In Croatia and Slovenia, the delays reflect mainly the former social (as opposed to state) ownership of these enterprises; in Poland, politically sensitive privatization has been particularly susceptible to frequent changes in government.

However, Poland, along with the Czech Republic and Slovenia, are the most advanced in the broader sense of privatization, namely easing the market entry of new entrepreneurial activities and investment; ensuring a climate of competition; and opening up the economy. Indeed, with the rapid growth of private small and mid-sized businesses in all of these countries, gross domestic output (GDP) is now generated mostly by the private sector. Private sector's share of GDP as of year-end 1996 ranged from a high of 75%-80% in the Czech Republic to a low of 45%-50% in Slovenia (see Exhibit 2).

INFLATION AND GROWTH

In the Czech Republic, Slovenia, Slovakia, and more recently, Croatia, the private sector has benefited from low single-digit inflation, minimal general government deficits (or even surpluses), and relatively stable exchange rates. As a result, growth has been strong from 1994 to 1996 in the first three countries, and recovered solidly in Croatia in 1996 (see Exhibit 3).

Exhibit 2: Private Sector Share of GDP 1996

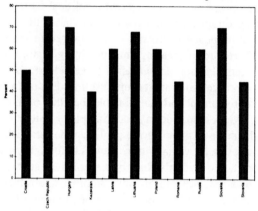

Exhibit 3: Consumer Price Inflation
Average Inflation

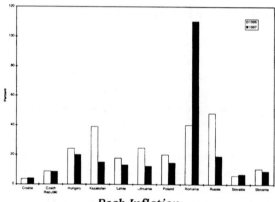

Peak Inflation

Exhibit 4: Real GDP Growth

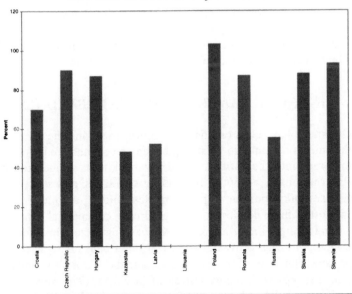

1996 GDP as a Percent of 1989 Levels

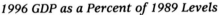

The most impressive recovery record belongs to Poland. Recovery there started earlier (1992), and Poland is the only transition economy with current real GDP higher than that of the pre-transition period — the estimated 1996 level of real GDP is 104% of the 1989 level. (See Exhibit 4.)

Poland's 1996 average inflation of about 20% is higher, however, than that of all other countries in the group except for Hungary. Persistent high inflation reflects insufficient relative price adjustment, inappropriate indexation of pensions, low financial intermediation, as well as inertia. The share of broad money to GDP is less than 40%, compared to 90% and 77% in the Czech and Slovak Republics, respectively. This translates into a lower tolerance for fiscally induced money creation; a given increase in base money as a percentage of GDP, is more inflationary in Poland than in the Czech Republic. As a result, fiscal prudence is needed all the more, and although Poland has succeeded in containing its general government deficits, it has been unable to cut them significantly below 3%.

Hungary provides a good illustration of the importance of financial stabilization. It has led all transition countries in establishing the role of the private sector, introducing competitive and open markets, and supporting evolution of market institutions. As a result, it is well ahead of other countries in attracting foreign investment. Still, its long-postponed social program adjustments, combined with banking sector bailouts, have reversed its growth, inflation, and balance-of-payments record. The situation improved in 1996, however, and Hungary was upgraded to investment grade in late 1996.

In all transition economies, enterprise restructuring has taken time, although significant cuts in subsidies to enterprises have been an important indicator of progress. Replacing and upgrading capital stock have begun more recently, with a marked recovery of investment in many countries, most notably in Poland, the Czech and Slovak Republics, and Slovenia. The high level of foreign direct investment in Hungary and the Czech Republic — and more recently in Poland — is an important source of both financing and modernization of these economies (see Exhibit 5).

FINANCIAL MARKETS AND INDEBTEDNESS

Financial markets have been broadened and deepened, and the legal and regulatory environments continue to be strengthened and rationalized. Specifically, all investment grade-rated countries adopted new banking laws and prudential regulations, internationally accepted accounting standards, and stricter disclosure requirements. Banks continue to play a modest role as providers of investment finance in most of these countries, although private commercial banks have come to play an increasingly important role in the banking sectors in Hungary, Poland, the Czech Republic, and Slovakia. Privatization of banks is lagging well behind overall privatization in all of these countries, and the sector's risk remains high in all of them, perhaps with the exception of Slovenia. (The most severe recent banking crisis occurred in Latvia and Lithuania in 1995, while a relatively large local bank failed in 1996 in the Czech Republic.)

To finance restructuring of their obsolete industrial sector, transition economies need to import capital and are, therefore, expected to run current account deficits. The size of the deficit is not a concern for Standard & Poor's as long as the imports are mainly capital goods bought by the private sector and financed mostly through direct investment.

Exhibit 5: Foreign Direct Investment
Percent of 1996 GDP

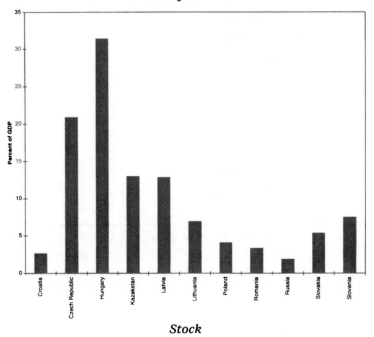

Stock

Exhibit 6: Per Capita GDP 1996 (U.S. Dollars)

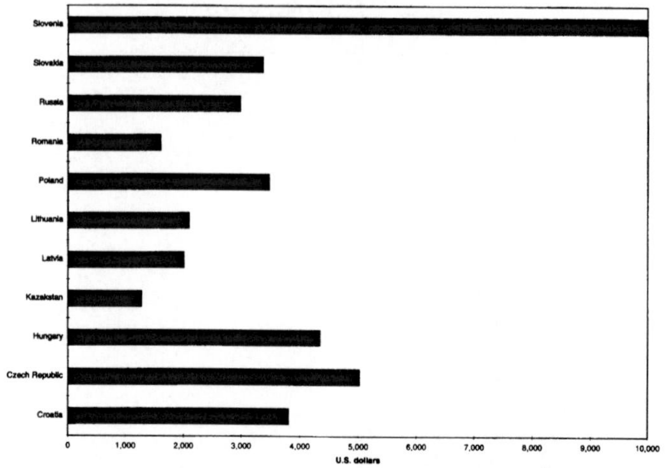

The internal and external indebtedness of the rated countries differ enormously, reflecting inherited foreign debt levels; different degrees of control over fiscal deficits more recently; and rescheduling history. Hungary and Poland are the most indebted countries, while the Czech Republic and Latvia are the least.

HIGHER RATED SOVEREIGNS

The debt of 'BBB' rated Latvia and the four 'BBB-' rated countries have characteristics that make timely debt service likely, although with a relatively low degree of assurance when compared to higher-rated sovereigns. While these countries represent a relatively diverse group, they all passed a tough and crucial threshold that distinguishes them from the speculative-grade category. Latvia's one-notch higher rating reflects the flexibility afforded by the country's low fiscal and external debt burdens compared to Poland and Hungary.

The Czech Republic and Slovenia are even better credits than the others. Not only are they the most developed and prosperous countries in the region (as reflected in their per capita income as shown in Exhibit 6), but in addition, most qualitative and quantitative indicators support the view that their industries and exports are more developed and more diversified than those of any other country in the region. In both, the political scene has been more stable and conducive to reforms than in other countries, notwithstanding recent inconclusive elections in Slovenia. Macroeconomic management has been exemplary, and policy consensus on structural reform has remained consistently strong. Last, but not least, the governments' financial positions are very strong, and both governments are net external creditors. All these factors reinforce each other, ensuring that the ability to address potential financial and/or economic stresses in these two countries is much stronger than in any other country within the group (see Exhibits 7 and 8).

Exhibit 7: Public Finances 1996
General Government Deficit/GDP (Excluding Privatization Receipts)

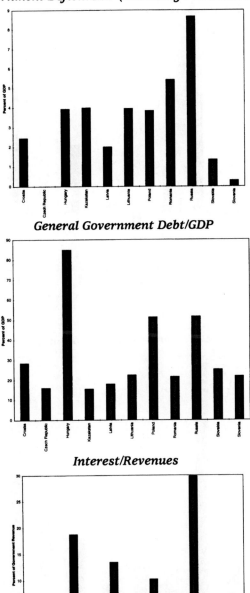

General Government Debt/GDP

Interest/Revenues

Exhibit 8: External Debt Indicators 1996
External Debt/Exports

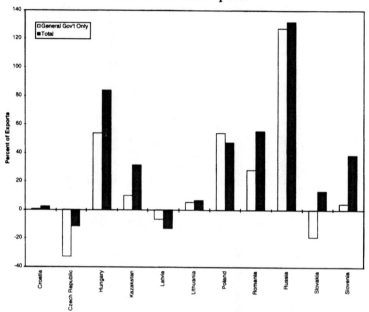

Net Interest Payments/Exports

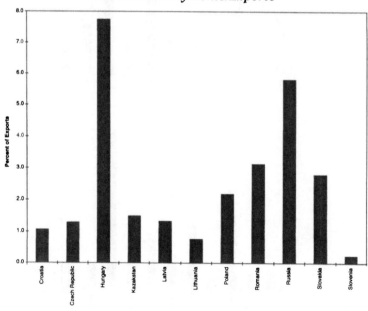

Exhibit 8 (Continued)
Debt Services

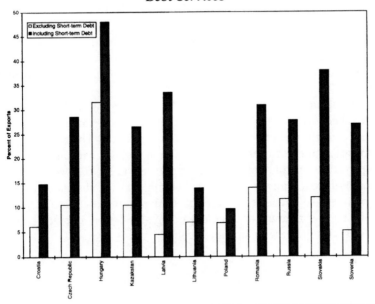

LESS ADVANCED TRANSITION ECONOMIES

The high-profile sovereign bond debuts in the international capital markets in 1996 included those of Romania, Russia, and Kazakstan, all rated 'BB–'. In EBRD terminology, all three are at "intermediate" stages of transition. Moldova, Kyrgyzstan, the Ukraine, and possibly Uzbekistan are the other intermediate reformers that are likely to approach the international capital markets soon.

The countries at this stage of transition have all moved decisively to strengthen product market competition by liberalizing most prices and foreign trade and by cutting back government subsidies and enterprises' access to soft credits from the banking system. They also have privatized many of their small companies and shops.

Russia stands out in the group of intermediate reformers by the quantitative indicator of large-scale privatization, which is higher than Poland's, for example. However, because Russian privatization accorded tremendous power to "insiders," the effectiveness of governance in these large privatized companies is very suspect. In general, the quality of management in these countries remains untested and seems to lack the "market memory" and "entrepreneurial behavior" that characterize the higher-rated countries.

Moreover, most of the intermediate reformers are significantly less adept than the advanced transition countries at restructuring enterprise and reforming financial institutions. The legal environment in these countries remains much weaker as well; laxity and lack of transparency are widespread, with obvious implications for economic decision-making and performance.

All these countries have been less successful in reducing their inflation as well, although 1996 witnessed significant improvements in Russia and Kazakstan. As a result, Kazakstan's dramatic decline in output was halted in 1996, and growth should be strong in 1997. In Russia, officially reported GDP continued to decline in 1996, but a recovery is expected in 1997.

Romania, which was the only early reformer within the group, loosened its financial control in 1996, a policy slippage that accelerated inflation, reversed economic growth, and undermined past reform efforts. The rapid expansion of credit to agriculture, recurrent interference in the foreign exchange market, stand-still in privatization, and corporate restructurings in 1996 leave the new center-right coalition government with the challenging task to substantially tighten economic policies and to accelerate reforms. In the short term, these policies will be costly in terms of a return to three-digit annual inflation, declining real output, and a significant increase in unemployment.

Chapter 8

Challenges in the Credit Analysis of Emerging Market Corporate Bonds

Christopher Taylor
Vice President
Emerging Markets Corporate Bonds
BT Securities

INTRODUCTION

Emerging market corporate bonds are an attractive asset class. That is, they have the potential to provide investors with attractive risk-adjusted returns. However, the asset class also raises unique challenges which require a disciplined approach to manage.

APPROACHES TO INVESTING IN CORPORATES

There traditionally have been two approaches to investing in emerging market corporate bonds: top-down and bottom-up. Neither approach is necessarily contradictory or mutually exclusive. However, in practice they have been treated as such. The *top-down approach* essentially treats investing in corporates as "sovereign-plus." The *bottom-up approach* sometimes has a tendency to treat emerging market corporates as "U.S. credits-plus." Investors have become more sophisticated in recent years — to a large extent due to the crisis in Mexico and the subsequent massive sell-off throughout Latin America — but there are still many inefficiencies. We believe that investing in emerging market corporate bonds can be most profitably done utilizing techniques learned with U.S. high-yield bonds, but the macro-environment and micro-factors unique to individual countries are also important.

Prior to the Mexican crisis, little attention was paid to corporate fundamentals. Most investment was "name lending" — the local blue chips would get loans at rates slightly above sovereign bonds. Hence the treatment of emerging market corporates as "sovereign-plus." Often this was justified since many of these blue-chips had credit ratios and characteristics which in the United States would have earned them investment-grade ranking. However, several times these investment decisions were made based on name and reputation, rather than sound credit decisions, and investors got stuck with low quality bonds.

Conversely, many investors bought these names based on their strong credit ratios and attractive yields relative to U.S. names with similar ratios. However, comparing ratios across borders obscures as much as it reveals. We believe that investors should pay close attention to ratios and other credit statistics. However, investors should also adjust for the fact that (1) emerging markets are inherently more volatile (thus ratios should be stronger), (2) inflation accounting distorts results (especially when inflation is increasing), (3) accounting standards are less rigid in many emerging markets, (4) the legal system is less developed and reliable in many of these countries, (5) recessions tend to be more severe, and (6) governments tend to intervene (and support their companies) more.

These factors should not deter investors from acquiring these bonds. We believe that investors are usually adequately compensated for these risks. However, it does mean that investors should be aware of these risks, and more to the point, on how to manage them.

EMERGING MARKET CREDITS VERSUS U.S. CREDITS WITH SAME RATING

In theory a BB rated emerging market bond should have the same default risk as a BB U.S. bond. In other words, the BB rating already incorporates sovereign risk. Most of the emerging market corporates that we look at have solid investment grade ratios for U.S. standards. Of course, these issuers are not based in the United States, they are located in a region where the economic and political environments are more volatile. This is why these issuers are rated BB rather than single or even double-A. However, to argue that a BB company should carry a premium relative to U.S. BB credits is discounting twice, since the BB rating already incorporates a penalty for sovereign risk. The solid investment grade ratios are what enabled these companies to survive even a drastic downturn such as occurred in Mexico and Argentina in 1995.

Most companies in Argentina and Mexico have just proven that they can easily survive even the most dramatic macro-economic turbulence. With an economic decline and liquidity squeeze equivalent to what the U.S. experienced during the 1930s, many of these companies managed to survive, often even without significant cash flow problems. We doubt that many U.S. single-B or even double-B companies would have been able to survive a downturn and liquidity squeeze so severe.

Of course, credit risk is not the only factor influencing bond pricing. Trading risk (e.g., volatility and liquidity) is another significant variable. Latin bonds are inherently more volatile and less liquid than U.S. high-yield bonds (although we can remember some instances less than a decade ago when U.S. high-yield bonds were rather volatile and illiquid). Any premium should be determined bond-by-bond, but even for the more liquid Latin credits we believe there should be a modest premium relative to U.S. credits with a similar default risk.

TIERING THE CREDIT

Traditionally, emerging market bonds have traded based on a company's reputation. However, reputation and credit strength may or may not be related. We recommend that investors rank credits in three categories based on standard credit risk measures (e.g., cash flow ratios, risk and volatility of industry, size of company, competence of management, etc.). Of course, many of the perceived blue chips will still be top tier credits if ranked by such a methodology, but this will not necessarily be the case. Short-term, companies which are perceived locally to be blue chips will probably trade better than those which have top-tier characteristics according to U.S.-style methodologies.

Longer term, however, especially now that many emerging markets are opening up to competition and slaying the inflation dragon, we believe that perception will sooner or later catch up with reality. Indeed, it is our observation that several Latin blue chips are not equipped to meet, or even survive, this new environment. Many blue chips became big, or remained big, not because of strong management. Instead, it was because of their political connections or high import barriers, and/or their ability to export thanks to high inflation and weak currencies, and/or because competitors could not emerge due to limited access to capital or lack of political connections. However, in a more stable environment with a healthier currency and better access to capital and lower import barriers and privatization, new competitors are emerging and management competence becomes the key variable.

In Argentina and Mexico — since they reformed earlier — many of the blue chips whose managements were incapable of dealing with the new environment have already been eliminated. In other countries (e.g., Brazil and Venezuela), we believe that there is still a significant divergence between companies which are locally viewed as blue chips and those that are top-tier credits based on more relevant credit guidelines. We caution that short-term U.S. investors could get frustrated since a significant part of emerging market trading is still dominated by "name trading." However, since the Mexican devaluation many market participants have become more sophisticated and more likely to do credit analysis. Over time, we continue to believe that the divergence between perception and credit reality will continue to close, and thus investors who today do their credit homework should outperform those who buy based on name trading.

Tier one credits are those that are constrained by the sovereign ceiling, meaning those that would be solid investment grade if they were located in a more stable environment. *Tier two credits* are not necessarily constrained by the sovereign ceiling. If they were located in a typical OECD country they would probably be BB or possibly borderline investment grade. Tier two credits tend to have some significant credit issues which bear watching, but not significant enough to cause a serious risk of default. *Tier three credits*, in contrast, have significant default and/or rescheduling risk. These credits should have a sizable risk premium, since in Latin America creditors have little recourse under local law in the event of default and local courts are somewhat inefficient.

JUDGING COMPANIES BY INFORMATION PROVIDED

Many investors are turned off from investing in emerging market corporate bonds by the historically pathetic levels of information these companies provided. There are still some companies which treat investors shabbily. (Often, not coincidentally, these companies are perceived blue chips whose credit fundamentals do not measure up to the perception.) However, we believe the level of disclosure has improved significantly since the Mexican devaluation. Many emerging market companies — especially the better managed ones — have learned to treat investors as a key constituency, rather than a nuisance to be tolerated. On the other hand, there are still quite a few poorly managed companies which do not provide their investors with even minimum acceptable information flow.

We believe that investors should demand a healthy premium for the bonds of companies which do not service their investors' legitimate information requirements properly. Lack of information flow and poor credit factors and poor management often go hand in hand. These companies are usually riskier, since foreign investors are usually the last to learn of any bad news. Also, the lack of information and bad news are usually correlated, since most companies would be more than happy to spread any good news. An unwillingness to open up to investors is often an indication of a traditional management which is incapable of changing with the times. And even if these uninformative issuers were good credits, we have learned that the bonds of companies which do provide good information to investors usually hold up better in a bear market and rebound faster in any recovery.

We have developed several rules of thumb. First, avoid private companies (i.e., ones that don't report to a stock exchange) unless their bonds are registered with the SEC or unless they have a New York based investor relations firm. With private companies it becomes very difficult to get hold of financial results once they take a turn for the worse. Private company bonds virtually always lag otherwise equivalent-risk bonds. Also, secondary trading tends to be very illiquid, especially in bear markets.

Second, demand a premium for issuers which do not have a New York based investor relations agency. Usually those companies which are not prepared to incur the expenses of an investor relations agency also have an unconstructive view towards investors (although to be fair we can also think of some exceptions that prove the rule). Often there is a close correlation between managements which treat investors as an important constituency (and thus usually have better performing bonds), and those which have the skill set needed to compete in a liberalized and rapidly changing economic environment. We should emphasize that there are several emerging market issuers which have excellent investor relations programs without having a New York based agency supporting them, but they are the exceptions.

Third, demand a premium for companies which do not file U.S. generally accepted accounting principles (GAAP) or at the least an annual U.S. GAAP reconciliation. In other words, demand a premium for 144A bonds over SEC-registered bonds. We are not necessarily saying that other GAAP's are less conservative. Indeed, we can point to examples where U.S. GAAP is too liberal (e.g., depreciation allowances) or too cumbersome (e.g., deferred taxes). However, at least U.S. GAAP is the devil the greatest number of investors know. Also, it seems to us to be the most comprehensive and the most thorough in disclosure.

We can think of several instances where a good cash flow company turned into a marginal one when statements were converted into U.S. GAAP — maybe because a "small" subsidiary or some parent company operations had to be consolidated or because a new policy on accounts receivable or inventory obsolescence or revenues accrual had to be recognized. Essentially what we're saying is that it is easier to have a higher degree of confidence in the companies which report under U.S. GAAP. Full U.S. GAAP numbers would be ideal, but an annual reconciliation is acceptable. Often companies once they have to show a reconciliation will change their local-GAAP policies so as to avoid too large a discrepancy between the two standards.

Nonetheless, we believe that investors should always check the reconciliation, just to understand the differences in what is reported quarterly (local GAAP) and what is filed at year-end with the SEC (U.S. GAAP). If the differences are only tax-related or (non cash) depreciation and amortization, one can have a high degree of confidence in quarterly numbers. If the differences are more substantial, investors should question management more thoroughly and take quarterly results with a grain of salt.[1]

Also, for a new issue the standards of due diligence and disclosure in the prospectus are much higher in an SEC-registered issue than in a 144A. We find that in most instances disclosure in 144A prospectuses is relatively limited. On the other hand, SEC-registered deals require a legal opinion regarding adequate disclosure, which forces the underwriter (and issuer) to do a much more thorough job in due diligence and disclosure. Therefore, we think investors should demand an adequate premium for 144A issues compared to SEC-registered deals. Of course, this premium should vary according to credit risk. If the issuer has high quality credit ratios, it should be very small. On the other hand, for high-risk credits this premium should be substantial.

---

[1] For example, we sometimes see instances where expenses which should be operating or cost of goods sold are reported as "other," thus distorting our EBITDA measurements; or where short-term liabilities are classified as long term, thus presenting a misleading picture of liquidity. Another common trick is capitalizing or deferring items which under U.S. GAAP would be operating expenses.

DEBT STRUCTURE MATTERS:
COVENANTS AND MATURITY PROFILE

We believe that many Eurobonds are poorly structured. If there are covenants at all, it is usually some useless maintenance ratio such as debt/capital. These ratios are not very meaningful even in the United States (after all, debt is repaid with cash, not with a capital ratio), but especially not in emerging markets where underdeveloped legal rules and/or inefficient local court systems make enforcement and/or recourse if these covenants are violated rather difficult. We can think of several instances where emerging market companies violated their debt/capital covenants and went right on paying dividends or making acquisitions. One example is BAESA, the bankrupt Argentine/Brazilian Pepsi bottler. Even though it is in violation of its Eurobond covenants, bond investors have gained absolutely no advantage as a result. The whole idea of covenants is to give investors leverage if things don't go as planned. Also, capital-based maintenance covenants give companies an incentive to incur off-balance-sheet debt or inflate their asset values. Since such debt is often secured and/or effectively has first claim on cash flows, these covenants effectively work against the interest of bondholders rather than protecting them.

These issues do not matter so much for blue chips with strong financial ratios (but not perceived blue chips with poor credit ratios). For top-tier credits, structure is relatively unimportant. However, for companies with weak ratios, emerging market investors should in our opinion pay more attention to structure, since this can have a significant impact in how a credit develops. Usually if an investor buys a second tier bond it is with the hope that the story will improve, or, if the yield is sufficiently attractive, that the story will stabilize. A well structured bond should give investors comfort that management won't take actions to worsen the credit, and gives investors leverage to prevent management from doing so. Instead, we have seen perceived blue chips with negative cash flow and an acquisition track record issue bonds without any covenants at all.

The key credit variables revolve around cash flow ratios. There is plenty of room for disagreement as to which particular ratio is best, but conceptually most analysts agree that some form of ratios which measure cash flow earnings relative to fixed cash payments (e.g., EBITDA/Interest or debt/EBITDA) provide the best measurement of credit risk. (In contrast, a capital-based ratio solely measures on-balance-sheet debt relative to historical investments — in other words, it is a backwards looking ratio). Thus, it follows that if one wants to create a covenant which best protects creditors, it should be a cash flow based ratio. Also, although one can never create a forward looking ratio, at least one can ensure that a ratio is as current as possible by requiring calculations on a pro forma basis. Most importantly, we believe that investors should require covenants that measure all fixed calls on cash flow, including off balance-sheet debt and mandatory preferred. Finally, any covenants should be self enforcing, which is crucial in a region where legal recourse is impractical.

The high-yield market has over the years developed effective covenants. It has learned how to tie management's hands if it doesn't meet its projections, without this adversely affecting bondholders or requiring major legal expenses by creditors. This is done by means of comprehensive "incurrence" tests. Essentially, some form of cash flow based ratio is chosen to measure management's projections of cash flow relative to future fixed obligations, with some margin for error. Essentially, management can do whatever it wishes, but if it wants to borrow or pay dividends or buy back stock or upstream money to its parent it must meet this ratio (on a pro forma basis). For example, a debt/EBITDA incurrence test in an issuer's covenant package is 4 times. On a historical basis this ratio was 3 times, but if management wanted to borrow more (e.g., to pay dividends) it would have to calculate the ratio based on the new debt level. It could incur as much debt as it wanted so long as the ratio remained below 4 times (usually known as "the ability to incur $1 of additional debt under the incurrence test"). This offers investors effective assurance that management's actions won't cause credit ratios to deteriorate beyond a certain point. If properly drawn, it makes it very difficult for management to borrow extra money for acquisitions or to pay dividends, etc.

Of course, general business risks could cause a credit deterioration, but no covenant can protect against such developments. Indeed, a maintenance covenant can worsen the situation by forcing management to focus on playing games (e.g., accounting tricks or off-balance-sheet liabilities) to avoid violating the covenant at the very time when they should be focusing on improving the business fundamentals.

Just as important for emerging market investors, where the legal system is not necessarily a reliable ally, incurrence covenants are self-enforcing. No bank will lend money or no board will declare dividends if that very act is a violation of the covenants. Under maintenance covenants, no such self-policing mechanism exists. The company is already in violation, so why shouldn't the board go ahead with other plans (e.g., pay dividends or pursue acquisitions), even if those cause further deterioration?

CRITICAL ROLE OF MATURITY PROFILE

One lesson we should have learned from the Mexican devaluation debacle is that short-term debt is bad. (Remember Tesobonos?) Commercial paper also proved itself to be a rather fickle source of finance for companies, while commercial bank debt could only be rolled over with difficulty — not to mention with significantly higher interest rates. We are encouraged that many Mexican firms have since improved their debt profile and retired shorter term debt, even if it costs them a few hundred basis points extra. Even in the U.S. commercial paper is usually not considered an appropriate and reliable source of capital for non-investment grade companies. Certainly in emerging markets, where capital availability is even more volatile, commercial paper must definitely be an inappropriate form of financing. It usually disappears just when it is needed most, i.e., during a major crisis.

We believe that those issuers which — despite the lessons of 1995 — still use high-risk short-term debt (in particular, commercial paper) should probably be avoided, even if other credit fundamentals appear sound. A willingness to tolerate a risky level of short-term debt says something about management, and in emerging markets we prefer to invest in well-managed companies. Most emerging markets have underdeveloped lending systems, with only short-tenor debt available. This debt usually automatically rolls over, becoming effectively long-term debt ("evergreen"). Thus, we can understand how traditional management got comfortable with high levels of short-term debt. However, this automatic "evergreen" does not apply to foreign debt, especially not commercial paper, where refinancing risk is significant. These are fickle, unreliable sources of financing, and companies which rely on them should be avoided.

Companies with bad ratios but no immediate refinancing requirements can usually muddle through. In contrast, during crises companies with stronger financial ratios but steep refinancing requirements can be pushed under. After all, a default is not caused by unfavorable financial ratios (unless there are those useless maintenance covenants) but rather by an inability to pay debt obligations. Thus, if there are no obligations coming due for a long time, the risk of default is reduced significantly, no matter how bad the ratios are in the interim. Debt structure (i.e., upcoming debt maturities) is in our opinion the most important credit variable in emerging markets, even more so than cash flow ratios.

A closely related issue is debt arbitrage. Many companies borrow in U.S. dollars to avoid steep local interest rates. However, the flip side of these high local rates is good returns on cash deposits. Thus, many companies overborrow hard currency and invest it in local instruments. During the good times this is a profitable strategy, but Mexican firms learned during December 1994 how risky this strategy is. We simply do not like companies which engage in such arbitrage! Not only is it risky when there are devaluations, it also sends some negative signals about management. It says that management likes to gamble, and also to some extent that management does not see many profitable investment opportunities in its core business. If management's core businesses were strong, it wouldn't be wasting its energy on non-core activities such as financial arbitrage.

BREACHING THE SOVEREIGN CEILING

As a general rule, we believe that virtually all emerging market corporates should trade at a premium to their sovereign bonds. However, in Argentina several of the top tier credits trade tighter than Argentine sovereign bonds. This is partly because of the stronger fundamentals of Argentine corporates and in several instances their ownership by strong foreign parents, but also due to Argentina's currency board.

The currency board makes exchange controls and/or restrictions less likely; therefore the theory behind the sovereign ceiling argument becomes less relevant.

The sovereign ceiling argument is essentially one of structural subordination. Simplistically, it says that if the sovereign needs foreign exchange it will have first call on hard currency, to the detriment of other creditors with hard currency debt such as corporates. Therefore, corporates should always carry a risk premium relative to sovereigns. (This is another reason why we do not like corporates with significant amounts of hard currency short-term debt or commercial paper: the sovereign is more likely to restrict access to foreign currencies for short-term obligations than it is for long-term debt, especially bonds.) In most countries the structural subordination argument is valid. With a currency board, however, the government essentially removes its first call on hard currency and therefore corporates are no longer structurally subordinated. The central bank is not "lender of last resort" to the government, and therefore the government no longer has a superior status structurally.

Of course, one should always be cautious about government risk. Currency boards were created by politicians and thus can be abolished by them. Therefore, one should focus carefully on the longevity of the currency board and its popular support. If one contracts with an insurance company in Bermuda or buys a mutual fund in the Bahamas — both of which have currency boards — sovereign risk is hardly an issue. This analyst does not even know what the economic or political risk in either country is, but that proves our point. If one is confident that a currency board will remain in place, local political and economic risk become almost irrelevant to the credit story.[2]

Of course, one is less secure in Argentina because the currency board has been in place for only five years while in Bermuda and the Bahamas there has been at least half a century of confidence building. Nineteenth century Latin America has plenty of examples of currency boards being abolished and/or manipulated once the going got tough. Therefore, one should always be more skeptical about Argentina than one would be in small Caribbean islands with a different legal and political tradition. Also, the currency board in Argentina has some weaknesses (e.g. 30% of reserves can be in the form of hard currency government bonds). However, we believe that the 1996 crisis has proven that the currency board has very solid across-the-board popular support in Argentina. Because of this, we remain reasonably confident that for the foreseeable future — or at least until most of the corporate Eurobonds which we cover have been safely retired — the currency board will remain in place. Thus, for very strong local blue chips there is justification for their trading through the sovereign ceiling. We note that recently one of the two key credit agencies accepted this argument and increased several companies' credit ratings to higher than that of the sovereign.

---

[2] Panama has gone one better, and does not have its own currency. Therefore, Panamanian corporates credit ratings should in theory be fully independent of the country's credit rating, just like in, say, New York IBM's credit rating is independent of the state government's.

STABILITY OF A COUNTRY'S CURRENCY

All other things being equal, we look for countries with historically stable currencies. We usually disregard whether the currency is short term over- or undervalued, since in the long run purchasing power parity usually holds. According to this theory, inflation usually catches up with a devaluation, thus in the longer term arbitrage risk (borrowing in hard currency, revenues in local currency) is relatively modest. However, countries with volatile currencies usually have more risk of dysfunctional macro-economic policies. In the short term these policies may actually benefit certain corporates (e.g., economic stimulation benefits companies which sell to the domestic market, while weak currencies benefit exporters and producers — usually commodities — whose prices are dollarized). However, long term (and often even short term) these policies increase cash flow volatility and cost of capital (or even reduce access to capital) and thus credit risk.

For example, in Mexico by 1997 inflation had already largely eroded the (alleged) short-term advantage of the December 1994 devaluation. In the interim, however, the government was forced to incur sharply higher interest rates and thus a severe recession in order to stem the resultant capital flight and inflation (which always follow devaluations). Thus, over a 2-year timeframe the currency arbitrage risk was minimal (inflation and thus unit prices caught up with the devaluation), but in the interim sales volumes collapsed and cost of capital skyrocketed. For some time this severely impacted some of the issuers' creditworthiness, even the exporters which were the alleged beneficiaries of the devaluation.

Our point is that for long-term bonds the currency mismatch (between local currency revenues and hard-currency borrowing) is not a major concern *per se*, since purchasing power parity usually holds (barring extreme exchange and price controls). However, countries with unstable currencies tend to have unstable macro-economic performances as well, and these are a major negative from a corporate credit perspective. One reason we are quite comfortable with Mexico at present is because since the devaluation debacle the government has learned its lesson and places a heavy emphasis on currency stability and avoids imbalances in the underlying macro economic fundamentals. In other words, the central bank has the upper hand over the economic growth advocates, and therefore economic growth — albeit slower at first — should become more stable and sustainable. Since stability and sustainability of cash flows (as opposed to short-term growth) is a key credit variables for corporates, conservative monetary policies are a significant positive.

We believe that one reason Argentine corporate bonds traditionally trade very tight relative to sovereign bonds is because with the currency board currency instability has been all but eliminated. Thus, the strength or weakness of the local currency is no longer a factor in corporate earnings, which makes them more predictable. Argentina has gone one step further and abolished inflation accounting (low inflation is fundamentally associated with a stable currency). This, of course, enhances the quality and reliability of earnings which should further reduce the risk premium required.

INFLATION ACCOUNTING

Inflation accounting makes it very difficult to truly understand what is going on in a company. Given that we all have time pressures, we prefer to invest in companies where we can easily and quickly understand what is going on. Also, given the complexities of inflation accounting, one is never quite certain whether one correctly understood what the numbers said. When we present an investment idea to investors, we prefer to be confident that we understand it ourselves; inflation accounting makes us somewhat less likely to stick out our necks. One rule of thumb we have developed is to disbelieve any numbers where inflation is above 50%, unless they have been translated into hard currency at the time of the transaction.[3]

In some Eastern European and Middle Eastern countries (e.g. Turkey) the income and cash flow statements are not restated, only the balance sheet. We find this methodology preferable to using comprehensive restatements as used in some Latin American countries. In our opinion the income statement is reasonably reliable so long inflation is modest; however, even with around 20% inflation the cash flow statement is distorted so as to make it almost meaningless.[4]

In Argentina, inflation accounting was abolished in 1995. In our opinion, this justifies a lower premium for their corporate bonds since we can easily and better understand the numbers, and thus are less likely to get caught by surprise. In Brazil, inflation accounting was abolished in 1996, but unfortunately most companies continue to use it. Worse, most companies do not separately disclose the inflation and devaluation component of their interest expense, making it virtually impossible to calculate true interest expense. Since the interest expense is a key variable in determining a company's credit risk, this is a significant negative for which investors should demand a significant premium.

In Mexico, inflation accounting still reigns with full force. Fortunately, however, inflation has come down significantly since the devaluation debacle. A big positive for Mexican corporates is their stock exchange's electronic database for reporting earnings. This database requires all Mexican companies to report relatively quickly (5 weeks after each quarter end, and 9 weeks after year end), and in relatively good detail. We believe this good level of disclosure helped many investors get comfortable with Mexican credits and helped in the relatively rapid rebound after the devaluation debacle. If Mexican reporting had been as slow as in Argentina or as uninformative and difficult to collect as in Brazil, we doubt many investors would have been willing to reenter the Mexican corporate sector after the devaluation — certainly not as rapidly as they did.

---

[3] Using average exchange rates for the period, not the period-end exchange rate as is the local convention.
[4] The whole point of a cash flow statement is to reconcile beginning and ending cash so one can understand the in- and outflows, but this is impossible if they all get restated based on inflation.

For Mexican and Brazilian credits, a key earnings variable is the strength of the local currency. Now that inflation is under control, the many companies which were able to compete based on their weak currency will have to start competing based on their core competencies. Many will not be able to not compete in this environment, and we believe investors should avoid these names altogether since their margins will only deteriorate. A good rule of thumb we have learned is to avoid companies which complain about the strength of the currency and loudly call for a devaluation, rather than proactively investing or restructuring so that they can compete regardless of the strength of their currency. Proactive companies will survive in the longer term (even if shorter term they have to borrow to finance these investments).

Also, with inflation coming down rapidly (which is directly related to a stable currency), cost control becomes a more important issue (e.g., often salaries rise to catch up with inflation), and operating margins no longer benefit from the inventory effect (i.e., inventory bought at lower prices results in lower cost of goods sold and better margins after the finished unit is sold at higher prices). This effects everyone's margins. Thus, investors should bet on companies which are focused on operating margins and results, not just top-line (sales) growth. We can think of several examples of companies which tried to grow (or acquire) their way out of uncompetitive cost structures that always failed.

EXPORTERS VERSUS DOMESTICS

For most countries, the corporate sector (and the economies, for that matter) can essentially be broken into two sectors: the dollarized sector and the non-tradeable sector. Roughly, in most Latin countries, a third to a half of the companies (and of the economy) is dollarized. In essence, producers in this sector base their prices on U.S. prices and/or international commodities. Thus, even though they may sell domestically and invoice in local currencies, they are reasonably hedged if they borrow in hard currencies. Products whose prices are dollarized include virtually all commodities such as mining products, chemicals, and paper, as well as internationally traded products such as autoparts, glass, electrical equipment and transportation services (e.g., shipping, airlines).

Note that this definition of "dollarized" includes a broader sector than just exports. The key is whether a producer has the *option* to export. For example, a paper or packaging producer may sell virtually all of its output domestically. However, if domestic prices were too low relative to international prices it could always shift sales abroad. Thus it has pricing power domestically, and therefore can tie its prices to international rates. Unless the government imposes major price controls, these companies are relatively hedged against devaluations.

The dollarized sector was traditionally the biggest beneficiary from devaluations or weak currencies in general. In dollar terms there was not much change in their revenues, but their local currency-based costs halved. (Of course, what they gain in better margins they usually lose in higher cost of capital and lower domestic volumes, but that's another story.) Going forward, as a general rule, we expect these dollarized producers to see tighter margins. In Argentina, which has had a fixed currency since the currency board was introduced, and in Mexico, which already had a period of stability and openness to competition prior to the devaluation debacle, most of the most vulnerable producers have already been eliminated.

In Brazil, however, this weeding out process has only just begun. From our observations, most of the vulnerable producers have not (yet) accessed the Eurobond market, but even the strongest producers will see a tightening of margins. Of course, on the positive side, the better run companies will be able to drastically lower their cost of capital and extend their debt maturities (in high inflation environments it was usually impossible to get financing beyond one year or even 6 months), thus largely offsetting the negative effects of tighter margins.

However, the uncompetitive firms (and their unions) usually put heavy political pressure on the government to devalue (or adopt economic policies which in the end will cause a devaluation). Also, one harsh side effect of this necessary restructuring is unemployment, which puts political pressure on the government to reflate the economy (and thus almost inevitably to devalue). All these pressures increase the risks for all of the country's issuers, even the strong ones, until the transition process is several years old and these uncompetitive firms have been restructured or eliminated. In Argentina, thanks to convertibility, this restructuring process is already largely complete, so these political pressures — and thus devaluation risk — are no longer severe. In Mexico to some extent, but definitely in Brazil, this will remain a risk for quite some time.

Assuming international commodity prices remain unchanged, revenues in dollar terms for these dollarized companies should be stable despite local currency instability. However, until inflation and interest rates decline to international levels (as has happened in Argentina), inflation and high real interest rates will continue to increase local currency-based costs. Thus, until the currency and inflation are totally stable, the strength (or weakness) of the currency and trends in inflation will remain key variables in companies' quarterly earnings and debt coverage ratios. Since this adds an extra element of instability and uncertainty — and thus risk — to companies' earnings, investors should ask for a risk premium for issuers in inflationary countries or those with high real interest rates.

Negative trends on margins from strong currencies can to some extent be offset if these companies can sell more value-added products domestically. Companies tend to export very commoditized products, but locally sell more customized products. As a general rule, domestic sales tend to have more value added and thus better margins. For instance, a paper producer might export standardized paper rolls but for domestic customers it may cut and/or coat the paper, thus increasing proceeds per ton by several hundred dollars. With more stable currencies and lower inflation often comes more confidence and higher disposable income, and thus a stronger domestic economy and more sales opportunities.

In addition, exports have higher transportation costs and generally command a somewhat lower price in the international market than locally due to the absence of tariff protection. (Although tariffs in the third world are declining, they are often still sizable.) As a very general rule, however, we do not believe that the higher margin domestic sales fully offset the negative impact of the stronger currencies on margins for dollarized companies, although we must admit that there are exceptions to prove our rule. The key is to do one's credit homework to thoroughly understand how each company is impacted by stronger currency and declining inflation on the one hand, yet benefits from stronger domestic spending and better access to capital markets on the other.

COST OF CAPITAL

Since Argentina has had a strong currency for most of this decade, the commodity producers have had to rely on cost cutting rather than a weak currency to remain competitive. However, thanks to the strong and stable currency, their cost of capital is below that of their Latin competitors. This is a significant advantage in the capital-intensive commodities business. For example, in steel Brazil would seem to have a natural advantage due to its low-cost iron ore deposits, which could pose problems for Argentine producers as Mercosur tariffs come down over the next few years. However, the low cost of capital in Argentina (relative to other Latin countries) could to a large extent offset this competitive disadvantage.

REGULATORY RISK

A final word of caution when investing in bonds of companies dependent on the domestic sector especially utilities: regulatory risk. Of course, this risk is present in the United States and European utilities, and telecommunication companies as well. Also, our concern is not necessarily the regulations *per se*. (Indeed, we would argue that in Argentina and Chile the regulatory regime is far advanced from those in the United States.) Instead, it is the process. In the United States, no matter how antiquated and cumbersome utility regulations may be, at least there is a clearly defined process which enables all to know how to participate and ensures some level of fairness. In contrast, it seems at times that the process in several emerging market countries is somewhat opaque and may be arbitrary.

This is a risk factor investors should get comfortable with, for it is entirely possible that all of the sudden a significantly different regulatory regime has been imposed with little or no warning — although to be fair we believe that most emerging markets seem to have learned that this scares off investors and are trying to amend their ways. Often, an agreed price increase is "waived by consent" in order to help the government's inflation control program. Fortunately, most utilities with bonds outstanding in emerging markets have strong coverage ratios, so these events only have a modest credit impact. However, for the few marginal utilities investors should certainly demand a premium to offset this risk. Unless a utility has strong support from an investment grade parent (or is sovereign owned), investors should always demand a reasonable risk premium compared to sovereign bonds.

SUMMARY

We believe that investors who use the skills gained in analyzing U.S. credits (bottom-up) can make significant risk-adjusted returns in emerging markets, since they understand how to analyze cash flows. This has not traditionally been a common skill in emerging markets, where top-down analysis has been the traditional approach. However, we have raised the above issues since there are also many factors unique to emerging markets, which sometimes we see U.S. investors not taking into account. Our point is that one should use high-yield style credit skills, but one should also be prepared for the unexpected. Do not assume that a Brazilian utility is just like a U.S. utility, but understand the differences as well. When all is said and then, however, use high-yield style disciplines. If you cannot get good information from management or get a good grip on cash flow, stay away from the bond altogether. On the other hand, if management is modern and informative, and helps you get comfortable with (which in our mind is usually synonymous with understanding) the risk, you can increase the probability of higher risk-adjusted returns.

Chapter 9

Relative Value Concepts Within the Eurobond Market

Peter J. Carril
Managing Director
Bankers Trust

INTRODUCTION

In the most basic sense, the term relative value constitutes the comparison of one bond to another. It quantifies the market terminology of rich and cheap, lending numerical representation to their meaning. The exercise of attempting to exploit the relative value between one bond or a sector of bonds versus another helps increase the market's pricing efficiency and thereby reduces, over time, those same opportunities. It is logical that a market's efficiency, as defined solely by its pricing mechanism, is greater as a market matures and participants seek to remove, or arbitrage, price dislocations. This can readily be seen in such markets as the U.S. Treasury market. At the other end of the bond spectrum is the emerging market (EM) Eurobond market. Relative value analysis can prove useful for the trader, investor, investment banker, and issuer. In this chapter, we will attempt to present applications for all these market participants.

GENERAL OVERVIEW AND TECHNICAL FACTORS

While it is difficult to place a precise number on the amount of outstanding Eurobond debt, some place the amount of Eurobonds from Latin American issuers alone at approximately $122 billion.[1] Eurobonds can be denominated in any currency. In this chapter, we focus our discussion on the U.S. dollar Eurobond market. The wide variety of outstanding Eurobond issues spread across varying industry, sector, and term structures offers an exceptional opportunity to compare and contrast different bonds. While the small initial issue size and tradable float of Eurobonds is often cited as a hindrance to effectively capturing seemingly large yield anomalies between bonds, there are many viable trade opportunities allowing the investor or portfolio manager to profitably position his investment thesis.

---

[1] See *Emerging Markets Investor* (March 1997), p.25.

No discussion of the EM Eurobond market would be complete without a brief mention of the peculiarities which drive and shape the market. In particular, the demand side of the price/yield equation has a strong, and very often overriding, determinant as to what currency, tenor, and basis point spread bonds are originally issued and traded in the secondary market. This may be a function of the relative immaturity of the market as the overall composition of the market is more demand driven than supply dictated. For example, the demand for high coupon Deutchemark bonds during 1995 and 1996 allowed the Republic of Argentina to issue 20- and 30-year bonds, substantially longer than the Republic was able to issue at that time in the U.S. dollar market. Another characteristic of the Eurobond market pertains to the small initial issue size of many of the bonds, which is often less than $50 million. Many first time issuers produce tighter spreads than one may anticipate because of their so called scarcity value. Other issuers have special cache because of their "window dressing" appeal or "museum" like qualities.

Certain relative value trades appear better on paper due to the strong technical position involving one particular Eurobond. In fact, these trades often result in profitable outcomes, but almost invariably succeed due to the movement of all the bonds *except* the one which is the most over-priced. An example would include Arg FRBs versus Arg 10.95s. This scenario often revolves around the comparison between a cheap non-Eurobond asset, typically a Brady bond, and an expensive Eurobond.

Care must be used when one attempts to (theoretically) arbitrage the expensive Eurobond versus the perceived-to-be-cheaper Brady asset. These cross market trades (i.e., Brady to Eurobond, collateralized to uncollateralized) have their own characteristics, and often subject the participant to unusually high profit/loss volatility. The analyses must include the payout of the shorted bond, often producing negative financing for the trade. If the shorted bond is difficult to borrow, any associated fee must also be included. The profitable outcome is due to the movement of the more liquid bond (Brady) against a less liquid bond (Eurobond) which remains in a tight trading range. The Eurobond, in reality, serves only as a cosmetic hedge, and introduces greater basis risk than the hedge instrument is intended to remove. Assuming that these trades are risk neutral is not entirely accurate due to the differences in liquidity between the two bonds. These trades only offer the "guaranteed, arbitragable profit outcome" when the expensive asset is held short to maturity. This is usually impractical and impossible.

PUTABLE BONDS

Bonds with put features offer their own difficulties in analysis, yet present their own relative value opportunities. The yield and spread of put bonds often illustrates investor's non-quantitative calculation of an issuer's ability to repay the bond at the put date. In mid-March 1996, for example, one could have purchased the putable Telcom Argentina 12.00% due 11/15/02 at $102.625. The yield to maturity was 11.42%. However, the yield to the 11/15/99 par put was 11.10%, producing a spread of 514 basis points (bps) over the U.S. Treasury 7.50% of 10/31/99. In this case the spread to put was marginally greater than the spread to maturity, yet the market was trading the bond to its final maturity. Putting the bond would result in an 2.625 point loss, which would prove problematic for many investors. Now, compare this with the non-putable Telcom Argentina 8.375% due 10/18/00 which was trading at a spread of 457 bps over Treasuries. The longer maturity Telcom offered a wider spread to the put date (514 bps) than the non-putable Telcom which has a longer final maturity. Investors could have purchased a bond which they could put earlier than the final date of the Telcom '00 yet also had the option to extend the bond to maturity. The extension from '99 to '02 was in a sense free. This anomaly resulted in the issuance of few emerging market Eurobonds with put features, as issuers felt they were not fairly compensated for the inclusion of a put feature. As one would have expected, by late December of 1996 this condition had been reversed and the spread to put of the Telcom '02 was appreciably lower than the spread to maturity of the non-putable Telcom '00.

Much analytical work has been devoted to the valuation of the put's option value, especially in the more mature U.S. investment-grade market. However, the overriding concern of many investors with putable bonds from non-investment grade issuers revolves around the *ability* of the issuer to have the financial resources to pay the investor at the put date *at the very point in time when the investor is exercising the put feature for credit deteriorating reasons.* The credit-specific decision as to whether to exercise the put feature usually takes place when the investor believes there is some likelihood that the issuer will *not* be able to repay the investor on the put date. Hence, traditional analysis used to quantify the option value which the issuer has granted the investor is overridden by the investors specific forward view of the creditworthiness of the issuer at the time of the first put date. The same analysis utilized to value investment-grade put bonds often produces an extraordinarily high valuation of the put option. In addition, many bonds have put features with put prices that are significantly below par (Banamex 9.50% due 04/06/00 are putable 4/06/98 at $95.480). This feature makes the sale of these bonds to investors problematic. It is cumbersome to explain that the purchase price paid for a bond is greater than its ending value at the put date even though putting the bond would produce the greater holding period return.

CONSTRUCTION OF A SOVEREIGN YIELD CURVE

The sovereign yield curve as depicted by each country's multiple bond representations is, in its simplest form, a series of the most *reliable* and independently trackable data points. It does not always quantify the sovereign risk associated with the term structure of a broader set of market constituency that quantify their risk parameters through other markets, namely the Brady market. Unlike the

Brady market which is deeper and broader but involves certain theoretical albeit unattainable stripped yield calculations, the Eurobond market offers a cleaner, more simplistic and attainable sovereign yield curve representation.

The construction of a usable, tradable, sovereign yield curve begins with the careful selection of that issuer's data points. The selection of these data points should involve the close evaluation of the characteristics discussed below.

Trading Liquidity

The choice of a bond which is infrequently traded for a data point is of little value, as it provides a point which is often too tight or too wide in spread. Bonds which have a small original issue size usually trade far *below* the natural or logical portion of the sovereign curve. Issues which have amortizing structures trade at a significant premium *above* where one might predict based upon other market conventions, most notably the high-grade market, due to the EM investor's disinterest in valuing the structure. Bonds with uneven coupons (e.g., 7.60%) which are more common from medium-term note issuers in the U.S. high-grade market trade at wider spreads, providing value for less liquidity-demanding investors. Investors can gain insight into the relative "tightness" of a bond (and hence its exclusion from the curve) by investigating its borrowing rate in the repo market. Because of the peculiarities of these bonds they should be avoided as data points.

Structure

EM bonds are issued in different forms and structures to meet the specific needs of the majority of the bond purchasers at the time of issuance. Bonds with direct sovereign guarantees placed in trust structures, as well as majority-owned (but not guaranteed) entities, regardless of the irrevocable nature of the direct guarantee, often trade between 8 bps (BNCE Huites) and 25 bps (CFE) above the sovereign curve. Agencies of sovereign government issuers trade between 3 bps (Nafinsa) and 10 bps (Banobras) above where the straight issues (UMS) trade. Issuers which produce perceived strategic resources (e.g., oil), often trade *through* the straight sovereign levels, such as Pemex in Mexico and Petrobras in Brazil.

Care must be used when constructing the yield curve to use similar data points. Issuers from entities which no longer issue bonds trade at relatively tight spread levels due to their scarcity level. Bonds which have step-up or non-cash features are usually not wise choices in constructing a curve. These bonds are of more use in measuring the market's compensatory requirements for nonconventional structures.

Once the bonds are selected we simply connect the data points to construct our curve. This method is chosen solely not for ease and simplicity. The use of a simple linear regression generated "best fit" line does not accurately capture the different slopes of the credit curve across its varying segments. This segmentation is what allows for trade opportunities as well as asset/liability management opportunities for issuers.

Exhibit 1: Argentine U.S. Dollar Sovereign Yield Curve

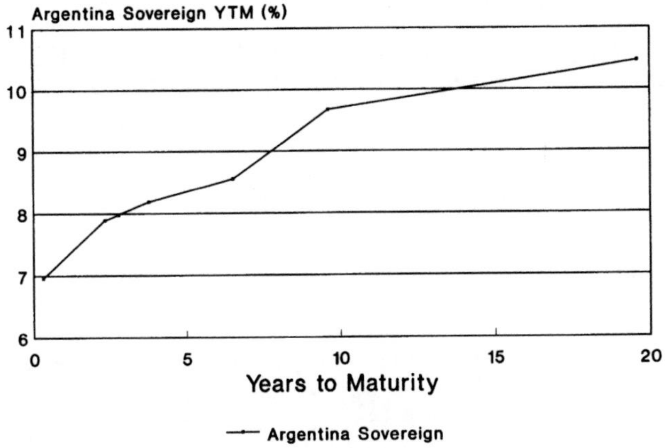

Argentina Sovereign YTM (%)

Years to Maturity

── Argentina Sovereign
Source: Bankers Trust Database

Exhibit 1 shows the Argentine U.S. dollar sovereign yield curve as it existed in May 1997.

SOVEREIGN YIELD CURVE TRADES

The slope of the yield curve should depict investors' preferences for short- and long-duration assets. By comparing the Eurobond yield curves of different countries at different points in time and placing them against the backdrop of the more developed and actively traded Brady market, we can identify trade opportunities.

Below we outline an Argentina-Mexico sovereign yield curve trade. The parameters of the trade are given in Exhibit 2. By comparing Argentinean par bonds and Mexican par bonds we observe that in mid-March 1996 the difference in spread was 217 bps. Due to the relatively higher volumes in the Brady market, we use this spread difference, and its magnitude, as an anchor for our calculations. Now, compare the Argentina 8.375% due 8/01/03 and the BNCE 7.25% due 1/01/04, both $1 billion global issues. Both were trading as general collateral in the repo market at the time of this analysis. Taking into account the differences in coupon and maturities, the spread differential in early March was 115 bps. Finally, the short-term Arg '01 to UMS '01 spread difference was 117 bps.

The logic of the trade is fairly straightforward. First we begin with the premise that the broad market (here defined as the Brady bond market) assesses a wider spread to Argentina than to Mexico. Thus if 10-year Argentinean-Mexican Eurobond sovereign spreads are 115 bps, it should follow that intra-country spreads of shorter tenor assets should be no greater than 115 bps. As observed above, the 5-year portion of the curve produced a 117 bps difference. Hence the trade is to buy Argentina 9.25% due 2/23/01 and sell UMS 9.75% due 2/06/01.

Exhibit 2: Parameters for an Argentina-Mexico Sovereign Yield Curve Trade of March 1996

Asset	Initiate Trade March 15, 1996		Reverse Trade April 26, 1996	
	Spread	Duration	Spread	Duration
Arg '01	573	3.98	395	3.90
Arg '03	586	5.29	400	5.38
Arg Par	1164	8.78	854	9.42
UMS '01	456	3.93	371	3.83
BNCE '04	471	5.58	384	5.59
Mex Par	947	9.30	661	9.81

Duration	Arg-Mex Difference (3/15/96)	Arg-Mex Difference (4/26/96)
3.8-3.9	117bps	24bps
5.3-5.6	115bps	16bps
8.8-9.8	217bps	193bps

Source: Bankers Trust Database

Exhibit 3: Gain/Loss on Bond on Argentina-Mexico Sovereign Yield Curve Trade of March 1996

Initiate Trade 3/15/96

> Buy $1,000,000 Argentina 9.25% due 2/23/01 at $90.25
> Sell (short sale) $1,000,000 UMS 9.75% due 2/06/01 at $96.25.

Reverse Trade 04/26/96

> Sell $1,000,000 Argentina 9.25% due 2/23/01 at $96.25
> Buy (repurchase) $1,000,000 UMS 9.75% due 2/06/01 at $99.00

We have neglected to duration-balance the trade due to the minor differences in durations between the two bonds.

Gain on Argentina '01	$962,500 − $902,500 = +$60,000
Loss on UMS '01	$962,500 − $990,000 = ($27,500)
Net gain	$60,000 − $27,500 = $32,500

To analyze the trade, we first look at the gain/loss on the bonds and then separately analyze the financing aspect of the trade. The gain/loss on the bonds is shown in Exhibit 3. Exhibit 4 analyzes the financing aspect of the trade.

Exhibit 4: Gain/Loss on Financing on Argentina-Mexico Sovereign Yield Curve Trade of March 1996

Long Argentina 9.25% due 2/23/01

Coupon interest: $10,534.72
Borrowing cost (includes A/I) at 5.25%: ($5,437.68)

Total: $10,534.72 − $5,437.68 = $5,097.04

Short sale UMS 9.75% due 2/06/01

Coupon interest: ($11,104.16)
Interest income at 5.00% on short sale proceeds: $5,533.34
Euroclear borrowing charge at 2.75% per annum: ($3,043.34)

Total: ($11,104.16) + $5,533.34 + ($3,043.34) = ($8,614.76)

Net gain/loss on financing = +$5,097.04 − $8,614.76 = ($3,517.72)

The result of this trade is:

Total gain/loss on Trade: +$32,500 − $3,517.72 = +$28,982.28

Annualized return: 25.45%

Obviously, it is unrealistic to think that this profit could be consistently transformed into a 25% annual return. However, we have assumed certain trade conditions which are not always in effect. These include the maximum 2.75% Euroclear borrowing charge. We have also assumed that the long Argentina position will not earn any incremental income by lending out the position in the general repo market. Finally, while these returns may pale against the high returns earned by simply pursuing an outright long strategy, they do produce returns with markedly lower volatilities and lower trade drawdowns.

The importance of including all borrowing charges in analyzing spread trades involving one particular bond that seems expensive compared to another cannot be overemphasized. This includes the fee to borrow the bond as well as the coupon which must be paid out on the borrowed (short) bond. To illustrate this point and the reduction in the earned return, we have produced another trade involving Argentina 01s and UMS 01s. In this case the spread between the two bonds collapsed even more. The trade begins on August 23 1996. Exhibit 5 summarizes the trade and the gain/loss on the bonds ignoring the financing cost.

Exhibit 5: Gain/Loss on Bond on Argentina-Mexico Sovereign Yield Curve Trade of August 1996

Initiate Trade 8/23/96

> Buy $1,000,000 Argentina 9.25% due 2/23/01 at $95.50
> Sell (short sale) $1,000,000 UMS 9.75% due 2/06/01 at $101.75

Reverse Trade 11/29/96

> Sell $1,000,000 Argentina 9.25% due 2/23/01 at $101.50
> Buy (repurchase) $1,000,000 UMS 9.75% due 2/06/01 at $103.625

Gain on Argentina '01	$1,015,000 − $955,000 = +$60,000
Loss on UMS '01	$1,017,500 − $1,036,250 = −$18,750
Net gain	$60,000 − $18,750 = $41,250

Exhibit 6: Gain/Loss on Financing on Argentina-Mexico Sovereign Yield Curve Trade of August 1996

Long Argentina 9.25% due 2/23/01

> Coupon interest: $24,666.67
> Borrowing cost (includes A/I) at 5.25%: ($13,204.59)
>
> Total: $24,666.67 − $13,204.59 = +$11,462.08

Short sale UMS 9.75% due 2/06/01

> Coupon interest: ($26,000.00)
> Interest income at 5.00% on short sale proceeds: $13,646.11
> Euroclear borrowing charge at 2.75% per annum: ($7,505.36)
>
> Total: ($26,000.00) + $13,646.11 + ($7,505.36) = ($19,859.25)

Net gain/loss on financing = $11,462.08 − $19,859.25 = ($8,397.17)

This trade produced a higher gain on the bond portion ($41,250) than our first trade ($32,500). However, the effect of the high cost of borrowing the bond and the payment of the coupon on the shorted bond will serve to reduce the earned return. The financing effect is shown in Exhibit 6. The result of this trade is:

> Total gain/loss on trade: $41,250 − $8,397.17 = +$32,852.83
>
> Annualized return: 12.32%

In the August 1996 trade, the spread contraction between the two assets is greater than for the March 1996 trade (116 bps versus 93 bps). Yet, we only earned $3,800 more on the trade and significantly less in percentage (annualized) terms. The difference is due to the combination of the Euroclear borrowing fee together with the payment of a high coupon (9.75%) over a longer period of time.

CORPORATE CREDIT CURVES-YIELDS AND SPREADS

An accurate, well defined corporate yield curve can provide a wealth of information. Some possible uses are:

1. Issuers can assess the current state of their outstanding debt as well as evaluate the market's ongoing reception of past issues.
2. Issuers can judge the underwriter's support of their issues in the secondary market.
3. Bankers can use the information to ascertain the optimal points along the credit yield curve which would be most receptive of additional issuance. Targeted data points can be tailored to fit the issuer's asset/liability needs.
4. Bankers can use the curve to help price new issues, and first time issuers can use the credit curve of a similar credit to help price their first time issue spread.
5. Investors and traders can take advantage of potential trade opportunities by visually spotting areas along the curve which have abnormally steep or flat areas.

The construction of a corporate credit curve involves the same guidelines which we used to construct a sovereign curve. The following example serves to illustrate.

Cemex is one of the most prolific and sophisticated issuers within the emerging markets. The construction of the curve begins with an delineation of their outstanding bonds. Exhibit 7 shows Cemex's outstanding bonds denominated in U.S. dollars. We have selected only these bonds shown in the exhibit to construct our Cemex corporate yield curve. The curve is plotted versus years to maturity in Exhibit 8.

Several items are readily apparent. The curve we have chosen has a more positive slope for the shorter term maturities compared to the longer term maturities. This accurate depiction quantifies the supply/demand imbalance of the issuer's desire to lengthen out the maturity profile and the desire of investors for a money market type product.[2] For maturities longer than seven years the curve is fairly flat as investors are indifferent between competing spreads over maturity points.

---

[2] After the devaluation of the Mexican Peso in January 1994, both sovereign and corporate issuers embarked upon an aggressive campaign to lengthen their maturity profiles. Investor preference, often led by flight capital, produced a fairly steep front-end yield curve.

Exhibit 7: Outstanding Bonds of Cemex

Issuer	Coupon (%)	Maturity	Original Issue Size (in millions of U.S. dollars)
Cemex	10.00	11/15/96	100
Cemex*	4.25	11/1/97	150
Cemex	8.875	6/10/98	1,000
Cemex**	10.00	11/5/99	150
Cemex	10.75	7/15/00	300
Cemex	8.50	8/31/00	250
Cemex	9.50	9/20/01	300
Tolmex	8.375	8/1/03	150
Cemex	12.75	7/15/06	300

* This bond is convertible into Cemex shares
** This bond was putable at $95.25 at 01/01/97

Exhibit 8: Cemex Spread Versus Years to Maturity

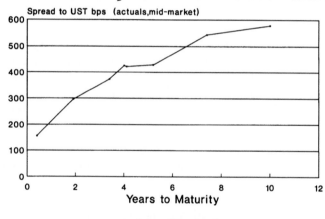

— Cemex $ Eurobonds
Source: Bankers Trust Database

The shape and form of the curve illustrates the interaction of investor demands for income (high coupon, high dollar price, high current yield) versus the desire for potential capital appreciation (low coupon, low dollar price, low current yield). This phenomenon was observed in mid-December 1996 and is demonstrated by comparing the following two bonds:[3]

	Price	Current Yield	Spread	Duration
Cemex 10.75% due 7/15/00	$103.5	10.39%	353bps	2.93
Cemex 8.50% due 8/31/00	$97.00	8.80%	335bps	3.09

[3] Bankers Trust Database-12/96

Exhibit 9: Cemex Stripped Corporate Curve

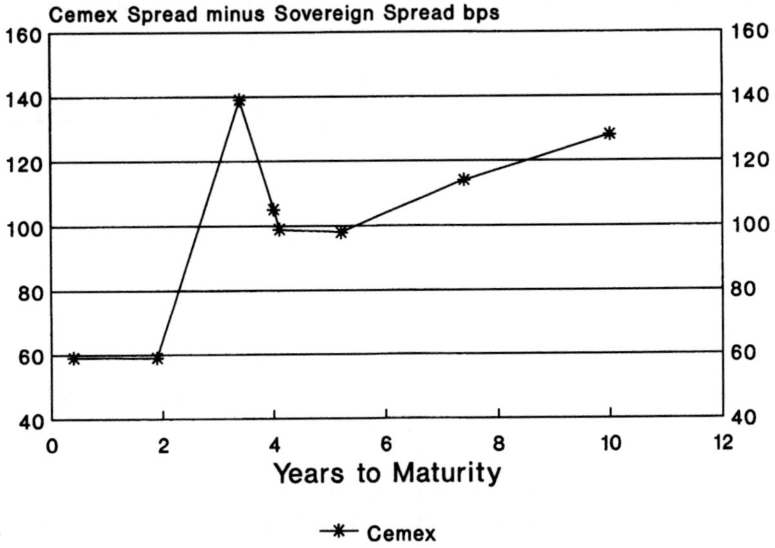

Cemex Spread minus Sovereign Spread bps

Years to Maturity

—*— Cemex

Source: Bankers Trust Database

Investors should be indifferent to owning the above two bonds with similar durations if the spreads are equal. However, the Cemex 8.5s with a slightly longer duration trade at a tighter spread than the Cemex 10.75s, demonstrating the market's preference, at this point in time, for lower absolute dollar price bonds.

CORPORATE TO SOVEREIGN SPREAD ANALYSIS

The spread at which an EM corporate trades is a function of several variables. Most notably is the market's assessment of the credit. The predominant driver of the spread is the sovereign component which, together with the corporate credit component, comprises the full spread. Extending our relative value analysis of corporate EM Eurobonds involves comparing the corporate curve against its sovereign curve to uncover areas, or points, of opportunity. By calculating the sovereign spread at that point along the curve, and then subtracting that sovereign spread from the total spread, we can assign a cleaner value as to how the market is pricing a particular credit. From our previous discussion, we place the two curves together and then subtract the two to produce the curve shown in Exhibit 9.[4]

As can be expected, it is reasonable to believe that investors would demand a greater yield spread as the term to maturity increases. This is a function in part of the market's perception of the ability and the intent of the issuer to repay their obligations

---

[4] Bankers Trust Database.

on a timely basis. Positive sloping spread curves assume a certain sense of monetary and fiscal "normalcy" with the issuing sovereign and respective corporate.[5] The following table demonstrates the differences between bonds of the same issuer:[6]

Bond	Spread to U.S. Treasury (bps)	Spread to Sovereign (bps)	Theoretical Spread to Sovereign
Cemex 98	206	16	N/A
Cemex 99	250	25	26
Cemex 00	293	63	36
Cemex 01	295	17	46
Tolmex 03	401	66	66
Cemex 06	439	84	86

By looking at the absolute spreads over U.S. Treasuries, one observes a modestly upward sloping spread curve with some flatness in the '00 to '01 portion of the curve. However, when the credit curve is overlaid against the Mexican sovereign curve, the tightness of the Cemex 01 issue is more readily observed. Investors who are interested in moving *in* along the Cemex credit curve can swap out of the Cemex 01 and into either of the Cemex 00 maturities and experience no reduction in spread to U.S. Treasuries. The relative value between the two bonds is more compelling when placed against the steepness in the Mexican sovereign curve, where the steepness of our Mexican sovereign Eurobond curve is 40 bps, compared with the 10 bps steepness in the identical area of the Cemex curve.

The importance of looking beyond the simple difference in spreads and factoring in the underlying sovereign spread between two corporate credits can be illustrated by the following example:[7]

Asset	Spread to U.S. Treasuries (bps)	Spread to Mexican Sovereign (bps)
Grupo Durango 12.00% 7/15/01	479	177
Grupo Durango 12.625% 8/01/03	520	120

By simply comparing the two bonds one could have concluded, incorrectly, that the slope of the Durango credit curve — as measured by the difference in spread between the 01s and 03s — was abnormally steep. The 41 bps difference between the two bonds was near the historical wide end of the trading range, prompting one to switch out of the Durango 01s and into the 03s. By looking *beyond* the simple spread difference and analyzing the slope of the underlying Mexican sov-

---

[5] During the Mexican Peso crisis, investors' concern over the immediate insolvency of the sovereign Mexico led investors to demand a significantly greater spread premium for the nearer term maturities, as those were the maturities which investors felt offered the lowest probability of principal repayment. Investors preferred the longer term maturities due to their rationalization that the issuer had more time to work out their short-term illiquidity problems. In periods of fiscal turmoil investors realize the "binary" nature of their investment decision which, if it matures soon, will be answered shortly.

[6] Bankers Trust Database-12/96.

[7] Bankers Trust Database-11/96.

ereign curve, one would have come to the opposite conclusion. In fact, the spread between the two bonds actually *widened* from 41 bps to 66 bps by late November 1996. Yet, the Durango 01 spread to Mexican sovereign came in from its wide of 177 bps to 152 bps along with a corresponding widening of the Durango 03 spread to sovereign, indicating that only now was the Durango 01, by this measure, relatively more expensive than the Durango 03. This trade opportunity was evident when one predicted that the slope of the Durango credit curve would begin to resemble the slope of the underlying sovereign curve.

The corporate to sovereign spread analysis can help uncover which points along the issuer's credit curve provide the best spread-advantaged areas for future issuance. (Obviously this neglects the non-monetary desires which issuers may require for their yield curve.) Steep, front end credit curves allow issuers to take advantage of the lack of short-term paper. Portions of the issuer's curve which have abnormal kinks, or bends, in their curve are areas for either future issuance (low spread points) or areas to avoid due to saturation (uneven bunching of maturities).

RELATIVE VALUE OPPORTUNITIES ACROSS OTHER MARKETS

By expanding upon our notion of stripped to sovereign spreads, we can quantify the relative value comparison of EM corporates with similar high-grade and high-yield bonds. By stripping the sovereignality from each corporate's spread, we can cleanly compare each market's assessment of strictly the credit component. By comparing just the credit component of both bonds we can uncover relative value opportunities across different markets. This analysis can often serve to signal the arrival, and exodus, of crossover money from the high-grade and high-yield markets.

The cornerstone of this analysis is to determine at what spread over U.S. Treasuries our target EM corporate credit would trade if it were in the U.S. marketplace. Drawing from our previous analysis, removing the sovereign spread component provides the raw materials to cleanly compare two credits in different markets. We begin by finding a comparable credit in the United States which best matches the characteristics of our selected EM credit. This is an inexact exercise at best because no two credits are exactly equal. However, selecting similar credits with respect to rating (unconstrained by any sovereign ceiling where applicable), industry, product visibility, free cash flow coverages and debt to capitalization, and equity matching can aid in the approximation of this analysis.

There are obvious shortcomings with this process. Attempting to find a similar U.S. corporate is difficult and involves a number of qualitative assumptions. The nuances and vagaries of the EM market distort the secondary market trading spreads. These influences have a greater impact in the EM market than in the deeper U.S. corporate market, where corporate capitalization and corporate familiarity often tend to outweigh individual corporate credit measurements.

Finally, in its purest sense, the determination of a corporate credit spread is the equilibrium point between buyers and sellers, and in a market which can be extremely inefficient, such as the EM market, this can produce extreme abnormalities. Many EM credits which trade through their predicted, or theoretical, value do so in large part as a function of the illiquidity of the market and the bond. This artificial *tightness* is difficult to reverse and often persists for long periods. The reversal of this collective investment outcome is dependent upon the rational, logical, and indifferent behavior of investors and their desire to avoid and reverse any economically non-optimal investment decision. Conversely, certain EM credits trade wide to their predicted value ranges due to the absence of strong investor sponsorship. This widening provides greater profitable investment opportunities than the (short) sale of abnormally narrow spread corporates.

One object of the comparison between two different bonds is to uncover relative value opportunities for those investors operating within the asset class of global high yield. Here, investors can switch out of one asset class, namely U.S. high yield, and into another, namely emerging markets, if they find similar credits at significantly wider spreads. Due to the subjectivity of the comparison process, it is often useful to include several assets with which to compare our target EM corporate credit. Investors can compare EM credits such as Durango in Mexico against similar credits in the U.S. including Stone Container and Gaylord Container. By comparing the pure corporate spread of each, investors can rank the relative attractiveness of each bond. However, strictly comparing the two can be misleading in an absolute sense. The comparative analysis must be placed in the context of the historical, relative ranges of all of the credits, each stripped of its representative sovereign component.

The ability to correctly predict when additional financial assets will migrate from one market to another is very problematic. When the shift is directed to the emerging markets the effect can be profound. The asset allocation from the U.S. high-yield market or other international high-yielding markets to emerging markets is often the result of relative value opportunities between the two markets. One way to monitor this relationship is to compare the U.S. high-yield market and the emerging markets to determine when one market is rich, or expensive, to the other. We can do this by comparing an index which best represents the composition and movements of each market. We chose two widely followed and well constructed indices, the JP Morgan Emerging Market Bond Index (EMBI) and the Merrill Lynch High Yield Index (MLHY), and compared the relative spread over U.S. Treasuries for each index.[8]

---

[8] This analysis also has flaws. The purpose of this exercise is to uncover when the participant of each market will be motivated to shift assets out of one market and into the other. While each index is constructed and rigidly maintained to encompass the widest constituency of the respective asset class, it assumes that all participants are able to freely invest in each included asset. This analysis also neglects historical changes with respect to duration. Finally, we are assuming that spread changes of each index efficiently reflect the improving or detoriating credit condition of the bonds in each index.

We have compared the two spreads to determine if one market is relatively expensive to the other. The emerging market index spread to U.S. Treasuries was very close to that of the U.S. high-yield market in late 1993 and early 1994. In fact, several new EM issuers were able to price their bonds at comparable spreads to similar credits in the United States, hence bypassing the EM sovereign spread for these issuers. The EM market was, on a relative value basis, expensive or overvalued to the U.S. high-yield market. An investor who would have shifted assets out of the EM market would have avoided the extreme spread widening which took place. The spread of EM to high yield kept widening during 1995 until it reached its maximum during late 1994 and early 1995. Indeed, during this period the EM market saw a significant influx of assets from the U.S. high-yield market. Many high-yield managers profited handsomely by allocating money into the EM market and enjoying the ensuing substantial price appreciation of these assets. Many portfolio managers who can actively allocate assets monitor this relationship to anticipate incoming flows from the more expensive market into the relatively cheaper market.

SUMMARY

The maturity of the emerging markets during late 1995 and through 1996 can be evidenced by the growing number of sovereign entities looking to exchange their collateralized Brady debt for long-term, uncollateralized Eurobonds. This, along with the ability of EM corporates to tap the market for longer maturities (often including innovative structures), provides the base product to profit from relative value abnormalities. Beginning with the solid foundation of a sovereign yield curve, investors and traders can effectively carry out their forward projections of the dynamics of the slope and direction of country curves. Since the sovereign component is critical to pricing a corporate's credit spread, the calculation and subtraction of the sovereign spread produces a clean valuation of the market's assessment of the pure, corporate credit risk. Finally, comparing the relative attractiveness of the EM market against other markets, including U.S. high-yield and other international high-yielding markets, can serve as a yardstick of the credit spreads available within the EM market. The continued growth and development of the Eurobond market should provide the practitioner of relative value analysis with a growing supply of return enhancement opportunities.

Chapter 10

Price Sensitivity and Risk Measures for Brady Bonds

Steven I. Dym, Ph.D.
President
Steven I. Dym & Associates

INTRODUCTION

Brady bonds are marketable securities created from defaulted bank loans to developing countries, under the auspices of then Secretary of the Treasury Nicholas Brady. These bonds come in a myriad of forms: collateralized and uncollateralized, fixed and floating rate, short and long term. While the bonds are denominated in a number of currencies, the bulk are dollar denominated, which is the concern of this chapter.

As with any non-governmental issue, Brady bonds must yield the U.S. Treasury rate plus a premium for credit risk. Thus, the bond's price will react to changes in the structure of U.S. yields and to movements in the market's perception of the issuing country's creditworthiness. Institutional investors, market makers, and traders need a precise measure of a Brady bond's responses to such changes. Positioning bonds in anticipation of shifts in these underlying variables is an important facet of the market, but becomes unmanageable without a concise measure of price sensitivity to such shifts. A dealer in Bradys may be comfortable with the credit risk of the firm's inventory, but a steep rise in U.S. interest rates will punish the portfolio even though the credit is unchanged. Hedging the U.S. interest rate aspect of the bond requires a measure of the bond's U.S. rate sensitivity. Finally, investors need to quantify their exposure to various markets. Separating a Brady's price sensitivity to U.S. interest rates and to credit risk is crucial in this regard.

This chapter presents such sensitivity measures in the familiar form of duration. By doing so it addresses the foregoing problems, as well as provides a basis for comparing Brady bond risk to that of other bonds. As a by-product of the analysis, the chapter also provides a new way to quantify the duration of floating-rate securities with credit risk. The risk measures developed here, therefore, are relevant to Eurobonds of developing countries as well, fixed and floating rate.

A substantial portion of this work was developed while the author was a consultant for Brinson Partners, Chicago, IL.

The format of the chapter is as follows. Formulas for price sensitivities, with corresponding durations, are presented for each of the four forms of Brady bonds: fixed or floating, with or without collateral. In each of the cases, the sensitivity measure is provided both for the U.S. interest rate component of the bond's yield, and for the credit risk component. Thus, there are eight measures in total. The algebraic derivations are tedious, but not complex, and are presented in summary form.

It is important to be aware that price sensitivity formulae are not measures of risk. A risk measure requires appending the volatility of the variable(s) to which the price is sensitive. The final section of the chapter shows how this is done. It also provides a comparison to corresponding risk measures for U.S. Treasury bonds and foreign currency denominated bonds of developed countries.

NOTATION

The following notation is used in this chapter:

P	=	price of bond
P_C	=	price of collateralized bond
C	=	coupon
m	=	maturity
y	=	yield to maturity
t	=	corresponding U.S. Treasury yield
tz	=	U.S. Treasury zero rate
r	=	bond credit spread over Treasuries
L	=	LIBOR
s	=	stated spread over LIBOR for floating-rate issues
Dur	=	standard duration measure
Dur_C	=	duration measure in presence of Treasury collateral

Thus, $y = t+r$. (In the context of floating-rate issues, r can be taken to represent the bond's discount margin.)

FIXED COUPON BONDS, NO COLLATERAL

A fixed-rate coupon bond with no collateral is the simplest type of bond, corresponding to the structure of a "plain vanilla" government bond. To review the interest rate-price relationship begin with the promised semiannual cash flows of the bond. (In this chapter we assume full coupon periods; that is, no accrued interest. Accommodating partial periods involves adjusting the maturity and duration by the fraction of the coupon period having elapsed.) The bond's present value is:

$$P = \frac{C/2}{1+y/2} + \frac{C/2}{(1+y/2)^2} + \frac{C/2}{(1+y/2)^3} + \dots + \frac{C/2+100}{(1+y/2)^{2m}} \tag{1}$$

where $y=t+r$. Notice that each of the cash flows are treated symmetrically in terms of their discount factor — the yield in the denominator equals the sum of the risk-free Treasury rate plus the risk premium. Thus, the bond's price sensitivity to these two variables will be the same.

First, write the standard duration formula:

$$\text{Dur} = \left[\frac{C/2}{1+y/2} \cdot 1/2 + \frac{C/2}{(1+y/2)^2} \cdot 2/2 + \frac{C/2}{(1+y/2)^3} \cdot 3/2 \right. $$
$$\left. + \ldots + \frac{C/2+100}{(1+y/2)^{2m}} \cdot m \right] /P \tag{2}$$

Taking the derivatives of bond price with respect to the two variables — the Treasury rate and the credit spread — we have the following well known price sensitivities:

$$\frac{\Delta P/P}{\Delta t} = -\frac{\text{Dur}}{1+y/2} \tag{3}$$

$$\frac{\Delta P/P}{\Delta r} = -\frac{\text{Dur}}{1+y/2} \tag{4}$$

Consider the (non-Brady) Republic of Argentina Eurobond of November 1 1999, paying a coupon of 10.95%. In early February 1996 it was yielding 8.55%, for a price of 107.5 (plus 2.85 of accrued interest). The interest rate on the interpolated U.S. Treasury note at that time was 5.08%, for a credit spread of 3.47%. Its duration using equation (3) was 3.11 years. Thus, a 10 basis point increase in either the Treasury rate or the credit spread will cause a 0.30% drop in the bond's price to 107.17.

FIXED-COUPON BONDS, PRINCIPAL COLLATERALIZED

The typical benchmark Brady bond — the "Pars" or "Discounts" — have their principal payments at maturity collateralized by U.S. Treasury zero coupons. This makes the cash flow of 100 in equation (1) riskless from a credit standpoint. As such, it should be discounted by the Treasury zero coupon rate for that maturity, without a premium for credit risk. For a fixed coupon collateralized bond, its present value therefore is:

$$P\_C = \frac{C/2}{1+(t+r)/2} + \frac{C/2}{(1+(t+r)/2)^2} + \ldots$$
$$+ \frac{C/2}{(1+(t+r)/2)^{2m}} + \frac{100}{(1+tz/2)^{2m}} \tag{5}$$

The lack of symmetry in the discount factors for the cash flows implies that were we to calculate yield to maturity in the standard way (as in equation (1)), the yield would be a blend of the credit spread and the Treasury rates, but would not be additive. Market convention is to subtract the last term from the price, which leaves the coupon cash flows to be discounted by the "stripped yield." (The terminology reflects the removal of the Treasury collateral from the bond.) r is then termed the "stripped spread."[1]

For example, Mexico's Par Brady bond, with a coupon of 6.25% and maturing December 31 2019, was priced at 67.375 in early February 1996. The interpolated Treasury bond yield at that time was 5.99%, while the Treasury zero was 6.53%. Solving for r in equation (5) produced a stripped spread of 6.96% and a stripped yield of 12.95%.

Treasury Yield Price Sensitivity

In order to arrive at a price sensitivity measure analytically similar to the standard method which uses duration, we define the duration of a principal collateralized bond, or "collateralized duration," in the following way:

$$
\text{Dur\_}C = \left[\frac{C/2}{1 + (t+r)/2} \cdot 1/2 + \frac{C/2}{(1 + (t+r)/2)^2} \cdot 2/2 + \ldots \right.
$$
$$
\left. + \frac{C/2}{(1+(t+r)/2)^{2m}} \cdot m + \frac{100}{(1+tz/2)^{2m}} \cdot m \cdot \frac{1+(t+r)/2}{1+tz/2} \right] / P\_C \quad (6)
$$

Notice that the final term receives more weight. Since it is riskless, it is discounted less heavily. And the "correction factor" $(1+(t+r)/2)/(1+tz/2)$ raises it somewhat more. This is as it should be — a change in Treasury yields will affect the bond considerably, as it is a factor in all the bond's cash flows, in particular the last one. But a change in the credit risk will have less of an effect on the bond's price, as it discounts only the coupon payments. Defined this way, the Mexican Par bond's collateralized duration is 12.51 years. (Duration calculated in the standard way would be 10.30 years.)

Specifying collateralized duration this way produces a very concise price sensitivity measure for the bond with respect to changes in the Treasury yield, exactly parallel to that for a non-collateralized bond, namely:

$$
\frac{\Delta P\_C / P\_C}{\Delta t} = - \frac{\text{Dur\_}C}{1 + (t+r)/2} \quad (7)
$$

---

[1] Technically, another factor enters the "stripped" calculations. The first two or three interest payments may also be collateralized for some Brady bonds, but with high grade money market instruments rather than Treasury zeros. Clearly, their discount factor should contain some sort of risk premium, albeit of lower order of magnitude than the bare coupons. It is a "rolling" guarantee, which means simply assigning the collateral to the nearby coupons is not entirely correct. Further, the precise circumstances which initiate payment of the collateral are complex. Some analysts, therefore, do not "strip" these interest payments from the bond. While not a perfect solution, this is the approach taken here.

The stripped calculations also ignore any "value recovery rights" (a call on the country's oil export revenues), if any.

For the Mexican Par, a 10 basis point increase in the Treasury yield causes a price decline of 1.17% to 66.58.[2]

Credit Spread Price Sensitivity

The collateralized bond's price sensitivity to changes in the credit spread is not symmetric with its Treasury rate sensitivity. The credit risk premium is only present in the discount factor for the coupon cash flows, so a change will have less of an impact on price. The sensitivity here takes the following form:

$$\frac{\Delta P\_C/P\_C}{\Delta r} = -\frac{\text{Dur}\_C - A/P}{1 + (t+r)/2} \tag{8}$$

where

$$A = m \cdot 100 \cdot \frac{1 + (t+r)/2}{(1 + tz/2)^{2m+1}}$$

Notice that the presence of the A/P term in the numerator of equation (8) reduces the impact of a change in the risk premium on the bond's price compared to a change in the Treasury yield of the same magnitude. (For the Mexican Par A/P=7.80.) A 10 basis point rise in the risk premium causes the bond's price to decline by only 0.46% to 67.06, well less than half the impact of the same basis point rise in Treasury yields.

FLOATING RATE BONDS, NO COLLATERAL

Calculating duration, hence price sensitivity, of a fixed coupon bond, even with some cash flows collateralized, is relatively simple, as shown above. What about issues with non-fixed coupons? If the bond is priced at par, then the process is again straightforward: duration equals the time until the next interest setting date, so that its price sensitivity is equivalent to that of a money market instrument. But Brady bonds typically trade far from par. The following discussion presents a general method of calculating durations and price sensitivities of floating-rate issues, regardless of their price, and whether they are Bradys or not. The next section adapts the method to collateralized bonds.

Consider first a non-government floating-rate note which pays, every six months, the then current 6-month LIBOR rate, L_i, plus a fixed spread, s. To arrive at the price, the market discounts each expected cash flow by the fixed long-term LIBOR rate, L, appropriate for the bond's maturity, plus the credit risk premium, r, for that point in time. It is important to note that while s is fixed for the life of the floater, r is market determined, and therefore will vary according to market conditions, just as yield to maturity or spot rates do. The bond's price thus reflects all the *expected* future values of L_i, and is determined by:[3]

---

[2] Implicit in this result is the assumption that the zero spot rate moves one-for-one with the Treasury coupon curve. A minor correction factor (available from the author) is necessary when this is not the case.
[3] Operationally, calculating the credit spread, r, requires substituting the prevailing fixed swap rate for LIBOR and solving for the credit spread that produces the market price.

$$P = \frac{100 \cdot (L_1 + s)/2}{1 + (L + r)/2} + \frac{100 \cdot (L_2 + s)/2}{(1 + (L + r)/2)^2} + \frac{100 \cdot (L_3 + s)/2}{(1 + (L + r)/2)^3}$$
$$+ \dots + \frac{100 \cdot (1 + (L_m + s)/2)}{(1 + (L + r)/2)^{2m}} \tag{9}$$

Calculating the effect of a change in LIBOR on the floater's price is complicated because both the cash flows in the numerator and the discount factors in the denominator will change. A way to get around this is by recognizing that if long-term rates, L, are completely determined by expected future rates, L_i, we can substitute L for all the expected L_i. (Alternatively, the cash flows can be "swapped" for a fixed coupon via an interest rate swap paying L fixed.) Doing so, and rewriting each cash flow as $L+s=(L+r)+(s-r)$, the bond's price can be presented as:

$$P = \frac{100 \cdot (L + r)/2}{1 + (L + r)/2} + \frac{100 \cdot (L + r)/2}{(1 + (L + r)/2)^2} + \frac{100 \cdot (L + r)/2}{(1 + (L + r)/2)^3} + \dots$$
$$+ \frac{100 \cdot (L + r)/2}{(1 + (L + r)/2)^{2m}} + \frac{100}{(1 + (L + r)/2)^{2m}} + \frac{100 \cdot (s - r)/2}{1 + (L + r)/2}$$
$$+ \frac{100 \cdot (s - r)/2}{(1 + (L + r)/2)^2} + \frac{100 \cdot (s - r)/2}{(1 + (L + r)/2)^3} + \dots + \frac{100 \cdot (s - r)/2}{(1 + (L + r)/2)^{2m}} \tag{10}$$

Recognizing that the first set of discounted cash flows are simply that of a bond paying a *fixed* coupon of $100 \cdot (L+r)$, the price can be rewritten further as:

$$P = 100 + \frac{100 \cdot (s - r)/2}{1 + (L + r)/2} + \frac{100 \cdot (s - r)/2}{(1 + (L + r)/2)^2} + \frac{100 \cdot (s - r)/2}{(1 + (L + r)/2)^3} + \dots$$
$$+ \frac{100 \cdot (s - r)/2}{(1 + (L + r)/2)^{2m}} + \frac{100}{(1 + (L + r)/2)^{2m}} - \frac{100}{(1 + (L + r)/2)^{2m}} \tag{11}$$

This can be finally simplified as:

$$P = 100 + P^* - \frac{100}{(1 + (L + r)/2)^{2m}} \tag{12}$$

where P^* is the price of a bond with coupon $100 \cdot (s-r)$, yielding $L+r$ and maturing in m years. While this bond also has a variable coupon, importantly it does not vary with LIBOR, so that its price sensitivity with respect to LIBOR (as well as its duration) is analytically calculable. This, in turn, means that getting a measure of price sensitivity (and duration) for the original bond is relatively easy. But before we do so, we must adapt this formulation to a Brady bond.

Brady issues trade off the U.S. Treasury curve. This means that the long-term Treasury yield, t, appropriate to the floater's maturity, replaces LIBOR as the yield in the denominator. To arrive at an equation like equation (12) rewrite each cash flow as $L+s=(L-t)+(t+r)+(s-r)$. Let $x=L-t$, the spread between the long-term LIBOR and Treasury yields. Then proceeding in exactly the same manner as above, we can write the value of the floater's cash flows as:

$$P = 100 + P^* - \frac{100}{(1+(t+r)/2)^{2m}}$$ (13)

where now P^* becomes the price of a bond with coupon $100 \cdot [x+(s-r)]$, yielding $t+r$ and maturing in m years.

Treasury Yield Price Sensitivity
Price sensitivity with respect to the Treasury yield is simply a matter of taking the derivatives of each of the three terms in equation (13):

$$\frac{\Delta P/P}{\Delta t} = -\frac{\text{Dur}^* \cdot P^*/P}{1+(t+r)/2} + \frac{100/P}{(1+(t+r)/2)^{2m+1}} \cdot m$$ (14)

where Dur* is the duration of an m year, $100 \cdot [x+(s-r)]$ fixed coupon bond, yielding $t+r$.

Consider the Venezuelan FLIRB (Floating Rate Interest Reduction bond), paying 6-month LIBOR plus $7/8\%$, maturing March 31, 2007. In February 1996, it was trading at 59.875. The corresponding Treasury yield was 5.69%. Using the (interpolated) 11-year swap rate of 6.05% for long-term LIBOR, this produced a credit spread of 8.50%. Then $x+(s-r)$ is -7.27%, which produces a bond price (P^*) of negative 18.4232 (without accrued interest) with a duration of negative 2.99 years.[4] Putting all the terms in equation (14) together, an increase of 10 basis point in the Treasury yield causes the floater's price to rise by 0.27% to 60.04.[5]

Credit Spread Price Sensitivity
The effect of a change in the risk premium on the floater's price is simpler, since the risk variable appears only in the denominator of the pricing equation (9). Substitute the fixed swap rate for LIBOR in the numerator to produce a "synthetic" fixed coupon equal to the swap rate plus the floater's spread over LIBOR. Then take the derivative with respect to r. The result is exactly equation (8), but where duration is that of a bond with the floater's maturity, yielding $t+r$ and a fixed coupon of $L+s$. For the Venezuelan FLIRB, duration is 6.62 years so that a 10 basis points rise in the risk premium will result in a 0.62% *decline* in price to 59.49.

---

[4] This bond is only being used to illustrate the methodology for floating-rate issues. In fact, the bond has an amortization schedule which will shorten its average life, hence durations and price sensitivities.

[5] This result assumes no change in the LIBOR-Treasury spread in response to the shift in Treasury yields ($\Delta x/\Delta t=0$). Allowing for changes in the spread results in:

$$\frac{\Delta P/P}{\Delta t} = -\frac{\text{Dur} \cdot P^*/P}{1+(t+r)/2} + \frac{100/P}{(1+(t+r)/2)^{2m+1}} \cdot m + \frac{\Delta x}{\Delta t} \cdot \frac{100}{P} \cdot Z$$

where

$$Z = \frac{1-(1+(t+r)/2)^{-2m}}{(t+r)/2}$$

FLOATING-RATE BONDS, PRINCIPAL COLLATERALIZED

There are no new complications in the case of floating-rate bonds that are principal collateralized. We already know how to alter the duration formula for a collateralized bond. And we have just presented a method for calculating price sensitivity to rate movements for floating-rate issues. Thus, a collateralized floater requires going through the same steps we did in deriving equation (13) for an uncollateralized floater, but recognizing that in the presence of collateral the final term is discounted using only the Treasury zero rate. This leads to:

$$P\_C = 100 + P\_C^* - \frac{100}{(1 + (t + r)/2)^{2m}} \tag{15}$$

where P_C^* is the price of a *collateralized bond* with fixed coupon $100 \cdot [x+(s-r)]$, credit risk premium r and maturing in m years.

Treasury Yield Price Sensitivity

Taking the derivative for price sensitivity with respect to the Treasury yield we have:

$$\frac{\Delta P\_C / P\_C}{\Delta t} = - \frac{Dur\_C^* \cdot P\_C^* / P\_C}{1 + (t + r)/2} + \frac{100 / P\_C}{(1 + (t + r)/2)^{2m+1}} \cdot m \tag{16}$$

where Dur^*_C is the collateralized duration (as defined in equation (6)) of an m year, $100 \cdot [x+(s-r)]$ fixed coupon bond, with corresponding Treasury yield t and risk premium r.[6]

Brazil's Discount bond is a floating rate, collateralized issue. It pays LIBOR + $^{13}/_{16}$% and matures April 15, 2024. In early February 1996, this bond was priced at 66.5. The corresponding Treasury was yielding 6.12%, with the appropriate Treasury zero 6.57%, for a stripped spread of 8.37%. Using the (interpolated) 28-year swap rate of 6.63% for long-term LIBOR, $x+(s-r)$ is -7.07%, which produces a collateralized (P_C^*) bond price of negative 31.6528 (without accrued interest) and a collateralized duration of negative 4.30 years. Using equation (16), an increase of 10 basis points in the Treasury yield causes the collateralized floater's price to decline by 0.12% to 66.42.[7]

Credit Spread Price Sensitivity

For the effect of a change in the credit spread on the collateralized floater's price, equation (8) can be used, but substitute the swap rate plus the spread for the fixed coupon in calculating collateralized duration. For the Brazil Discount issue, a synthetic fixed coupon consisting of the 6.63% swap rate plus the spread of $^{13}/_{16}$% produces a bond with a collateralized duration of 11.89 years. A 10 basis points increase in the credit spread causes the floater's price to drop by 0.47% to 66.18.

---

[6] The statement in footnote 3 applies here as well.

[7] Here, too, we need to add the extra term as explained in footnote 5 to recognize any changes in the LIBOR-Treasury spread caused by the movement in rates.

COMPARATIVE MEASURES OF RISK

We can define risk for a bond as the standard deviation of its relative price movements.[8] Since Brady bond prices are functions of two variables, $P(t,r)$, we have:

$$VAR(\Delta P_{Brady}/P_{Brady})$$

$$= Dur_t^2 \cdot VAR(\Delta t) + Dur_r^2 \cdot VAR(\Delta r) + 2 \cdot Dur_t \cdot Dur_r \cdot COV(\Delta t, \Delta r) \quad (17)$$

where VAR and COV are variance and covariance, and where we have suppressed the $1+(t+r)/2$ term in the divisor (or, alternatively, redefined duration in "modified" form).[9] Dur_t and Dur_r are the Treasury yield and credit spread price sensitivities, respectively, as defined above, and will differ according to whether the bond is collateralized or not, fixed or floating rate. Risk is the square root of this variance. Note that only in the case of fixed, un-collateralized Brady bonds or developing country Eurobonds will the two price sensitivities be equal (as in equations (3) and (4)). In that case equation (17) collapses to:

$$VAR(\Delta P_{Brady}/P_{Brady})$$

$$= Dur^2 \cdot [VAR(\Delta t) + VAR(\Delta r) + 2 \cdot COV(\Delta t, \Delta r)] \quad (18)$$

How should a portfolio manager think about these risk measures? One way is to compare them to the risk of similar maturity U.S. Treasury bonds. Since there is obviously no credit risk we can write:

$$VAR(\Delta P_{U.S.}/P_{U.S.}) = Dur^2 \cdot VAR(\Delta t) \quad (19)$$

Compare the structure of the simple Brady or Eurobond in equation (18) to the Treasury bond in equation (19). The former will have a higher yield, somewhat lowering the duration. The Eurobond will carry a higher coupon, further lowering duration, but this will not be the case for the Brady. In any case, the addition of the variance of the risk premium significantly adds to the total variance as given by equation (18), hence to the bond's risk, and will almost certainly swamp the effect of the possibly lower duration. The covariance term's contribution depends on its sign. While this will be a function of the particular country and the market environment at any point in time, history points to an expected positive correlation.[10]

If the Brady bond has one of the other three structures, the comparison is between equations (17) and (19). The presence of collateral, if any, in the Brady raises the Treasury duration, since, as explained earlier, the last cash flow receives

---

[8] This is developed in S. Dym, "Measuring the Risk of Foreign Bonds," *Journal of Portfolio Management,* Winter 1991.

[9] We also continue with the assumption in footnote 2.

[10] Even in a negative correlation case, it is unlikely for the net effect to be a reduction in total variance since for this to be true it must be the case that $COV(\Delta t, \Delta r) < 0.5 \cdot VAR(\Delta r)$.

more weight. But, for the same reason, the spread duration is lower. For floating-rate issues, of course, Treasury duration is reduced (and sometimes negative), with collateral mitigating this effect. Thus, variance and risk depend on the structure of the bond, the country and the market environment, and require a case by case analysis.

It is instructive to make a final comparison with foreign currency denominated bonds of developed, or industrialized, nations. From the perspective of the U.S. investor, the bond's value, $P_{foreign}$, is P/e, where P is the bond's price in foreign currency terms, and e is the exchange rate, measured in units of the foreign currency per U.S. dollar. Since we are dealing with government issues, it is safe to ignore the credit risk, as we did with U.S. Treasury bonds. For these assets, therefore, foreign exchange risk in a sense replaces credit risk. Thus:

$$\mathrm{VAR}(\Delta P_{foreign}/P_{foreign})$$
$$= \mathrm{Dur}^2 \cdot \mathrm{VAR}(\Delta t) + \mathrm{VAR}(\Delta e/e) + 2 \cdot \mathrm{Dur} \cdot \mathrm{COV}(\Delta t, \Delta e/e) \quad (20)$$

where t is now the yield of the foreign government bond and Dur its duration. Can we compare equation (20) for foreign industrialized country bonds to equations (17) or (18) for developing country bonds? Foreign exchange rates tend to be quite volatile and, depending on the country, can account for upwards of two thirds of a foreign bond's overall risk.[11] Just as with developing country bonds, foreign bond risk depends on the country and the market environment, as well as on the specific bond's duration. Hence, while we cannot make any generalized statements about comparative risk across the various categories of bonds, this analysis allows the trader or investor to pinpoint which parameters are relevant, and how they would enter into an overall risk measure.

---

[11] This estimate is from Dym, "Measuring the Risk of Foreign Bonds."

Chapter 11

Local Fixed Income Arbitrage

Marcelo Castro
Vice President
U.B.S. Securities

Efstathia Pilarinu, Ph.D.
Vice President
Bankers Trust Securities

INTRODUCTION

This chapter discusses relationships that hold for local fixed income securities. The two basic risks, interest rate and foreign exchange risk, are quantified. The arbitrage relationship between local interest rates and LIBOR is discussed in frictionless markets and in markets with capital control restrictions. The behavior of local interest rates versus local dollar interest rates is also examined.

The relationships are then applied to three case studies. The first case study is on Ecuadorian sucre-denominated but dollar-indexed bonds. The second case study is on a hedged portfolio of Mexican Cetes with Coberturas. The last case study is on hedging the foreign exchange risk, the slippage risk present in a dual exchange rate system, and convertibility risk in a Brazilian portfolio.

INTEREST RATE RISK VERSUS FOREIGN EXCHANGE RISK IN LOCAL FIXED INCOME SECURITIES

Local fixed income instruments in emerging markets entail many types of risks which may not be present in other developed international fixed income markets. Liquidity considerations are important, since in many of the aforementioned local markets no market makers exist and secondary market trading is thin and usually one way. Counterparty risks, settlement risks, and custody risks are also considerable when dealing with very low capitalization brokerage companies or even with local exchanges that have been operating for a very short period. Convertibility risk is another major consideration, since foreign exchange controls can be (and have been) imposed in emerging market countries. Event risk, resulting from shocks to the financial system (e.g., a banking crisis, a sudden change of regulations, etc.), can make repatriation of foreign capital difficult or impossible.

All of the above risks are not easily quantifiable. In contrast, the risk due to changes in local interest rates and the risk due to changes in the foreign exchange rate can be measured for any local fixed income security. A simple example is a 1-year zero-coupon (discount) Treasury-bill (T-bill) denominated in a foreign currency. The price of the T-bill in a local currency assuming a 30/360 daycount is:

$$P = \frac{1}{(1+y)} \tag{1}$$

where

P = price
y = yield

The dollar price is:

$$\$P = \left[\frac{1}{(1+y)}/Fx_0\right] \tag{2}$$

where

Fx_0 = foreign exchange rate
$\$P$ = dollar price

The change in the dollar price for a unit change in the yield assuming an unchanged foreign exchange rate is equal to the product of the foreign exchange rate times the dollar price squared, as shown below:

$$\frac{\partial \$P}{\partial y} = -\frac{\$P}{(1+y)} = -\$P^2(F_{x_0}) \tag{3}$$

The change in the dollar price for a unit change in the foreign exchange rate is equal to the ratio of the dollar price over the foreign exchange rate as shown below:

$$\frac{\partial \$P}{\partial Fx} = -\frac{1}{(1+y)(Fx^2)} = -\frac{\$P}{Fx} \tag{4}$$

The change in the dollar price for a unit percentage change in the foreign exchange rate is equal to the ratio of the dollar price over the foreign exchange rate times the initial foreign exchange rate as shown below:

$$\frac{\partial \$P}{\partial((Fx - Fx_0)/Fx_0)} = \frac{1}{Fx_0}\left(\frac{\partial \$P}{\partial Fx}\right)$$

$$= -\frac{1}{Fx_0}\left[\frac{1}{(1+y)(Fx^2)}\right] = -\frac{\$P}{Fx_0(Fx)} \tag{5}$$

Exhibit 1 shows the percentage price change of the 1-year T-bill for a given change in local interest rates (assuming the exchange rate remains unchanged) and for a given percentage change in the exchange rate (assuming local rates remain unchanged). The convexity of the percentage price change with respect to yield is negligible since the tenor is relatively short. For example, a 200 basis point (bp) drop in local interest rates results in a 1.68% price appreciation. (See the dashed line in Exhibit 1.) A 200 bp rise in rates results in 1.63% price depreciation. On the other hand, a 2% devaluation of the currency results in a 1.96% price drop (assuming yields are unchanged). An equal currency appreciation results in a 2.04% price increase.

It should be clear that the effect of rising local interest rates can be offset from an appreciating (i.e., strengthening) currency. Similarly, the effect of a devaluation in the currency (i.e., a weakening) can be offset by a drop in local interest rates.

Exhibit 2 shows the percentage price change of a 1-year T-bill as a function of a simultaneous change in both yield (measured in basis points) and foreign exchange (percentage change). For example, if rates rise 100 basis points (bps) and the currency appreciates 1%, there is only a 0.18% price appreciation. If rates rise 400 bps and the currency appreciates 4%, the price appreciation is 0.83%. The percentage price change is slightly convex with respect to yield and currency changes. For example, a 400 bp drop in rates coupled with a currency devaluation of 4%, results in a price depreciation of 0.55% which is lower than the symmetric appreciation of 0.83%.

Exhibit 1: Percentage Dollar Price Change as a Function of a Change in Yield (Assuming Constant Foreign Exchange) and as a Function of a Change in Foreign Exchange (Assuming Constant Yield)

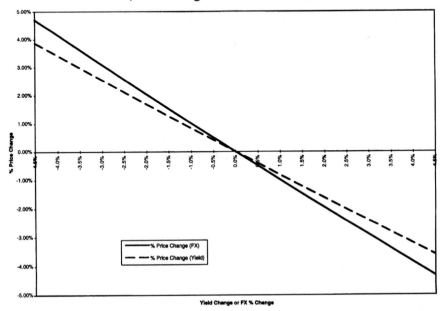

Exhibit 2: Percentage Dollar Price Change as a Function of Changes in Yields and in Foreign Exchange

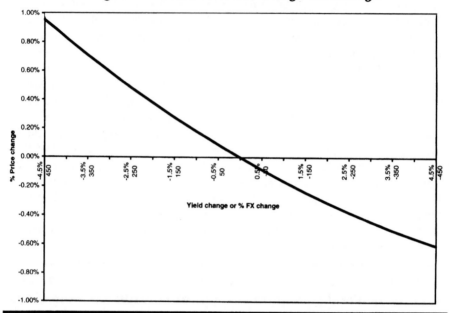

WHY LOCAL RATES MAY DIFFER FROM LIBOR

The interest parity states that assuming no restrictions on capital flows and no arbitrage opportunities, the domestic interest rate in any foreign country should satisfy the following relationship:[1]

$$(\text{LIBOR} + s)t = \frac{(1 + i)^t}{(1 + \hat{e}_t)} - 1 \tag{6}$$

where

LIBOR	=	London Interbank Offered Rate
s	=	the foreign country risk spread
i	=	the domestic interest rate in the foreign country
t	=	time
$\hat{e}_t$	=	the expected devaluation of the local currency versus the international currency, in period t

---

[1] For t greater than one year, LIBOR should be compounded. Therefore, equation (6) should be rewritten as:

$$(1 + \text{LIBOR} + s)^t = \frac{(1 + i)^t}{(1 + \hat{e}_t)}$$

We will use the linear rate version, as depicted in equation (6), because we are dealing with short-term capital flows.

The right-hand side of equation (6) represents the interest rate earned in U.S. dollars[2] by investing in the local market and hedging currency risk. The left-hand side represents the cost of funding in dollars, taking into account country risk. Therefore, any inequality in equation (6) would represent a perfect arbitrage situation: if the domestic interest rate in dollars is greater than LIBOR plus the country risk spread, money would flow indefinitely into the country to capture the interest rate differential. Alternatively, if the local interest rate in dollars is lower than the international benchmark plus the country risk spread, foreign investors and local participants will realize that they are not being properly compensated for accepting the risk of investing in the local market, and will exit the country until international reserves are exhausted.

Equation (6) is restrictive for policymakers who may want to independently conduct monetary and exchange rate policy. The most frequent situation is when the Central Bank wants to maintain a high interest rate in an economy with a currency peg or a band system on foreign exchange. This can result in a spread over LIBOR higher than what the market attributes as the country risk. As a consequence, foreign capital starts flowing into the country to take advantage of the high spread. In the short run, the increase of foreign capital inflows can cause an appreciation of the currency and a drop in the local interest rate. To prevent this, the Central Bank may purchase the excess dollars and print money, which is then sterilized by selling local currency denominated bonds. Sterilization operations, however, cannot be performed repeatedly without inconveniently increasing the amount of domestic public debt.

Another solution is to impose some form of capital controls. Such restrictions can reduce the dollar inflows and, at least for some time, enable the central bank to control both the currency and interest rates. Therefore, equation (6) may not hold in markets with capital controls, thus creating opportunities for local fixed income arbitrage. Capital controls usually have been imposed in the following forms: taxes on earnings, upfront fees, and minimum tenor requirements.

Taxes on Earnings

Taxes on earnings are withholding taxes imposed on earnings to reduce the flows of foreign capital into the local market. To include the effect of withholding tax on earnings, equation (6) should be rewritten as follows:

$$(\text{LIBOR} + s)t = \frac{[(1 + i)^t - 1](1 - \text{tax}) + 1}{(1 + \hat{e}_t)} - 1 \qquad (7)$$

where tax = tax rate on earnings.

The difference between equation (6) and equation (7) is the term

$$[(1 + i)^t - 1](1 - \text{tax})$$

which represents the after-tax earnings in the local market.

---

[2] It is assumed henceforth that the foreign investor obtains funds in U.S. dollars.

Upfront Fees

Upfront fees are an initial cost that foreign investors have to pay to enter the local fixed income market. The fees are usually payable on the foreign exchange, as the investor sells dollars to buy the local currency. Brazil adopted such a system in 1993. The Brazilian authorities established several types of investments, each one with its own upfront fees (these are called "Imposto sobre Operações Financeiras" — IOF). The Brazilian IOF has varied according to the levels of local interest rates and foreign capitals. Under such a system, it is important to determine the break-even period of time required to recover the initial investment, including upfront fees.

As an example, let's assume the upfront fee is 5%, and that the investor obtains funding at LIBOR plus 100 bps. An initial investment of $100 will result in $5 of upfront fee. Therefore, the total initial investment is $105. Let's assume that the local bonds yield 12% per annum in dollars after taxes. Assuming that the investor's horizon is one year, the initial $100 will be worth $112. Dividing $112 by the initial investment of $105, we obtain an annual return of 6.67%. Assuming LIBOR at 5.5% per annum (p.a.), the 1-year dollar return in the local market is only 12 bps higher than the investor's funding cost of 6.5% p.a.

Was it a bad investment decision? It depends on the investor's investment horizon. Notice that for the second year the position can be rolled-over without any additional upfront fee. Once the upfront fee has been amortized, the investor has a free option to roll over the position. The option value depends on the forward local interest rate in dollars for the second year, as well as the volatility of such a rate. In practice, experience has shown that the trade just described is not regarded as attractive. Yet, sometimes a favorable combination of both high local interest rate in dollars and low upfront fees may lead to a break-even period of less than 6 months.

For the case of capital controls with both upfront fees and withholding taxes on earnings, equation (6) should be revised as follows:

$$(\text{LIBOR} + s)\bar{\imath} = \frac{[(1+i)^{\bar{\imath}} - 1](1 - \text{tax}) + 1}{(1 + \hat{e}_t)(1 + \theta)} - 1 \tag{8}$$

where

θ = upfront fee
$\bar{\imath}$ = investment horizon

Minimum Tenor Requirements

Some countries impose a minimum period during which remittances are either prohibited or heavily taxed. Sometimes, even within the minimum tenor the investor is able to capture high rates, although the longer-than-desired minimum tenor may limit the amount of risk the investor is willing to take. There are other situations where the investor likes the country risk, but since the return is not so attractive, a shorter maturity would be preferable. Here, assessing the future level of local rates is key: once the minimum tenor is reached, the position attains daily liquidity. If, at that moment, high rates still prevail, the initial investment in the country would have paid off.

Another consideration regarding markets with minimum tenor requirements is whether or not an investment in local fixed income securities grants access to other local instruments that would otherwise be barred to foreign investors. A franchise in local swaps, options, and equities can represent an important competitive advantage, and may justify an investment in local securities at not really attractive returns.

How Local USD Interest Rates Change

We just demonstrated that the local interest rate in dollars may differ from the risk-free international rate plus a risk spread due to taxation and maturity constraints. We define the local interest rate in dollars as $i_{us\$}$, so that:

$$i_{us\$} = \left[\frac{(1+i)^t}{(1+\hat{e}_t)} - 1\right]\frac{1}{t} \tag{9}$$

It is interesting to observe how $i_{us\$}$ behaves. In the previous section, it was shown how capital restrictions cause substantial divergences between the $i_{us\$}$ and LIBOR. Generally, when currency risk is low, $\hat{e}_t$ follows the expectation of the inflation differential, and $i_{us\$}$ will be as high as the real interest rate is expected to be. As currency risk increases, $\hat{e}_t$ will start trading at a spread over the inflation rate; in other words, those who demand a currency hedge have to pay a premium to convince speculators to go long the local currency. In this situation, other things being equal, $i_{us\$}$ tends to decrease — the more expensive hedge reduces the foreign investor's gains. However, local interest rates can be so high that, despite the more expensive hedge, $i_{us\$}$ remains high. Finally, when currency risk is deemed extremely high, $i_{us\$}$ tends to be always low, regardless of the level of local interest rates; a negative $i_{us\$}$ is rare, but has been observed for short periods of time.

The relationship just described assumes that there is no credit risk involved in hedge instruments nor in dollar-linked bonds issued by local governments. In times of extreme distrust regarding the government capacity to pay, the credit risk may play an overwhelming role, and cause a very high $i_{us\$}$ in government dollar-linked bonds.[3] On the other hand, the effect of an increase in credit risk on $i_{us\$}$ traded in derivative markets (e.g., currency swaps) is less clear; usually market players become very selective with their counterparties, and, as result, liquidity disappears.

Exhibit 3 shows the 90-day $i_{us\$}$ in Brazil. The market was extremely volatile during the Mexican Crisis (December 1994 to March 1995). As the demand for hedge increased, $i_{us\$}$ dropped. Meanwhile, the Brazilian domestic interest rate increased almost 20% p.a., from January 1995 to March 1995. (This is not shown

---

[3] In the Mexican crisis of December 1994 - March 1995, Tesobonos yielded as much as 40% in dollars, due to the lack of international reserves to pay redemptions.

in Exhibit 3.) The volatility in the local interest rate also explains the sharp ups-and-downs of $i_{us\$}$. After July 1995, the market perceived the crisis as petering out. The demand for hedging dropped much faster than the domestic interest rate, and $i_{us\$}$ climbed to 24% p.a. For the remainder of 1995 and for 1996, the downtrend in local real interest rates was the main determinant in driving $i_{us\$}$ down. There have been some jittery moments at the end of July 1996 Mr. Cavallo's resignation from the Argentinean Ministry of Finance and in November 1996 when the markets showed concerns with the trade balance. In both events, $i_{us\$}$ dropped a couple of 100 bps and later rebounded, as the view on the local currency improved.

CAPTURING THE INTEREST RATE DIFFERENTIAL: THREE CASE STUDIES

The definition of arbitrage is a risk-free trade with a positive payoff in all scenarios. Opportunities of such arbitrage in local markets are either rare or costly. As noted earlier, trading in local markets involves convertibility risk, custody risk, currency risk, local interest rate risk, changes in taxation, changes in regulations, credit risk, and execution risk. The main ingredient of the recipe of local fixed income trading is to determine which risks have to be hedged, and which do not.

The first case study discusses a widespread instrument, local currency denominated dollar-indexed bonds. The second and third cases involve derivatives and hedging techniques. Because of the greater complexity of these two cases, we will adopt the following steps:

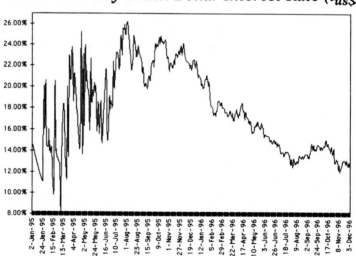

Exhibit 3: 90-Day Brazil Dollar Interest Rate ($i_{us\$}$)

Source: Bankers Trust, Brazilian Mercantile Exchange

1. Formalize the payoffs of each instrument, as well the payoff of the whole basket of instruments. We will call the latter the *payoff function*. Amounts and quantities need not be specified at this time.
2. Find quantities and amounts that make the payoff function insensitive to changes in the currency and interest rate.
3. Substitute these quantities into the payoff function and find the *payoff of the hedged position*.
4. Formalize the initial investment.
5. Find the yield of the trade by dividing the payoff of the hedged position by the initial investment.
6. Judge the trade idea, understanding how the parameters change and how they affect the final yield.

Case Study 1: The Two Sides of a Foreign Currency Denominated Dollar-Linked Securities

A foreign denominated but dollar-linked security has a purchase price and cash flows (coupon and principal) denominated in the foreign currency. However, these cash flows are indexed to the foreign exchange rate of the currency to the dollar.

For example, a 1-year zero-coupon security denominated in sucres (Ecuadorian currency) can be dollar linked in the following way: the security carries a "forward" foreign exchange rate $(Fx_{forward})$[4] which is set at issuance. At maturity, the principal amount paid in sucres is increased by the devaluation percentage of the sucre above the preset forward level. If the currency has appreciated relative to the forward level, then the principal payout is unchanged.

The following equation shows the price in sucres of a 1-year sucre denominated but dollar-linked security with a preset forward exchange rate $(Fx_{forward})$:

$$P = \frac{\left[1 + \max\left(0, \frac{Fx - Fx_{forward}}{Fx_{forward}}\right)\right]}{(1 + y_{sucres})} \tag{10}$$

The sucre price is equal to the principal payout in sucres, which is the sucre face amount at issuance adjusted by any devaluation above the forward foreign exchange rate level, and then discounted by the sucre yield (y_{sucres}). From equation (10) it can be seen that the payoff of the dollar-linked security entails the payoff of an option on the foreign exchange rate.

As shown below, the dollar price of the security (P) is equal to the face amount (in sucres) at issuance divided by the preset forward exchange rate and then discounted by the dollar yield (y_{dollar}):

$$\$P = \frac{P}{Fx_0} = \frac{(1/Fx_{forward})}{(1 + y_{dollar})} \tag{11}$$

---

[4] The preset "forward" foreign exchange rate level is not necessary equal to the forward foreign exchange rate. Usually, the issuer (sovereign) sets this level based on inflation expectations.

Exhibit 4: Sucre Principal Payout and Dollar Principal Payout of a Dollar-Linked Security as a Function of the Foreign Exchange at Maturity

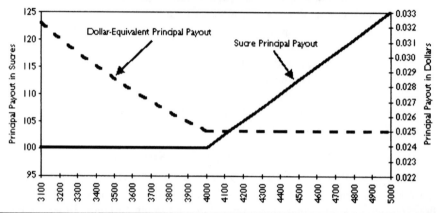

Exhibit 4 shows the principal payout at maturity of a zero-coupon 1-year dollar-linked security with 100 sucres face at issuance in sucres and the dollar equivalent for various foreign exchange levels. In this example, the forward foreign exchange rate is set at 4,000 and the spot level at issuance is 3,200. For all currency levels lower than 4,000, the payout is 100 sucres. The dollar equivalent is at least $0.025 (=100/4000) and increases (above $0.025) as the currency strengthens relative to the 4,000 level. For currency levels weaker (higher) than the forward level, the payout in sucres is over 100 (increased by the amount of the devaluation from the 4,000 level). However, the dollar equivalent is constant at $0.025.

Exhibit 5 shows the sucre and dollar return of the dollar-linked security for various exchange rate levels. It is evident from Exhibits 4 and 5 that the dollar-linked security, ignoring default scenarios, guarantees a minimum dollar yield or return which is based on a foreign exchange rate equal to that preset at issuance (i.e., the forward). The security described above also offers full participation in any appreciating scenario up to the forward level.

At issuance, the sucre yield of the security in the example above is 40% (based on equation (10)) and the dollar yield is 12% (based on equation (11)). As long as the sucre is below the forward level (4,000) at maturity, the investor earns a 40% sucre return which translates to a dollar return equal to or greater than 12%. If the sucre devalues above the forward level (4,000), then the sucre return increases above the 40% and the dollar return is fixed at 12% (see Exhibit 5).

Depending on the investor's profile, the relevant yield may be either the sucre yield or the dollar yield of a sucre-denominated dollar-linked security. However, the implied sucre rate of the dollar-linked security may be quite different than the sucre rate of a comparable sucre-denominated security. Under such a scenario sucre investors may earn higher sucre returns from sucre-denominated securities. Also dollar investors holding sucre-denominated but dollar-linked securities may sell their securities at very low dollar rates (but high implied sucre rates) and thus earn a significantly high dollar return.

For example, a 1-year sucre-denominated dollar-linked security issued at a 12% dollar yield implies a sucre rate of 40% given a foreign exchange rate of 3,200 at issuance and a 4,000 forward level. Let's assume that after a month (1) the foreign exchange rate has devalued to 3,300 and (2) local interest rates have dropped from levels around 40% to levels around 30% but dollar rates are unchanged. Under such a scenario of constant dollar rates (12%), the implied sucre rate of the dollar-linked security drops to 34.5% because of the currency devaluation. Sucre investors can earn a higher sucre rate by purchasing dollar-denominated securities at sucre rates (34.5%) considerably higher than those of sucre-denominated securities (30%).

Exhibit 6 shows the implied sucre yield for two sucre-denominated but dollar-linked securities (one at a 10% dollar yield and the other at a 12% dollar yield) under various foreign exchange rate scenarios. Furthermore, from the point of view of a dollar investor that holds a sucre-denominated security, the returns can be very high in a scenario as the one described above. Consistent with the reduced sucre market rates (30% in our example), the dollar investor may offer the sucre-denominated securities at a 30% implied sucre rate which is equivalent to an 8% dollar yield. This would result in a 400 bps interest gain (12% original yield).[5]

Exhibit 5: Sucre Return and Dollar Return of a Dollar-Linked Security as a Function of the Foreign Exchange at Maturity

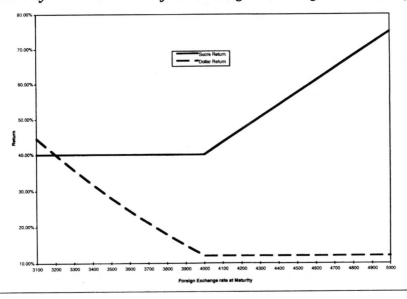

---

[5] It should be mentioned that at the same time the currency has devalued in our example by 100 sucres or 3.125% which actually reduced the net dollar gain.

Exhibit 6: Sucre Returns of Two Dollar-Linked Securities with 10% and 12% Dollar Yields as a Function of the Foreign Exchange Rate at Issuance

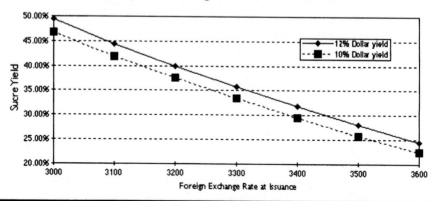

Case Study 2: Cetes Hedged with Coberturas — The Tax Nuance

Cetes are zero-coupon bonds with a nominal value of 10,000 Mexican pesos that trade on a discount yield and an actual/360 day basis. For example, the price of a 91-day Cetes that trades at 30% p.a. is 9,295.12.[6] The example described involves the purchase of USD 1 million equivalent of Cetes which is hedged with Coberturas. Coberturas are forward contracts on the Mexican exchange rate. Coberturas settle in pesos and are subject to taxation. This creates an additional hedging problem, as we shall see below.

Step 1: Assessing Payoffs in Dollars at Maturity

The Cetes payoff is equal to the proceeds in pesos (i.e. quantity times face value), converted into dollars using the free market spot rate two business days before the Cetes maturity. The spot rate settles in 48 hours. Alternatively, the investor could wait until the Cetes maturity to buy dollars at the cash peso rate. However, due to the characteristics of the Cobertura, this would result in an undesired two days exposure to the peso.

Mathematically, the Cetes payoff can be expressed as follows:

$$\text{Cetes payoff} = \frac{10{,}000Q}{e_{n-2}} \tag{12}$$

where

Q = quantity of Cetes with 10,000 pesos face each

e_{n-2} = free market spot exchange rate two business days before the Cetes maturity (n is the Cetes maturity date)

---

[6] Cetes Price $= 10{,}000 \div \left(1 + 30\%\left(\frac{91}{360}\right)\right) \approx 9{,}295.12$

Cobertura contracts are settled in pesos, by the difference between the preset spot rate $(\bar{e}_0)$ and the free official spot exchange rate, two business days prior to the liquidation of the contract $(\bar{e}_{n-2})$. Cobertura gains are subject to a withholding tax. The Cobertura payoff can be expressed as follows:

$$\text{Cobertura payoff} = \frac{A(\bar{e}_{n-2} - \bar{e}_0) - A(\text{tax})[\max\{\bar{e}_{n-2} - \bar{e}_0; 0\}]}{e_{n-2}} \quad (13)$$

where

$\bar{e}_{n-2}$ = the free official spot exchange rate two business days before the Cetes maturity. (It is calculated daily by the Bolsa Mexicana de Valores as a weighted average of spot market rates)

$\bar{e}_0$ = preset peso rate, agreed between the counterparties at the closing of the Cobertura

A = amount of the Cobertura contract (expressed in dollars)

tax = tax on the Cobertura gains[7]

Therefore, the combined payoff of a position of Cetes and Coberturas is the sum of the individual payoffs given by equations (12) and (13):

$$P = \frac{10{,}000Q + A(\bar{e}_{n-2} - \bar{e}_0) - A(\text{tax})[\max\{\bar{e}_{n-2} - \bar{e}_0; 0\}]}{e_{n-2}} \quad (14)$$

where P = payoff function.

Notice that e_{n-2} and $\bar{e}_{n-2}$ are normally correlated: the former is the rate that the investor can actually buy dollars, the latter is the rate that the Cobertura contract pays. The execution risk can be expressed by the ratio α, where

$$\alpha = \frac{e_{n-2}}{\bar{e}_{n-2}}$$

Substituting α in equation (14), we can express the payoff function P as depending on a single variable, $\bar{e}_{n-2}$:

$$P = \frac{10{,}000Q + A(\bar{e}_{n-2} - \bar{e}_0) - A(\text{tax})[\max\{\bar{e}_{n-2} - \bar{e}_0; 0\}]}{\alpha\, e_{n-2}} \quad (15)$$

The tax on the Cobertura, represented by the term

$$A(\text{tax})[\max\{\bar{e}_{n-2} - \bar{e}_0; 0\}],$$

poses a problem locking in fixed returns in dollars, as we shall see below. Notice that it represents a call option on the peso/dollar rate $\bar{e}_{n-2}$ at the strike $\bar{e}_0$. The

---

[7] At the time of this writing, this tax had already been eliminated. However, the impact of taxation in fixed income arbitrage is a recurrent issue in emerging markets. For this reason, the present example is still worth discussing.

simplest way to solve the arbitrage problem is to purchase an amount "A(tax)" of call options with identical characteristics. However, it is difficult to find such an option in a real market situation. Therefore, we will proceed with the analysis by assessing the taxation risk in different scenarios and deciding how it should be handled. For this purpose, equation (15) should be rewritten as follows:

$$P = \frac{10{,}000Q + A(1-\text{tax})(\bar{e}_{n-2}-\bar{e}_0)}{\alpha\bar{e}_{n-2}} \qquad \text{for } \bar{e}_{n-2}>\bar{e}_0$$

and (16)

$$P = \frac{10{,}000Q + A(\bar{e}_{n-2}-\bar{e}_0)}{\alpha\bar{e}_{n-2}} \qquad \text{for } \bar{e}_{n-2}<\bar{e}_0$$

Step 2: Determining the Hedge Ratio

In order to determine the amount of Coberturas necessary to hedge the Cetes currency risk, we differentiate the payoff function P in equation (15) with respect to the foreign exchange $\bar{e}_{n-2}$ and set it to zero. Equation (17) shows the amount of Coberturas (A) required to hedge Q amount of Cetes

$$A = \frac{10{,}000Q}{(1-\text{tax})\bar{e}_0} \qquad \text{for } \bar{e}_{n-2}>\bar{e}_0$$

and (17)

$$A = \frac{10{,}000Q}{\bar{e}_0} \qquad \text{for } \bar{e}_{n-2}<\bar{e}_0$$

Equation (17) shows that, if the peso does not devalue during the holding period, then the amount of Coberturas should be equal to the amount of Cetes on maturity, converted into the preset exchange rate. However, if the peso devalues, part of the Cobertura gains will be taxed, and the initial amount of Coberturas should be higher for the Cetes position to remain hedged.

Step 3: Finding the Payoff of the Hedged Position

Substituting the amount of Coberturas determined by equation (17) into equation (16) we obtain the payoff of a perfectly hedged position:

$$\text{Payoff of hedged position} = \frac{10{,}000Q}{\alpha\bar{e}_0} \tag{18}$$

Equation (18) assumes a correct forecast of the direction of the peso at maturity ($\bar{e}_{n-2}$): whether the Coberturas were purchased assuming either a devaluation or an appreciation of the peso. That happened to be the right assumption. We will discuss the case of incorrect forecasts later.

Step 4: Determining the Initial Investment

The initial investment in dollars is equal to the amount of pesos spent on the purchase of Coberturas, plus the present value of Cetes. This amount is converted into dollars at the rate e_0. Notice that "cob," in the equation below, is the premium that the investor has to pay for the Cobertura; the term that multiplies "cob" is the amount of Coberturas, given by equation (17).

$$\text{Initial investment} = \left(\frac{10,000Q}{\bar{e}_0(1-\text{tax})}\text{cob} + \frac{10,000Q}{\left(1+\dfrac{id}{360}\right)}\frac{1}{\bar{e}_0} \right) \quad \text{for } \bar{e}_{n-2} > \bar{e}_0$$

and   (19)

$$\text{Initial investment} = \left(\frac{10,000Q}{\bar{e}_0}\text{cob} + \frac{10,000Q}{\left(1+\dfrac{id}{360}\right)}\frac{1}{\bar{e}_0} \right) \quad \text{for } \bar{e}_{n-2} < \bar{e}_0$$

Step 5: Calculating the Return of the Trade

The return of the trade as a percentage of the initial investment, is calculated as follows:

$$\text{Return} = \frac{\text{Payoff of the hedged position}}{\text{Initial investment}} - 1$$

From equations (18) and (19) and substituting $\alpha = e_{n-2}/\bar{e}_{n-2}$

$$\text{Return} = \left(\frac{\text{cob}}{\bar{e}_0(1-\text{tax})} + \frac{1}{\left(1+\dfrac{id}{360}\right)} \right)^{-1} \left(\frac{e_0}{\bar{e}_0}\right)\left(\frac{\bar{e}_{n-2}}{e_{n-2}}\right) - 1 \quad \text{for } \bar{e}_{n-2} > \bar{e}_0$$

and   (20)

$$\text{Return} = \left(\frac{\text{cob}}{\bar{e}_0} + \frac{1}{\left(1+\dfrac{id}{360}\right)} \right)^{-1} \left(\frac{e_0}{\bar{e}_0}\right)\left(\frac{\bar{e}_{n-2}}{e_{n-2}}\right) - 1 \quad \text{for } \bar{e}_{n-2} < \bar{e}_0$$

Step 6: Judging the Trade Idea

It is noteworthy that the tax on the Cobertura changes the return. Moreover, the hedge ratio depends on the direction of the peso. Since Mexican inflation is higher than U.S. inflation, the peso has a natural tendency to depreciate. Therefore, the longer the period of the trade, the more likely a nominal devaluation of the peso is.

Another subtle, but yet important factor, is that the term $(e_0/\bar{e}_0)$ $(\bar{e}_{n-2}/e_{n-2})$ shows the execution risk. If the actual foreign exchange rate is different from the official rate as calculated by the Bolsa Mexicana de Valores, the return will be different. As an example, if the actual peso rate at maturity (e_{n-2}) is 7.60, and the official rate $(\bar{e}_{n-2})$ is 7.55, the return will drop 0.658%. In a 6-month trade, this represents a reduction of more than 130 bps in the annualized rate of return.

Exhibit 7: Cetes Plus Coberturas Trade Returns*

	Hedging for 15% tax			Not Hedging for 15% tax	
Amount of Coberturas:	11,764,706		Amount of Coberturas:		10,000,000
Initial investment:	9,653,684		Initial investment:		9,435,223

Peso	USD Payoff	USD Yield (a)	USD Payoff	USD Yield (b)	Yield Difference (b)-(a)
5.00	9,569,412	-1.73	10,000,000	11.84	13.57
5.25	9,673,950	0.42	10,000,000	11.84	11.42
5.50	9,768,984	2.36	10,000,000	11.84	9.48
5.75	9,855,754	4.14	10,000,000	11.84	7.70
6.00	9,935,294	5.77	10,000,000	11.84	6.07
6.25	10,000,000	7.10	9,992,800	11.69	4.59
6.50	10,000,000	7.10	9,935,385	10.49	3.39
6.75	10,000,000	7.10	9,882,222	9.37	2.28
7.00	10,000,000	7.10	9,832,857	8.34	1.24
7.25	10,000,000	7.10	9,786,897	7.37	0.28
7.50	10,000,000	7.10	9,744,000	6.47	-0.62
7.75	10,000,000	7.10	9,703,871	5.63	-1.46
8.00	10,000,000	7.10	9,666,250	4.84	-2.25
8.25	10,000,000	7.10	9,630,909	4.10	-2.99
8.50	10,000,000	7.10	9,597,647	3.41	-3.69
8.75	10,000,000	7.10	9,566,286	2.75	-4.35
9.00	10,000,000	7.10	9,536,667	2.13	-4.97
9.25	10,000,000	7.10	9,508,649	1.54	-5.56
9.50	10,000,000	7.10	9,482,105	0.98	-6.11
9.75	10,000,000	7.10	9,456,923	0.45	-6.64
10.00	10,000,000	7.10	9,433,000	-0.05	-7.14

* The USD yield multiplies the return of the trade, as described in equation (20), by 360/182.

Exhibit 7 shows a hypothetical trade of Cetes and Coberturas that took place on July 6, 1995. It illustrates the difference in returns due to the 15% tax, ignoring execution risk. Market prices were taken from Bloomberg Financial Markets.[8] The assumptions are:

Initial peso (e_0) = Cobertura peso rate $(\bar{e}_0)$ = 6.22
Cobertura premium (cob) = 0.770
Cetes rate (i) = 43.50% p.a.
Tenor (d) = 182 days
Quantity of Cetes (Q) = 6,220
Tax on Cobertura (tax) = 15%
e_{n-2} = $\bar{e}_{n-2}$ (i.e., no execution risk)

Using the equations above, the results are reported in Exhibit 7.

The exhibit shows that the additional hedge for the tax may reduce the USD yield substantially. Yet, leaving the position unhedged for the tax causes the USD yield to drop as the currency devalues. As the peso approaches the rate of 7.25 pesos/USD, the investor would be better off if the position is completely hedged. The decision of hedging clearly depends on the investor's expectations. In the above example, the peso value at maturity (January 2, 1996) closed at 7.665, which would have led to a 7.10% annualized return for a position hedged for the tax, and 5.91% for a position not hedged for the tax.

Another important risk to be considered is credit risk of the Cobertura, which is typically sold by a private Mexican financial institution. The correlation between a major devaluation of the peso (where the Mexican counterparty would owe money to the foreign investor) and a deterioration in the creditworthiness of the Mexican counterparty should not be ignored. Other minor risks are convertibility, a change of regulations (for example, if the Mexican government increases the tax on the Cobertura), and custody risk (where the Cetes and Coberturas are held). This trade bears no interest rate risk if it is held to maturity. However, unwinding the trade earlier certainly entails interest rate risk.

Case Study 3: Brazilian Tourist Exchange Rate

After July 1994, the Brazilian stabilization plan led to very high domestic interest rates. To avoid a massive inflow of short-term capital, the Brazilian government imposed several restrictions on foreign investments in local fixed income. Yet, all restrictions were aimed at the commercial exchange rate, whereas the tourist exchange market remained free. By mid-1995, foreign investors realized that the Brazilian Central Bank was targeting the Brazilian Real (R$) in the tourist market as well. The perception of currency stability, along with very high domestic rates, triggered an investment boom in the Brazilian tourist rate market. On August 11, 1995, the Central Bank increased restrictions on local fixed income instruments, and, among other measures, established a 7% upfront fee (called IOF[9]) on new investments in the tourist market.

However, the legislation still allowed transfers of money between accounts in the tourist market — the so-called non-resident accounts (CC5 accounts). Moreover, the legislation allowed Brazilians to pay external liabilities, such as imports and dividends, by depositing the equivalent R$ amount in foreign investors' CC5 accounts. Soon a market developed to buy and sell cash held in CC5 accounts; as a consequence, instead of paying the 7% upfront fee determined by the Central Bank, foreign investors could acquire the right to exchange dollars for R$ by paying a fee determined by the market, which ranged from R$ 0.0020 to R$ 0.0050. This transaction was locally referred as "purchase of space in the CC5 account."

This situation lasted until December 1995, when the Central Bank called the main dealers and told them to stop doing such transactions, because they were caus-

---

[8] As a proxy to the Cetes rate, the example uses the "Mexico Bank repo 182 days" — code MXBA182D.

[9] "Imposto sobre Operações Financeiras."

ing substantial dollar inflows that had to be sterilized, thus disrupting monetary policy. In the meantime, this situation offered an opportunity of what was perhaps the closest thing to a perfect arbitrage. Foreign investors were able to "purchase space in the CC5 account," exchange dollars for Brazilian currency (R$), and buy short-term local bonds such as BBCs and LTNs. Most of the investors hedged the local bonds for the currency risk, some also hedged for the slippage risk, and very few bought convertibility protection. After incurring all taxes, the costs of purchasing "CC5 space," and hedging, the investor could still earn spreads over LIBOR as high as 600 bps in a 6-month timeframe. Tenors shorter than that did not yield a similar return because foreign capital had to remain invested for some time in local bonds to amortize the upfront costs, such as the "purchase of space in the CC5 account."

The case described below involves hedging three major risks: (1) currency risk, (2) change in the premium between the tourist rate and the commercial rate ("slippage risk"), and (3) convertibility risk. The methodology is the same as in the first case study.

Before we go through all the steps, the following considerations about the Brazilian market are worth noting. First, money market funds are remunerated on a business days basis. For instance, from Friday to Monday, government securities pay only 1-day interest. The interest rate benchmark is *cdi*, which is the overnight rate for interbank deposits. The *cdi* bears a very close relationship to the *selic*, which is the Brazilian equivalent of the U.S. fed funds rate. Both *selic* and *cdi* overnight rates are quoted on a 30-day rate basis. As an example, a *cdi* of 4.50% is equivalent to an actual overnight rate of 0.15%.

Second, everyday the Central Bank publishes the closing quote for both the commercial and the tourist exchange rates through the electronic system of the Central Bank, at the code "Ptax800 - offer rate." These are the exchange rates governing currency swaps, as we shall see below.

Third, the R$ spot rate settles in two days if the investor is buying government bonds. For corporate bonds and derivatives, the settlement is in one day. Consequently, if a foreign exchange transaction is executed to settle government bonds on the following day, the spot rate should be deflated by one overnight rate. Analogously, if a foreign exchange transaction is executed to settle government bonds on the same day, the spot rate should be deflated by two overnight rates. This concept will be evident in equations (21) and (28) below.

Finally, virtually all currency swaps refer to the Ptax800 exchange rate with 1-day lag. Therefore, to avoid currency risk, the investor has to buy dollars and sell R$ one day prior to the swap maturity. Since this case involves a great deal of variables and parameters, the notation used is summarized in Exhibit 8.

Step 1: Assessing Payoffs

This case study assumes that the investor is able to close the foreign exchange transaction at the Ptax800 rate. Therefore, the model disregards execution risk in the foreign exchange market at maturity. To avoid mismatch with the currency swaps, the purchase of dollars must be executed the day before maturity $(n-1)$. The Ptax800 tourist rate is then represented as e^f_{n-1}. Applying the definition of premium between the tourist rate and the commercial rate we have:

$$e^f_{n-1} = (1 + \phi_{n-1})e_{n-1} \tag{21}$$

Exhibit 8: Notation Used in Case 3

e_t	=	ptax800 – offer rate for the commercial rate at day t
e^f_t	=	ptax800 – offer rate for the tourist rate at day t[a]
$\tilde{e}^f_0$	=	actual tourist rate that the investor sells dollars and purchases R\$, at the beginning of the trade
cdi_t	=	cdi overnight rate at day t. To simplify the equations, the cdi will already be divided by 30.
$\overline{cdi}$	=	average cdi overnight rate in the period of the trade[b]
α	=	the average percentage of the benchmark cdi that a government security yields[c]
$CC5$	=	the market fee for foreign investors to exchange dollars for R\$ at the tourist rate
ϕ_t	=	$\dfrac{e^f_t}{e_t} - 1$ (i.e., the premium between the tourist and commercial rate)[d]
ϕ^e	=	the expected premium on date $n-1$ that can be locked in through currency swaps
$i_{us\$}$	=	the USD domestic interest rate in currency swaps (commercial rate vs. accrued cdi) to hedge the currency risk
$i'_{us\$}$	=	the USD domestic interest rate in currency swaps (commercial rate vs. accrued cdi) to hedge the slippage risk
$i^f_{us\$}$	=	the USD domestic interest rate in currency swaps (tourist rate vs. accrued cdi) to hedge the slippage risk
n	=	tenor of the trade, expressed in calendar days
w	=	tenor of the trade, expressed in working days
ψ	=	annualized cost of convertibility hedge
A	=	the initial R\$ amount of local bonds
A'	=	the initial R\$ amount of the swap to hedge the currency risk
A''	=	the initial R\$ amount of the swap to hedge the slippage risk
P	=	the final proceeds, after taxes, converted into dollars
p^{hedged}	=	the payoff of the hedged position
tax	=	15% withholding tax on bond earnings

[a] The Tourist rate is also called "Floating rate," therefore the choice of the superscript f.

[b] By definition, $\overline{cdi} = \left[\prod_{j=0}^{n-1}(1 + cdi_j)\right]^{1/w} - 1$

[c] Government securities should yield 100% of cdi, but due to transaction costs and scarcity factors, the investor usually earns a percentage of the cdi close to 99.50%.

[d] Notice that ϕ_t is the premium that the tourist rate trades relative to the commercial rate; ϕ_t is usually positive (i.e., the tourist exchange rate trades weaker than the commercial rate), but during the period we of this case study, ϕ_t was indeed negative due to the substantial supply of dollars at the tourist market.

The investor will purchase local bonds that yield a percentage (α) of the local benchmark *cdi*. As the bonds mature, the investor pays the withholding tax and rolls over the position, until the final maturity of the trade. The tenor of the bonds should be short enough to avoid divergences between the yield of the bonds and the benchmark *cdi*, caused by changes in the local interest rate.[10] To simplify, we will assume that the investor purchases bonds equivalent to a R\$ amount A, which yield the average daily rate $\alpha(\overline{cdi})$, compounded over w business days. Further, the total withholding tax is due at the end of the trade, as opposed to at the maturity of each bond.[11] The bond payoff is then converted into dollars using the tourist rate of the previous day, deflated by one overnight rate, as explained above:

Local bond payoff

$$= (A[([1 + \alpha(\overline{cdi})]^w - 1)(1 - \text{tax}) + 1]) \div \frac{e^f_{n-1}}{(1 + cdi_{n-1})} \quad (22)$$

Substituting equation (21) into equation (22):

$$\text{Local bond payoff} = \frac{A[([1 + \alpha(\overline{cdi})]^w - 1)(1 - \text{tax}) + 1](1 + cdi_{n-1})}{(1 + \phi_{n-1})e_{n-1}} \quad (23)$$

The commercial rate versus *cdi swap* (US/DI swap), traded at the Brazilian Futures Exchange (BM&F), pays the difference between the return of a USD-linked investment at the rate $i_{us\$}$, and an investment at the daily *cdi* rate. The payoff converted into dollars using the exchange rate e^f_{n-1} as defined in equation (21) is

$$\text{US/DI swap payoff} = \frac{A'\left[\left(1 + i_{us\$}\frac{n}{360}\right)\frac{e_{n-1}}{e_{-1}} - \prod_{j=0}^{n-1}(1 + cdi_j)\right]}{(1 + \phi_{n-1})e_{n-1}} \quad (24)$$

Analogously, the tourist rate versus *cdi* swap (USf/DI swap) pays the difference between the return of a tourist USD-linked investment at the rate $i^f_{us\$}$, and an investment at the daily *cdi* rate. The payoff is:

$$\text{USf/DI swap payoff} = \frac{A''\left[\left(1 + i^f_{us\$}\frac{n}{360}\right)\frac{e^f_{n-1}}{e^f_{-1}} - \prod_{j=0}^{n-1}(1 + cdi_j)\right]}{(1 + \phi_{n-1})e_{n-1}} \quad (25)$$

Equations (23) and (24) show that the bonds and the US/DI swap follow the *cdi* overnight rate. Therefore, a proper amount A' of US/DI swaps can hedge the currency risk of local bonds.

---

[10] There are ways to hedge this interest rate risk using interest rate futures. Yet, the strategy of buying short-term bonds simplifies the example without altering the conclusions.

[11] This could make a significant difference in terms of tax deferral should the trade have a long tenor (n). For the purposes of the current example, however, such a difference is negligible.

The second risk to be hedged is the change in the premium between the tourist and commercial exchange rate ("slippage risk"). It is possible to set a forward on the premium (ϕ^e) through opposite positions of US/DI swaps and USf/DI swaps, both with the same amount A''. From equations (24) and (25), such a payoff (premium payoff) can be formalized as follows:[12]

$$\text{Premium payoff} = \frac{A''\left(\left(1 + i_{us\$}^f \frac{n}{360}\right)\frac{e_{n-1}^f}{e_{-1}^f} - \prod_{j=0}^{n-1}(1 + cdi_j)\right)}{(1 + \phi_{n-1})e_{n-1}}$$

$$- \frac{A''\left(\left(1 + i'_{us\$}\frac{n}{360}\right)\frac{e_{n-1}}{e_{-1}} - \prod_{j=0}^{n-1}(1 + cdi_j)\right)}{(1 + \phi_{n-1})e_{n-1}} \quad (26)$$

With some rearranging we have:

$$\text{Premium payoff} = \frac{A''}{e_{-1}^f}\left(1 + i_{us\$}^f \frac{n}{360}\right)\left(1 - \frac{1 + \phi^e}{+ \phi_{n-1}}\right) \quad (27)$$

where

$$1 + \phi^e = (1 + \phi_{-1})\frac{\left(1 + i'_{us\$}\frac{n}{360}\right)}{\left(1 + i_{us\$}^f \frac{n}{360}\right)} \quad (28)$$

The last risk to be hedged is the convertibility. The convertibility hedge is an insurance policy. If an event of non-convertibility occurs, the investor receives a predetermined USD amount. In this case study, the USD amount should be equal to P, defined as the sum of all payoffs — local bonds plus swaps — as follows:

$$\text{Convertibility premium} = \psi\left(\frac{n}{360}\right)P \quad (29)$$

Finally, from equations (23), (24), and (27), we can build the payoff function P:

$$P = \text{Local bond payoff} + \text{US/DI swap payoff} + \text{Premium payoff} \quad (30)$$

Step 2: Determining Hedge Ratio

Equation (30) shows the payoff of a portfolio comprising local bonds and currency swaps. However, the amount of swaps A' and A'' is still not balanced with the amount A of local bonds, so that the portfolio is hedged for currency risk and

---

[12] The reason to distinguish i_{us} and i'_{us} is that the currency and slippage hedges may be closed with different counterparties, and i_{us} may change from one trade to another.

slippage risk. In order to determine the right amounts of A' and A'', we should differentiate the payoff function P with respect to the exchange rate at maturity (e_{n-1}) and the premium at maturity (ϕ_{n-1}):

$$\frac{\partial P}{\partial e_{n-1}} = 0 \Rightarrow A' = A\frac{[((1 + \alpha(\overline{cdi}))^{w} - 1)(1 - \text{tax}) + 1](1 + cdi_{n-1})}{(1 + \overline{cdi})^{w}} \quad (31)$$

and

$$\frac{\partial P}{\partial \phi_{n-1}} = 0 \text{ and } \frac{\partial P}{\partial e_{n-1}} = 0 \Rightarrow A'' = A'\frac{\left(1 + i_{us\$}\frac{n}{360}\right)}{\left(1 + i'_{us\$}\frac{n}{360}\right)} \quad (32)$$

Step 3: Finding the Payoff of the Hedged Position

Equations (31) and (32) represent the relationship between the swap amounts A' and A'', and the amount of local bonds, A, that hedge the portfolio for changes in the exchange rate and the premium. Substituting them into equation (30) we find the payoff of the hedged position P^{hedged}:

$$P^{\text{hedged}} = \left(\frac{A}{e_{-1}}\right)\left(\frac{[((1 + \alpha(\overline{cdi}))^{w} - 1)(1 - \text{tax}) + 1](1 + cdi_{n-1})}{(1 + \overline{cdi})^{w}}\right)$$

$$\times \left(\frac{\left(1 + i_{us\$}\frac{n}{360}\right)}{(1 + \phi^{e})}\right) \quad (33)$$

Step 4: Determining the Initial Investment

At the beginning of the trade, the investor sells dollars at the current market rate $(\bar{e}_0^f)$, minus a market fee $(cc5)$, to have the R\$ amount A credited in a CC5 account. Since the purchase of bonds is to be executed on the same day, the exchange rate must be discounted by two overnight rates (cdi_0). Therefore, the actual exchange rate will be:

$$(\bar{e}_0^f - cc5)/(1 + cdi_0)^2$$

In addition to the purchase of the local bonds, the investor has to pay for the convertibility insurance. As per equation (29), the insurance cost ψ is applied over the amount to be hedged; in this case, the payoff of the hedged position (P^{hedged}). The initial investment is then:

$$\text{Initial investment} = A \div \frac{(\bar{e}_0^f - cc5)}{(1 + cdi_0)^2} + \psi\frac{n}{360}P^{\text{hedged}} \quad (34)$$

Step 5: Calculating the Return of the Trade

The return in the period is given by

$$\frac{P^{hedged}}{\text{Initial investment}} - 1 \tag{35}$$

From equations (33) and (34) and with some rearrangement we arrive at:

Return

$$= \left(\Omega \left(\frac{e^f_{-1}(1+cdi_0)}{(\bar{e}^f_0 - cc5)} \right) \left(\frac{(1+cdi_0)}{(1+cdi_{n-1})} \right) \left(\frac{(1+\phi^c)}{(1+\phi_{-1})} \right) \left(\frac{1}{\left(1 + i_{us\$}\dfrac{n}{360}\right)} \right) + \psi \frac{n}{360} \right)^{-1} \tag{36}$$

where

$$\Omega = \frac{(1+\overline{cdi})^w}{[([1 + \alpha(\overline{cdi})]^w - 1)(1 - \text{tax}) + 1]} \tag{37}$$

Step 6: Judging the Trade Idea

Two risks were left out of the analysis above — credit risk on the Brazilian Futures Exchange and execution risk on the foreign exchange at maturity. All other determinants of the trade are represented in equation (36). It is worth discussing the meaning of each term in the equation.

Ω is the ratio of the gross return over the net return of Brazilian money market funds. In practice, the net return is always lower, due to transaction costs (α) and taxes (tax). Notice that the higher Ω is, the lower the return of the trade. Furthermore, the minimum value Ω can attain is 1, in the case of no transaction costs ($\alpha = 1$) and no taxes (tax = 0).

The second term of equation (36), $e^f_{-1}(1 + cdi_0)/(\bar{e}^f_0 - cc5)$, represents the ratio of the theoretical initial exchange rate e^f_{-1} over the exchange rate the investor actually receives $(\bar{e}^f_0 - cc5)/(1 + cdi_0)$. Usually, the latter is less favorable than the theoretical exchange rate, causing this term to be higher than 1, and thereby acting against the investor. Occasionally, in days when R\$ weakens, this term may work on the investor's behalf.

As mentioned at the outset of this case, purchases of government bonds entail a loss of one overnight rate, which should be recovered at maturity. This is expressed by the third term of equation (36) — $(1 + cdi_0)/(1 + cdi_{n-1})$. Notice that the initial overnight rate, cdi_0, can be either greater or less than the final overnight rate, cdi_{n-1}. Shortly we will see that this effect is negligible in a low inflation environment, when local overnight rates show low volatility.

The fourth term of equation (36) — $(1 + \phi^c)/(1 + \phi_{-1})$ — is the difference between the initial premium of the floating rate over the commercial rate (ϕ_{-1}), and the forward premium set via currency swaps (ϕ^e). Therefore, the cost of hedging slippage risk increases as the forward premium ϕ^e diverges from the initial premium ϕ_{-1}.

The fifth term of equation (36),

$$1 \Big/ \left(1 + i_{us\$}\frac{n}{360}\right),$$

represents the domestic USD interest rate. Finally, $\psi\dfrac{n}{360}$ is the premium to hedge convertibility risk.

Two terms in equation (36) — the final overnight rate cdi_{n-1} and Ω — should be treated as variables since they are unknown when the trade is executed. The cdi_{n-1} hardly presents a problem because in a turbulent scenario, the overnight rate should go up, which would then increase the return of the trade. Factor Ω is more problematic, as a rise in the overnight rate causes an increase in taxation and, as a result, reduces the net return of Brazilian money market funds. Furthermore, Ω also depends on α — the percentage of the benchmark cdi earned by the investor. This percentage may vary at each rollover of local bonds, adding uncertainty about the return of the local bonds. One way to lock such a return is to buy bonds that coincide with the maturity of the trade. However, this is not always possible.

The following numerical example illustrates this point. The trade has a 180-day tenor, whereas the bonds liquidity at that time was concentrated around 50 days. Therefore, the investor could not avoid running rollover risk. Exhibit 9 shows market rates in October 1995, a period that was especially favorable for this trade. This hypothetical trade took place on October 9, 1995, maturing on April 8, 1996. The market parameters on that date were:

Ptax800 floating rate (e^j_{-1})	= R\$ 0.9542
Ptax800 commercial rate (e_{-1})	= R\$ 0.9590
Therefore, the Ptax800 premium (ϕ_{-1})	= −0.50%
182-day forward premium (ϕ^e)	= 1.00%
Floating exchange rate $(\bar{e}^j_0)$	= R\$ 0.9542
Overnight rate (cdi_0)	= 0.14167% p.d.
Upfront fee to purchase R\$ at the floating rate $(cc5)$	= R\$ 0.002
Premium of convertibility insurance (ψ)	= 2.00% p.a.
Tenor of the trade (n)	= 182 days
USD interest rate in the first US/DI swap $(i_{us\$})$	= 21.75% p.a.
USD interest rate in the second US/DI swap $(i'_{us\$})$	= 21.70% p.a.
number of Brazilian business days comprised in the trade (w)	= 121
withholding tax (tax)	= 10.00%

Three variables still have to be defined — the average overnight rate for the 121 business days of the trade $(\overline{cdi})$, the percentage of the benchmark (CDI) that the investor earns (α), and the final overnight rate (cdi_{n-1}). As a simplification, we conservatively assumed that the final overnight rate is equal to the average overnight rate $(\overline{cdi} = cdi_{n-1})$. α usually ranges from 98.5% to 100% of CDI. Since the actual α was unknown at the initiation of the trade, a conservative assumption should again be made. For the purposes of this illustration 98% of cdi

was assumed. Therefore, the return of the trade depended on one variable — the average overnight rate $\overline{cdi}$. A sensitivity analysis may show how a rise on the $\overline{cdi}$ increases the amount of taxes, with negative impact on the return. Before that, however, it is worth going through the execution of the trade.

On October 9, 1995, the actual exchange rate was R$ 0.9542 minus R$ 0.002, adjusted for two overnight rates of 0.14167% (because the investor had to purchase local government bonds on the same day). As a result, the actual exchange rate was R$ 0.949508. Assuming a USD 10 million investment, the investor should have bought Brazilian bonds worth R$ 9,495,080.00.

The investor would then close a swap to hedge the currency risk, receiving 21.75% p.a. plus currency depreciation and paying CDI. Assumptions of α, $\overline{cdi}$, and cdi_{n-1} are necessary to determine the amount of the swap; α has already been determined above. Let's assume 0.1500% for the $\overline{cdi}$ as well as cdi_{n-1}, and later see how errors in this forecast might affect the return of the trade. Substituting these values in equation (31), the amount A' of the swap is R$ 9,320,628.33.

Exhibit 9: Brazilian Market Rates in October 1995

Date t	R$ Commercial e_t	R$ Tourist e_t^f	Premium ϕ_t	Overnight Rate cdi_t
Oct-02-95	0.9555	0.9505	−0.52	0.14467
Oct-03-95	0.9585	0.9535	−0.52	0.14433
Oct-04-95	0.9585	0.9535	−0.52	0.14433
Oct-05-95	0.9585	0.9535	−0.52	0.14367
Oct-06-95	0.9590	0.9542	−0.50	0.14233
Oct-09-95	0.9585	0.9545	−0.42	0.14167
Oct-10-95	0.9585	0.9540	−0.47	0.14233
Oct-11-95	0.9585	0.9535	−0.52	0.14233
Oct-13-95	0.9585	0.9535	−0.52	0.14233
Oct-16-95	0.9585	0.9540	−0.47	0.14233
Oct-17-95	0.9585	0.9565	−0.21	0.14333
Oct-18-95	0.9590	0.9568	−0.23	0.14533
Oct-19-95	0.9593	0.9585	−0.08	0.14533
Oct-20-95	0.9613	0.9605	−0.08	0.14567
Oct-23-95	0.9615	0.9595	−0.21	0.14567
Oct-24-95	0.9617	0.9600	−0.18	0.14467
Oct-25-95	0.9617	0.9596	−0.22	0.14433
Oct-26-95	0.9625	0.9610	−0.16	0.14400
Oct-27-95	0.9622	0.9613	−0.09	0.14267
Oct-30-95	0.9617	0.9608	−0.09	0.14200
Oct-31-95	0.9619	0.9595	−0.25	0.14033

Additionally, the investor would buy a forward on the premium between the tourist and commercial rate (ϕ^e) at 1%. As pointed out in equations (27) and (28), this is done through a combination of two currency swaps — one paying foreign exchange (fx) devaluation at the commercial rate plus a spread and receiving CDI and one receiving fx devaluation at the floating rate plus a spread and paying CDI. Let's assume that the investor purchased the forward on the premium with another counterparty, and that the spread on the commercial rate swap $i'_{us\$}$ changed to 21.70%. Therefore, according to equation (28), the spread in the floating rate $i^f_{us\$}$ should equal 18.439%, resulting in a forward premium ϕ^e of 1%. Finally, equation (32) sets the amount of the combination of swaps A'' at R\$ 9,322,751.46.

At that point, the investor had already converted the USD 10 million into local currency, purchased local bonds, and closed swaps to hedge both the currency risk and slippage risk. The last risk to be hedged is the convertibility risk. In this example, it costs 2% per annum over the insured amount, which should be what the investor expects to receive at maturity, namely, the payoff of the hedged position (P^{hedged}). Substituting our assumptions, including the assumed values for $\overline{cdi}$ and cdi_{n-1}, into equation (33) we find USD 10,680,999.27. Therefore, the investor should pay 2% p.a. on 182 days over that amount, which equals USD 107,996.77.

Finally, the investor should assess the return of the trade. If the assumptions of $\overline{cdi}$ and cdi_{n-1} turned out to be correct, the trade would yield 5.669% in USD, or 11.21% annualized. However, the assumptions of $\overline{cdi}$ and cdi_{n-1} could be wrong. In this case, the return would vary in several ways.

It has already been pointed out that the return of the trade is negatively affected if the overnight rate increases. The reason for that is the increase in taxation. Yet, underestimations of $\overline{cdi}$ also provoke less intuitive relationships: the higher taxation reduces the final proceeds, and, as a consequence, the investor ends up overhedged for currency risk and slippage risk. In other words, the hedge amounts were calculated for a given impact of taxation on the final proceeds. As the nominal return of the bonds increases, the tax impact is magnified. As a consequence, the investor should have closed a smaller amount of currency swaps. Indeed, equations (31) and (32) point out that, as the average overnight rate $\overline{cdi}$ increases, the amount of swaps A' and A'' should decrease.

The "overhedge effect" due to errors in the assumptions for $\overline{cdi}$ cause the investor to become short the local currency. In a stress-case scenario, this is a desirable effect, because an upsurge of inflation followed by a rise of local interest rates should increase the probability that the currency devalues faster than inflation. To sum up, the overhedge effect increases the uncertainty over the return of the trade, but also mitigates the investor's loss in a stress-case scenario.

Exhibit 10 illustrates this point. The curve "theory" shows the annualized return of the trade assuming no errors for the $\overline{cdi}$ and cdi_{n-1} forecasts. The curve "numeric simulation" shows the return of the trade when $\overline{cdi}$ and cdi_{n-1} were initially assumed to be 0.15%, and the actual overnight rate ranges from 0.05% to

1%. Additionally, the real effective exchange rate devalued 10%.[13] The exhibit shows that, as the scenario deteriorates and the overnight rate increases, the numeric simulation performs better than the theory. Nevertheless, the local currency can also act against the investor's overhedged situation. In fact, the gap between the two curves shows how critical the exchange rate becomes, once the forecast of the average overnight rate $\overline{cdi}$ turns out to be wrong.

Some considerations should be made on the cost of hedging. The question of whether the investor should really hedge a position for currency, slippage, and convertibility risks remain beyond the scope of this chapter. Yet, pure arbitrage situations are extremely rare in the real world. The present case study, for example, is not a perfect arbitrage, since it implies exposure to the domestic interest rate. An intuitive way to assess the cost of hedging is to recalculate the return of the trade, altering each of its components one at a time, such as withholding tax, future premium, etc. Following this methodology, Exhibit 11 shows how much upside the investor gives away with each one of the components of the trade, as specified in equation (36). The currency hedge was excluded from this analysis because the discussion about currency risk is beyond the scope of this chapter.

We can see that the heaviest cost is the withholding tax that reduces the return by 3.42%. The hedges for slippage risk and convertibility risk add up to 5.38%. The investor has to decide whether or not these hedges are expensive, based on his or her view of the local market. After thorough research, the investor might eventually decide not to put on the hedges, thus enhancing the return of the trade. Then, it should be clear that the trade departs from the initial arbitrage concept, as it acquires more speculative characteristics.

Exhibit 10: Return of the Trade versus Average Overnight Rate ($\overline{cdi}$)

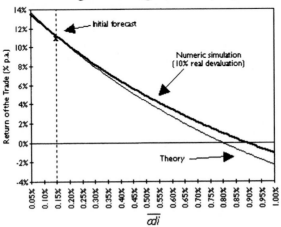

---

[13] The inflation rate was assumed equal to the annualized overnight rate less a 22% spread to account for the real interest rate.

Exhibit 11: Sensitivity Analysis of the Return of the Trade

Determinants of the trade	Percent annualized	Assumptions
Swap rate	21.75	
Withholding tax	3.42	tax = 0
Slippage hedge	3.12	$\phi_{-1} = \phi^e$
Convertibility hedge	2.26	$\psi = 0$
Bonds transaction cost	0.69	$\alpha = 100\%$
CC5 market fee	0.43	$cc5 = 0$
Ptax 800 effect	0.29	$\bar{e}_0^f = e_{-1}^f(1 + cdi_0)$
Overnight rate mismatch	−0.02	$cdi_{n-1} = cdi_0$
Cross residual effect	0.35	
Total costs	10.54	
Net return of the trade	11.21	

SUMMARY

The cases studies discussed are a representative sample of the nuances and the idiosyncrasies that arise in local fixed income trading. The inefficiencies of these markets introduce additional risks that may not be captured by employing traditional valuation techniques. Frictions (e.g., capital restrictions) may further complicate seemingly simple payoff structures.

Deep knowledge of local market conditions (regulatory, policy, political issues, etc.) is a prerequisite to a successful trading strategy. Arbitrage opportunities can be identified once all parameters are taken into account.

Chapter 12

The Emerging Markets Repo Market

Jonathan S. Cooper
Managing Director
BT Securities Corporation

INTRODUCTION

The market for repurchase agreements (repos) and reverse repurchase agreements (reverse repos) in emerging markets (EM) debt instruments started in the early 1990s as Mexican banks and other financial institutions used their newly exchanged Brady bonds as collateral for loans from American and European banks. Through repos,[1] these institutions could borrow at rates lower than those associated with certificates of deposit or other forms of unsecured funding. Transactions were documented as purchases and forward sales rather than secured loans, with margin calls triggered upon a decline in the value of the "purchased" bonds (relative to the cash advanced plus accrued interest). Documentation was on a "one-off" basis and replete with loan covenants. Spreads were often above LIBOR plus 300 basis points and 30% haircuts were common. For the American and European banks acting as lenders, the risk of default was mitigated by the U.S. Treasury component of the Brady bonds taken as collateral. Although not easily realized, the U.S. Treasury component gave credit departments comfort that there was "salvage value" should the obligor default. No more than half a dozen banks were actively lending dollars through reverse repos, and only the top tier Mexican banks had access to such credit.

As other countries issued Brady bonds or other externally traded debt, financial institutions in those countries became active in the EM repo market. Argentine and Brazilian counterparties, holding both long-term investment and short-term speculative positions, began to take advantage of lower funding costs on reverse repos. The repo market remains driven by the business of financing clients' long positions, although relative value trades (where a counterparty is long one bond and short another, financing both sides) and covering of outright short positions are also commonplace.

---

[1] The term "repo" is used generically throughout this chapter, referring to both reverse repos and repos.

STANDARD DOCUMENTATION

The development of master agreements, whereby all repos between two counterparties are governed by a single agreement (as opposed to one agreement per transaction basis), expanded the EM repo market into a volume business. The most commonly used master agreement for EM repo is the Global Master Repurchase Agreement (GMRA) developed by the Public Securities Association (PSA) and the International Securities Market Association (ISMA). The GMRA, which is also known as the PSA/ISMA Agreement (after its sponsors), is based to an extent on the PSA Master Repurchase Agreement (the PSA Agreement).

The PSA Agreement, governed by New York law, was historically used to document repos on U.S. Treasuries and agencies between broker/dealers and their clientele; however, an International Annex has been developed which will broaden the use of the PSA Agreement for international repos. Differences between the PSA/ISMA Agreement and the PSA Agreement include procedures for handling default, varying agency provisions, and market based differences in margin calculations. In addition, the PSA Agreement includes provisions addressing the regulated status of certain U.S. entities.

The PSA/ISMA Agreement, governed by English law, was initially drafted to facilitate standard documentation for the growing repo markets in Bunds, Oats, and other non-dollar sovereign securities; however, it quickly became the most commonly used agreement for repos involving EM instruments. There are two reasons for this. First, to satisfy regulatory concerns, broker/dealers or banks that book EM repos had used entities domiciled outside of the United States. Second, the EM repo market has adopted many of the market practices and style of trading from the London-based non-dollar repo markets. A single PSA/ISMA Agreement can be used to book both EM and non-dollar repo trades.

Many operations groups supporting EM repos are located in London. The business revolves around bonds that (typically) clear through the European depositories, Euroclear or Cedel, making European based operations groups the natural choice to control settlements.

Although most EM repos are actually booked outside of the United States, the EM repo trader community is, for the most part, located in New York. This stems from the fact that repo desks follow cash trading. Traditionally, trading in EM cash instruments has been centered in New York due to the market's initial focus on Latin American credits. The large European dealers, however, have often located their trading units in London and, with cash markets expanding into Eastern Europe and developing Asia, EM repo trading is inevitably becoming more global.

THE INTER-DEALER MARKET

The acceptance of the master agreements by banks and broker/dealers has allowed an inter-dealer market to develop. Like the U.S. or European repo markets, one dealer who is long a bond (either because it is funding a client's position or because the trading desk owns an issue) can lend the bond to another dealer. In return, the borrower will collateralize the repo with cash. The cash earns a below market interest rate, the exact level depending on the scarcity value of the underlying paper. By financing a client, typically at LIBOR plus levels, while simultaneously lending out the client's bonds to another dealer, often at sub-LIBOR levels, the repo dealer is paid on both sides of the transaction. It should come as no surprise that counterparties, seeking to finance bonds with scarcity value, have learned that the financing rates should reflect this scarcity value, and any net spread (extracted by the broker/dealer) should only reflect compensation for credit intermediation.

General Collateral Market

The EM inter-dealer market has also developed a general collateral (GC) market. GC is a tool for dealers to finance long positions in bonds which have no scarcity value (and hence cost more to finance). In the U.S. Treasury repo market, GC funding rates are similar across broker/dealers, and are normally below the rates of typical short term inter-bank funding. Conversely, GC in the EM repo market trades at levels higher than short-term inter-bank funding rates, making it attractive (as a way to fund long positions) only to non-bank dealers who otherwise have LIBOR-plus funding costs. The result is a funding advantage to commercial banks and subsidiaries that have access to inter-bank funding (allowing them to avoid borrowing in the GC market altogether). Investment banks, who by definition cannot access the inter-bank funding market, often engage in repos with their client base to finance their own positions. However, many of the traditional clients who invest cash in repos are restricted as to the type of collateral they may accept, limiting themselves to U.S. Treasuries or other highly rated securities. As a result, non-bank dealers have fewer funding alternatives and are often forced to the GC markets, paying a premium to inter-bank rates to fund their EM positions. Initially, the market priced the funding differential as high as 50 basis points (which was often higher than the rate at which investment banks could borrow cash unsecured from the banks). However, this premium has been arbitraged out by banks who use their inexpensive funds to lend to investment banks. The funding advantage of banks over investment bank competitors has decreased as a result of this arbitrage and has contributed, at least in part, to the overall narrowing of spreads in the marketplace.

Because the seller of collateral in a GC repo has the right to specify which paper they will deliver, and many EM issues are illiquid, the broker/dealer community has agreed to a market practice which specifies (unless otherwise agreed between the two parties to the trade) what is acceptable general collateral. GC is defined as "U.S. dollar denominated sovereign or sovereign guaranteed issues that clear through Euroclear/Cedel and whose issue size is at least U.S. $1 billion."[2] This precludes instruments such as Russian Ministry of Finance bonds, non-sovereign Eurobonds, and small tranches of Brady bonds.

Covering Short Positions

A securities funding transaction can be structured in a number of ways, repo being one method. However, when covering a short position, there are few alternatives to the repo market. The primary alternatives are Cedel and Euroclear which offer automatic securities lending services at hefty premiums. When a short position is limited to a period of one or two days, the operational cost of covering the short position through a repo may exceed the premium charged by the depository. However, on trades exceeding one or two days, the most efficient method of accessing bonds for the purpose of covering a short sale is often through the repo market.

When bonds are available to be lent by the depositories, a cap is placed on the scarcity premium that can be charged in the inter-dealer repo market. Dealers will choose between the inter-dealer market and the depositories, and use the less expensive option. However, the availability of bonds at depositories may change frequently. For paper in high demand, sudden and unpredictable changes in the availability of the bonds can cause painful dislocations in the repo market.

Leveraged Investors: Hedge Funds

In the mid 1990s, another class of investors began to take advantage of the opportunities in the EM repo market: hedge funds. As naturally leveraged investors, hedge funds needed counterparties to finance their investments. Often holding long positions on EM bonds, the hedge funds were a boon to the EM repo community by providing a steady flow of bonds to bonds to finance. Broker/dealers earned money by lending cash at a positive spread to their cost of funds. While the underlying bullishness in the market had been rocked from time to time, numerous hedge funds saw tremendous value in the EM market and ran large long positions. However, much of the profit from pure directional trades came at increasing risk, culminating in the Mexican liquidity crisis of late 1994. At that time, many of the directional players turned away from pure long side trading and toward trading spreads — long one bond and short another, betting on the bonds' relative values. Other fund managers who focused exclusively on playing spreads, often assisted by state-of-the-art computer programs, entered the EM cash and repo markets. In addition, many broker/dealers exported the arbitrage expertise they developed in their U.S. Treasury dealer operations to their EM desks and began to run what amounted to internal hedge funds with substantial spread positions. While funding client or house long positions is a straightforward exercise, lending out bonds to cover short positions is much more difficult. Cash is fungible, bonds are not.

Being short an EM bond creates a need to borrow the paper. Ideally, the broker/dealer is long the paper, either holding the bond in inventory or providing financing to a client on that bond, and is totally self-contained. But if that is not the case, the repo trader must access the inter-dealer market and bid for the specific issue in order to cover the short position. Often, the bond that is being shorted is expensive on a relative basis to other securities (including other EM

---

[2] Emerging Markets Traders Association, "Emerging Markets Repo Market Practices," December 6, 1996.

bonds or U.S. Treasuries). The probability that the broker/dealer is long paper that is considered expensive in the market is low. Thus, in this "Catch-22" situation, the repo desk will often be long the paper it doesn't need, and short the paper it requires. When too many cash market traders do the same trade (shorting an expensive bond and going long a cheap bond) the shorted bond becomes scarce in the repo market and expensive to borrow. Forced to lend cash at lower and lower rates in order to attract a counterparty to lend the bond, the cost of the repo passed on to the cash trader increases. In the end, the effect of the repo costs on the total return of the cash trade can be substantial. Purely technical factors may also affect the market. Exhibit 1 shows that the Brazil EI bonds traded with great scarcity value on two occasions in the sample series. The more extreme instance (the period surrounding October 1996) was a result of market and technical factors both moving in the same direction.

CONTROLLING THE RISK

Modifying the PSA/ISMA Agreement

Many market participants have tailored their PSA/ISMA Agreements to mitigate certain risks associated with EM repo. Annexes to the master agreements frequently include termination clauses based on (1) changes in the value of the underlying securities (typically by more than 20% relative to the purchase price); (2) material adverse changes in the general economic, political or financial conditions of the issuing country of the underlying securities; or, (3) policies of the United States making it inadvisable or impractical (in the opinion of the buyer) to proceed. Other clauses allow for cross-defaults to other standard master agreements covering other products, most notably the ISDA Master Derivatives Agreement. Many of the EM specific provisions, onerous by the standards of the U.S. Treasury or European sovereign repo markets, are actively negotiated by the counterparties.

Exhibit 1: Brazil EI Repo versus 1-Month LIBOR

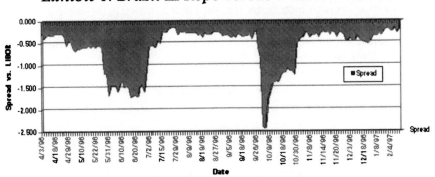

Source: Liberty Brokerage Inc., Bankers Trust Company

"Two-Name Paper"

Credit departments around the globe look at the non-investment grade status of EM bonds and participants with some trepidation. Repo is considered "two name paper," meaning both the counterparty and the collateral mitigate the risk inherent in the trade. However, when either the collateral (e.g., U.S. Treasuries) or the counterparty is highly rated, the importance of the other "name" diminishes. The combination of often volatile bonds and non-investment grade clients makes the traditional analysis of repo somewhat suspect.

Although some exceptions exist in EM repo, the underlying paper is typically non-investment grade. The volatility pattern of EM bonds is typified by periods of relative calm, punctuated by short spurts of volatility. The risk of "price gapping" created by this pattern is especially troublesome for repo trades. Counterparties, particularly those with their primary operations in the same country as the issuer of the underlying instrument, present a risk unique to the repo market. If the correlation between the financed bonds and the repo obligor is considered high (i.e., if the bonds default, the chances are that the repo counterparty will have financial difficulty as well or visa versa) the comfort from taking collateral can be small. The most extreme case of a dangerous correlation would be lending cash to a client, and taking, as collateral, the bonds issued by that client. The volatility of the underlying instruments, combined with the risk of high correlation between those bonds and the repo obligors, make these transactions very credit intensive.

The major difference between the EM repo markets and the non-dollar or U.S. Treasury repo markets is the credit component. The profits that dealers are able to extract in the non-dollar or U.S Treasury repo business are typically from creating timing mismatches, anticipating client or dealer flows, and/or betting on interest rates (cumulatively referred to as running a "matched book") and not from credit intermediation. In EM repo, financing a non-investment grade counterparty's investment in non-investment grade bonds and lending those bonds in the repo market (or vice-versa), resembles running a matched book. In reality, however, the EM repo dealer, who acts as principal on both sides, has just performed a classic credit intermediation; the spread earned is the compensation for taking credit exposure. The risk of confusing a credit-remote matched book and a credit intermediation business is very real, resulting in spreads which can be out of line with the counterparty risk absorbed.

Pricing the Risk

Pricing the risk in EM repo is a difficult task. Analysts often compare a repo transaction to selling a put struck at the repurchase price of the repo. This approach is incorrect since the repo won't necessarily create a loss (from the perspective of the broker/dealer) simply by virtue of the underlying bond's decline in price (in the case of a reverse repo, or rise in price if a repo). The counterparty must default *and* the underlying bond must move against the dealer to create a loss. This is, in effect, a compound option with the components being the credit status of the counterparty and the volatility of the underlying instrument. To the extent the two are closely correlated, credit officers often liken the transaction to an unsecured term loan and seek spreads which reflect unsecured risk. This approach ignores the value of over-collateralization, daily mark to markets, and margin calls. By marking to market daily and having the right to make daily margin calls (if necessary), the effective duration of the trade is shortened to the delivery cycle for additional collateral or cash plus a liquidation period (should the counterparty default on the margin call).

Haircuts and Over-Collateralization

One way to mitigate counterparty and collateral risk is to obtain haircuts (or its corollary, over-collateralization) from counterparties. For example, if a client wishes to enter into a reverse repo on a bond worth $100, and the broker/dealer advances $90 against that bond (e.g., a 10% haircut), a 10% cushion is built into the transaction. The bond's value must decline by 10% before the broker/dealer is at risk. Clearly, the larger the haircut, the less the risk. In the early days of EM repo, haircuts of 20% or 30% were not uncommon. Competitive pressures, lack of recent market shocks, and better technology have contributed to shrinking haircuts.

The Four Elements of Risk

The vast majority of risk assumed in an EM repo is found in four aspects of the transaction: (1) counterparty credit; (2) liquidity of the underlying bond; (3) margin maintenance; and, (4) legal implications.

The first factor to be understood is the risk associated with the credit quality of the counterparty. Counterparties to EM repos differ greatly in their credit quality — with ratings ranging from AAA to B. While it is true that repo is "two name paper," the first name is always the counterparty. Without a default by the counterparty, the collateral cannot be liquidated.

The second aspect of the transaction to be closely monitored is the stability and liquidity of the underlying bond. The volatility of the paper and susceptibility to shocks must be understood. For example, short-term paper carries greater risk, as it must be rolled over frequently. This was borne out in the 1994 Mexican liquidity crisis. Broker/dealers or banks who financed Tesobonos, the short-term Mexican government issued dollar-linked paper, saw their collateral become completely illiquid as the threat of default loomed. Like the Tesobonos, Mexican Brady bonds fell in value, but did not exhibit the same evaporation of liquidity seen in the short-term bonds.

The third important factor in addressing risk is the ability to accurately mark to market the underlying bonds in a timely manner and, when appropriate, make margin calls or liquidate positions. Having the technology necessary to track large numbers of trades and report exposures is crucial to controlling risk. Equally important is being part of an organization that is an active participant in the cash markets. This provides direct access to accurate prices and timely liquidation in the event of a default. Last, but certainly not least, is understanding the legal implications of an EM repo.

LEGAL ISSUES[3]

The legal and regulatory implications of an EM repo may be complex, particularly when dealing with foreign counterparties. Therefore, it is critical that a party obtain appropriate legal advice and be satisfied as to tax and accounting treatment prior to engaging in any transactions. The following is a general discussion of several of the many issues to consider when entering a repo transaction generally, and, in particular, with foreign counterparties.

Financial institutions engaging in repo should be aware of regulatory restrictions in their own jurisdictions that may affect their ability to enter into financing transactions. Additionally, parties should be well-versed in the treatment of repos under the governing law of the contract; for instance, parties negotiating the PSA/ISMA Agreement must consider the treatment of repos under English law, while parties using the PSA Agreement must consider treatment under New York law. Whenever a party wishes to enter into a transaction or master agreement with a counterparty whose assets or main place of business is in another jurisdiction (including the main office of an off-shore branch), the party needs to consider the laws of that jurisdiction. As jurisdictions treat repo differently, a party must analyze the legal risks to which it might be exposed in each jurisdiction.

When dealing with a foreign counterparty, in each case, a party negotiating a master repo agreement needs to determine whether:

1. the master agreement is legal and enforceable against the counterparty. This includes determining whether the terms of the agreement are enforceable against the counterparty under the governing law of the contract and whether the governing law will be recognized and enforced under the laws of the counterparty's jurisdiction;
2. the counterparty has the legal capacity and authority to enter into the agreement;
3. the party can in fact obtain the property rights (such as the repo securities or margin) it intends to acquire under the terms of the agreement and can enforce these rights against the counterparty or third parties:
4. the party can exercise its remedies upon default as specified in the agreement including in the event of insolvency of the counterparty;
5. any market conventions exist which may affect the way the transactions are conducted;

---

[3] The author thanks Katarina Dimich for her assistance in writing this section.

6. there are any special tax or accounting issues; and,
7. there are regulatory or other legal restrictions in entering into repo transactions with the international counterparty.

More specifically, a party should consider the following: (1) how is the transaction characterized in the counterparty's jurisdiction — as a sale or a secured loan? If it is considered a secured loan, how is the security interest perfected and can the buyer deal freely with the securities including lending them to other counterparties? If it is treated as a sale, how is it treated for tax purposes and can transactions be netted?; (2) can the counterparty post securities with a market value above the amount of cash financing extended (i.e., haircuts)?; (3) can the counterparty be marked to market during the term of the repo?; and, (4) in the event of the counterparty's bankruptcy, is close-out netting enforceable? Often the answers to these questions are far from clear.

In certain jurisdictions, a repo may be treated as a type of sell/buyback; there is no master agreement and the securities would not be marked to market. In some jurisdictions, the governing law of the contract will be recognized; however, in others, local custom and rules pertaining to financing transactions may be applicable if the assets or parties are located on-shore. Although generally branches are subject to the same restrictions as the main office, jurisdictions may vary as to whether local rules apply to off-shore branches.

Bankruptcy treatment is perhaps the most complex legal issue to be addressed prior to engaging in cross-border repo transactions, particularly in the emerging markets. While a foreign jurisdiction may recognize and honor the governing law of the master agreement prior to bankruptcy, once a counterparty files for bankruptcy protection in its own jurisdiction, the bankruptcy laws of that jurisdiction will likely be observed. Therefore, understanding the foreign jurisdiction's insolvency regime is important. In many countries, for instance, banks and corporations undergo different insolvency procedures and treatment.

For both regulatory and risk management purposes, the enforceability of close-out netting provisions in a master agreement, in the event of a counterparty's insolvency, will need to be considered. Close-out netting provides that upon a counterparty's bankruptcy, all delivery and payment obligations under a master agreement are accelerated, aggregated, and set-off so that only a net sum is payable by or to a counterparty. This protection is particularly significant in jurisdictions where greater credit concerns exist and unfortunately, in many EM jurisdictions, close-out netting in bankruptcy is not permitted. Initiatives are underway in certain jurisdictions to amend the bankruptcy codes.

As stated above, in many countries, once a counterparty has filed for bankruptcy, the ability of a non-defaulting party to accelerate its outstanding transactions, terminate the agreement, and net its positions may be limited. Additionally, participants should be aware of any applicable pre-bankruptcy periods wherein payments to a particular counterparty may be voided as preferences.

To complicate things further, some bankruptcy courts may consider the law of the jurisdiction where the assets are held (for instance, Belgium, if the assets are held in Euroclear) or may apply the law of the contract for characterization purposes (i.e., a secured loan or a purchase/sale) and then apply its own bankruptcy laws as to priority of payments.

In summary, it is critical that EM repo participants understand the legal aspects of engaging in repo transactions prior to entering into a transaction or master agreement. In some cases, due to lack of precedent, there is no clear answer as to how a foreign court will treat a transaction. Nevertheless, it essential that a party obtain legal advice from counsel in each jurisdiction where it intends to do business and weighs the risks involved.

The EM repo market shares many of the features seen in other repo markets around the globe. To be sure, an efficient repo market complements an efficient cash market, and visa versa. However, just under the covers lay many idiosyncrasies which are ignored at one's peril.

Chapter 13

The Economics of Retiring Brady Debt

Robert S. Gay
Managing Director
Bankers Trust Securities

INTRODUCTION

In April 1996, Mexico ushered in a new phase to the workout of the developing country debt crisis of the 1980s. With the launch of a much-heralded global bond exchange, about $1.75 billion in new uncollateralized bonds were swapped for Par and Discount bonds that were issued in March 1990 as part of the restructuring of past-due commercial bank loans under the Brady Plan. When the new deal was done, Mexico actually had retired on net almost $1 billion of marketable debt and had reduced its debt service by perhaps $150 million over several years. The transaction also marked the first of several steps toward reshaping the country's external finances, including the lengthening of maturities on marketable debt and early repayment of expensive U.S. loans that were made at the time of the peso crisis in early 1994. International investors subsequently rewarded Mexico's sensible debt management strategy by drastically bidding down spreads on sovereign debt.

On the surface, it seems bizarre that any country would want to retire 30-year debt with low coupon payments, usually about 6% per annum in U.S. dollars. Few industrialized countries qualify for such attractive terms let alone developing ones. Obviously, these complex Brady instruments have some unusual features that, when combined with the volatility and imperfections of most emerging markets, can make early retirement both feasible and worthwhile under certain circumstances. One of the key features that distinguishes Brady bonds from other sovereign debt is their collateral, which was designed to assuage investors' fears about repayment of principal and interest. The oddity of the collateral, often in the form of zero-coupon U.S. Treasury bonds, is that its value accumulates over time, making the securities themselves gradually more valuable even if sovereign creditworthiness does not change at all. Moreover, investors and the sovereign issuers tend to value the collateral differently. A sovereign entity, for example, can sell the collateral for cash when a Brady bond is defeased, whereas an investor generally cannot capture in full this value without resorting to somewhat

171

171

sophisticated financial machinations that in themselves entail additional market risk. In short, the investor audience is limited somewhat by the peculiar character-istics of these securities.

Although differences in valuations open the door to potential mispricing that would facilitate a sovereign debt buyback or exchange, there are other essen-tial pre-conditions to a successful and economical swap. Namely, the country must: (1) have sufficient fiscal credibility to issue uncollateralized long-term debt at a yield well below the so-called "stripped" spread on existing Bradys; (2) have enough accumulated collateral underlying the Bradys to make it worth capturing that value by retiring the bonds; and, (3) have some profitable use for the freed collateral. We will examine the interplay of these pre-conditions and how they affect various countries' decision to retire Brady debt. First, however, the next section gives a brief overview of the Brady market and a description of some of the generic instruments. Aficionados may wish to skip this section.

THE BRADY PLAN: SECURITIZATION OF A DEBT CRISIS

U.S. Treasury Secretary Nicholas Brady announced the novel market-based strat-egy to redress the developing country debt crisis of the 1980s in March 1989. His initiative, referred to as the Brady Plan, had several innovative features that would leave an indelible mark on the securities that ultimately would be issued. First, the plan recognized that many debt nations would not be able to repay in full the extensive loans made primarily by international commercial banks in the late 1970s and early 1980s. In many cases, the money had been spent on ill-advised projects that turned sour when world interest rates soared and commodity prices collapsed or was squandered on subsidies to inefficient state enterprises.

Under the Brady framework, creditors agreed to reduce their claims for principal and past-due interest in exchange for new securities with credit enhance-ments (i.e., collateral) so that they could be more easily sold to end-investors (see Exhibit 1). Second, international financial institutions including the IMF and World Bank provided financing for the down payments on collateral to back the new securities. Third, debtor countries in return were required to maintain an eco-nomic adjustment program sanctioned by the IMF in order to receive new loans. Usually the IMF plan — complete with an agenda of market-oriented reforms, including reducing trade barriers and privatizing state enterprises and targets for economic performance, notably on government budget balances — would be nego-tiated prior to setting the terms for the exchange of old bank loans for new securi-ties. With the first Brady exchange by Mexico in 1990, a new asset class was born.

By April 1997, 16 countries had completed Brady plans, as shown in Exhibit 2. The face value of outstanding bonds exceeded $168 billion. As commer-cial banks sold off the bonds to an ever-wider investor base throughout the world, trading volume soared to US$1.58 trillion in 1995, or roughly 60% of the total turnover of all emerging country debt instruments. The Brady packages and instruments vary by country, but most provided a choice of securities with below-market interest rates at the outset (*Pars* and *FLIRBs*) and others that had floating rates with a negotiated discount on the principal loan amount (*Discounts*). Exhibit 3 outlines the terms of a typical Brady Plan package for these common instruments.

Exhibit 1: Evolution of the Brady Debt Market

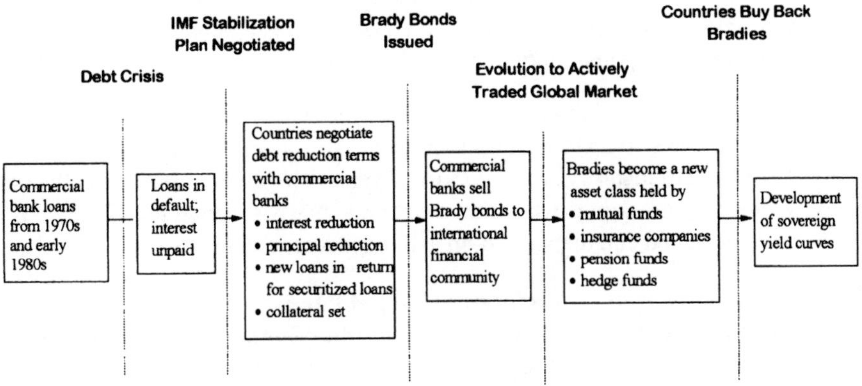

Exhibit 2: Countries with Brady Bonds

Country	Issue Date	Amount Issued (in US$ billions)
Mexico	1990	32.1
Costa Rica	1990	0.5
Venezuela	1990	17.6
Uruguay	1992	1.1
Philippines	1992	4.5
Nigeria	1992	2.1
Argentina	1993	24.3
Jordan	1993	0.8
Brazil	1994	57.1
Dominican Republic	1994	0.5
Bulgaria	1994	5.1
Poland	1994	7.9
Ecuador	1995	5.4
Albania	1995	0.1
Panama	1996	3.4
Peru	1997	6.0
Total		168.5

Exhibit 3: Typical Brady Plan Instruments

Reduced Interest Rate Bonds

Par Bonds: Old loans are exchanged for Par bonds at face value, but the interest rate is fixed well below market rate. Collateral, mostly in the form of zero-coupon U.S. Treasury bonds, is included and is financed by reserves, the IMF and World Bank. Interest collateral usually covers the next 12-18 months of payments. Maturities are 25 to 30 years with a bullet payment at maturity. A few Par bonds (Mexico, Venezuela, Nigeria) have additional enhancements ("value recovery rights") based on high oil exports or prices. Maturity is 30 years.

FLIRBS (Front-Loaded Interest Reduction Bonds): These bonds have low initial interest rates that step up to market levels over 5 to 7 years. Interest rates then float over LIBOR until maturity, usually 15 to 17 years. There is no principal collateral, and interest collateral ends when the interest rate reaches market levels. There is a 7-year grace period and then a step-up amortization schedule.

Reduced Principal Bonds

Discount Bonds: Principal (face value) of debt is reduced by a negotiated amount, usually 30% to 45%, but the interest rate varies with market levels, typically LIBOR plus $^{13}/_{16}$%. Like Par bonds, Discount bonds have U.S. Treasury collateral on principal and a few interest payments. Maturities are 30 years with a bullet payment.

Converted Loans with Additional Lending

New Money and Debt Conversion Bonds (DCBs): Creditors agree to provide new loans in return for the right to convert old loans into marketable bonds. These bonds have interest rates that "float" with market levels, usually LIBOR plus $^{7}/_{8}$%, and they amortize over their 15-to 18-year life after a 5-10 year grace period. There is no collateral.

A few features of the Brady bonds encourage early retirement if market conditions are right. First, the collateral attached to the Par and Discount bonds, which was meant to be a credit enhancement at issuance, also becomes a source of untapped cash as its value accumulates over time. Only the issuer can "capture" this value by defeasing the bond and selling the collateral; for investors, the collateral is solely a residual claim in the event of default. In the extreme, Brady bonds become entirely U.S. Treasury risk at maturity, because the zero-coupons ultimately are equal in value to the final bullet payments. At some point, as the value of the collateral grows and the remaining life of the Brady bonds shortens, sovereign issuers inevitably will find it worthwhile to retire the bonds. The only surprise has been that the various conditions for a profitable buyback have come together so soon during the life of these instruments.

Second, for most Brady packages, the cost of debt service steps up, usually during the first 7 to 10 years, as initial below-market interest rates are phased out or postponed amortization payments come due. For example, the Front Loaded Interest Reduction Bonds (FLIRBs) issued by Venezuela, Brazil, Bulgaria, Panama and Peru typically carry fixed rates during the first 7 to 10 years that step up from low levels of 3% to 5% per annum and then convert to floating-rate notes. Of greater concern for sovereign debt management are the sliding schedules, or grace periods, for amortization payments. Apart from Pars and Discounts, which repay principal at maturity, most Brady instruments have grace periods on amortization payments ranging from 3 to 10 years, including the FLIRBs, Debt Conversion (DCBs), Past-Due Interest (PDIs), and New Money Bonds. When those grace periods end, countries must come to grips which the added burden of debt service in their fiscal budgets or the added interest expense of issuing new marketable debt to cover the amortization payments. By 1996, the issue of escalating external debt service once again had become a major consideration for some of the early issuers of Brady bonds including Mexico, Argentina, and Venezuela.

POTENTIAL BENEFITS OF DEBT RETIREMENT

Although various features of Brady bonds including accumulating collateral, coupons that step up over time, and delayed amortization, make them candidates for early retirement, few countries are motivated to retire long-term debt unless there is a compelling rationale to do so. Most Finance Ministers who make the final decisions on debt management probably would list similar objectives for their financing strategy. At the top of the list, however, they would require that transactions to retire debt also must achieve some savings on debt service and hence government expenditures. Indeed, the principal reason why excessive indebtedness poses a problem is that debt service eats up too much government revenue, leaving too little left for other worthy social goals. The whole point is to relieve pressure on the government's budget, just the way a corporation would pay off or refinance debt in order to improve its cash flow, thereby enhancing its ability to pay and perhaps even its credit rating. Other considerations undoubtedly play a role in sovereign debt management. For heavily indebted countries, reducing the large stock of debt in itself might be a worthy goal, but in practice any buyback would have to eliminate future debt service payments or to spread them out over time in order to make the transaction "saleable" to government decision makers who wish to see tangible benefits and preferably during their tenure in office.

Another common motive is to extend maturities beyond the 2 or 3 years to which indebted countries are often limited. Indeed, issuance of long-term debt can represent a milestone in the development of a country's capital market, because it alleviates the risks associated with constantly having to refinance a preponderance of short-term debt. These refinancing risks can be substantial if world interest rates increase dramatically, as they did in the early 1980s, thereby causing debt service to soar when government tax receipts probably are dwindling, or in the extreme if global capital markets close their door to indebted issuers, as was the case after the Mexican peso crisis of December 1994. A related motive is to develop a sovereign yield curve with an array of long- and short-term debt — a strategy that greatly helps to even out debt service payments, to minimize the budgetary costs of external shocks from world interest rates, and to better plan government expenditures on infrastructure and social programs.

Perhaps the least appreciated potential benefit of a broad and deep capital market, for either external or internal debt, is to provide pricing benchmarks for corporate issuers who often are the principal source of foreign exchange earnings. In most countries with the exception of a few with dominant state enterprises, such as the national oil companies of Venezuela and Nigeria, the private sector generates the lion's share of foreign currency that ultimately is used to pay external debt service. Thus, efficient, low-cost access to capital markets contributes to corporate profitability and in turn sovereign creditworthiness. This ancillary benefit of sound sovereign debt management normally is ignored, because the payback to public finances is neither immediate nor direct enough to pique the interest of most policymakers.

THE ARITHMETIC OF A BRADY BUYBACK:
A CASH FLOW MODEL

Of the various potential benefits mentioned above, by far the most compelling rationale for retiring or exchanging Brady debt is to save on debt service expenses in the government's budget. Without such savings, other arguments, including establishing a yield curve and benchmarks, will fall on deaf ears. This focus on a single objective — cash savings — also has the advantage of providing a simple analytical framework for assessing the viability of either a debt exchange or straight buyback. Namely, a model of the net change in cash flow from these transactions can go a long way toward determining whether retiring Brady debt would be both economical for the issuer and attractive to investors.

Let us first define the monetary savings of a buyback as government expenses on debt service — interest due plus amortization of principal — over the remaining life of any given Brady bond less those for a Eurobond with a fixed coupon and principal repayment at a maturity date close to that of the Brady. This framework closely imitates the change in cash flow experienced by the government in a debt exchange, but can easily be modified to cover a repurchase with the proceeds from an asset sale, such as the privatization of a state enterprise. Including amortization payments as part of the savings is debatable. They clearly can be a drain on the government's cash flow if new debt cannot be raised in the market, as was the case for many Latin American countries in early 1995, and many fiscal budgets of reforming countries seem to presume this worst-case scenario. In any event, as long as the new debt is presumed to be a debt service expense at maturity, the calculation of net savings is a good barometer of a worthwhile transaction. An appropriate discount rate should be used to arrive at a present value for the future stream of net cash savings on debt service. Not surprisingly, government officials seem to be more interested in the undiscounted cash savings over the next five years than they are in the theoretically pure calculation of present values.

Several other assumptions also are required. First, the country must have sufficient credibility, especially on fiscal discipline, to be able to issue uncollateralized long-term debt. The assumed market yield on a new issue to replace a collateralized Brady should be somewhere between the theoretical return after the value of any collateral is removed conceptually (the so-called "stripped" yield) and the yield to maturity with the collateral attached (the "blended" yield). Investors will demand something more than the blended return they currently would earn in order to get them to accept a swap. The issuer also should be willing to pay somewhat more than the blended yield, because it actually can realize the higher stripped yield at redemption by selling the attached collateral. Floating-rate instruments also require a future scenario for global interest rates. Finally, one must make some assumption about what the issuer does with the proceeds from the sale of collateral, if any. Usually one would assume the money is spent on retiring more debt, preferably of the expensive, short-term variety.

CONDITIONS FOR A SUCCESSFUL EXCHANGE

On the surface, it seems plausible that most Brady countries would be delighted to dispose of these complex and inefficient instruments, especially when they begin to repay principal. In practice, however, conditions are rarely ripe for a windfall transaction for issuers. Markets are savvy enough to sense a windfall in the making and quickly arbitrage the opportunity away. Nonetheless, a number of golden opportunities presented themselves during 1995 and 1996, but only a few countries were sufficiently fleet afoot to take advantage.

Here are some rules of thumb on the basic conditions that make a Brady debt exchange (or buyback) attractive to the sovereign issuer and yet palatable for investors. First, the deeper the discount on the price of a Brady bond, the greater the amount of debt and debt service that will be eliminated. This observation is simple arithmetic. When an instrument's market price is only 60% of its face value, as often was the case for the Par bonds of Mexico, Venezuela, and Brazil shown in Exhibit 4 during the early and mid-1990s, a country's Treasury could eliminate $1.67 worth of debt (face value) and the attendant debt service by issuing $1 worth of new bonds. That leverage can override a very substantial difference in coupon rates on the two instruments. Prices, of course, are discounted heavily for a reason. Countries either did not have the means to pay off debt or did not have sufficient credibility to issue long-term instruments, especially during the early years of the IMF-sanctioned stabilization plans. As economic performance improved and countries mended their public finances, prices rose in concert.

Exhibit 4: Prices of Selected Latin American Par Bonds

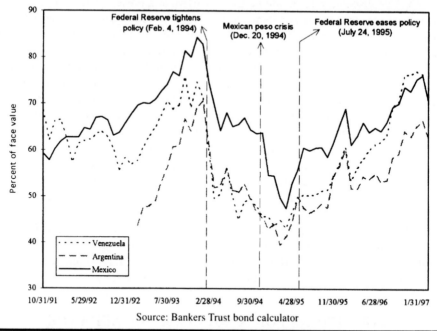

Source: Bankers Trust bond calculator

An intriguing episode, though, was the collapse in prices to as low as 35 to 45 cents per dollar of face value at the depths of the Mexican peso crisis in March 1995. At those levels, the economics overwhelmingly favored a buyback, but that option either was not feasible or not considered because other pre-conditions were not satisfied. Mexico, for example, was technically insolvent, because its foreign currency reserves had been depleted in defending the peso at an overvalued level, and investors were not willing to renew about $29 billion in short-term debt that was coming due that year. Temporary loans from the United States and international agencies defused the liquidity crisis, thereby permitting Mexico's expeditious return to the capital markets and setting the stage for the Brady exchange less than a year later in May 1996.

Other Brady countries did not take advantage of this temporary mispricing of the entire market for various reasons. Venezuela was still laboring under capital controls and the costly bailout of its banking system in 1994. Argentina was forced to pay cash for all debt service and could not use reserves because of their role as backing for the peso monetary base under its currency board system. Poland's Brady plan was only several months old in early 1995, and buying back debt that had just been issued probably seemed like a strange idea. The Philippines and Brazil were the most viable candidates. Both probably were deterred by high market interest rates at the time. Brazil in particular missed an extraordinary opportunity. Reserves were soaring, as the *Real* Plan introduced in July 1994 had wiped out hyperinflation literally overnight, but could not easily be used to retire debt because of legal restrictions. There also was little pressure to reduce external debt service which was minimal at the time. All these countries would get a second chance in 1996 as market interest rates for emerging country debt plummeted amidst a wave of excess global liquidity.

A second consideration is the value of the accumulated collateral underlying the Bradys which effectively reduces the net cost of a buyback. Exhibit 5 shows the estimated value of both the interest and principal collateral in the Pars and Discounts. For the early issuers of Bradys — Mexico, Venezuela, Philippines and Nigeria — collateral had grown to 21% to 25% of the face value of the bonds by April 1997. This represents a substantial hidden reserve of cash that could be tapped. The value of the collateral, usually in the form of zero-coupon U.S. Treasury bonds, varies with U.S. interest rates but otherwise sets a gradually rising floor under the price of the Brady bonds. What is relevant for the buyback analysis is the net cost of retiring Bradys, or the market price net of the underlying collateral value. Recall, however, that Pars and Discounts also have relatively low coupon rates, so interest cost per unit of debt invariably increases after an exchange because market rates for an emerging country are unlikely to ever be as low as those on most Bradys. A buyback becomes viable when the net price is low enough to permit the country to buy (and retire) far more Brady bonds than it issues in Eurobonds with higher coupons. In short, the key relationship in a buyback is that between the discounted price on the Brady net of collateral and the cost of new funding.

Exhibit 5: Value of Collateral in Selected Brady Bonds

Country	Type of Brady	Maturity	Amount Outstanding (billions $US)	Bid Price per $100 Face Value (4/2/97)	Interest Collateral (millions of $US)	Principal Collateral (millions of $US)	Total Collateral (% of Face Value)
Argentina	Par	3/31/23	12.5	62.75	303.6	1,953.1	18.1
	Discount	3/31/23	4.3	80.31	139.9	672.0	18.9
Brazil	Par	4/15/24	10.5	62.56	282.5	1,535.1	16.8
	Discount	4/15/24	7.3	80.50	233.3	1,067.2	17.8
Bulgaria	Par	7/28/24	1.9	59.63	81.0	272.8	18.6
	FLIRB	7/28/12	1.7	42.75	36.0	0.0	2.1
Ecuador	Par	2/28/25	1.9	41.25	44.4	262.9	16.2
	Discount	2/28/25	1.2	65.25	46.1	166.1	17.7
Mexico	Par	12/31/19	17.9	70.69	628.9	3,470.9	22.9
	Discount	12/31/19	11.4	87.50	637.4	2,210.5	25.0
Nigeria	Par	11/15/20	2.1	63.50	59.2	383.8	21.1
Poland	Par	10/27/24	0.9	53.13	0.0	132.2	14.1
	Discount	10/27/24	2.7	97.50	0.0	383.4	14.1
Philippines	Par	12/7/17	1.9	84.75	20.7	426.6	23.7
Venezuela	Par	3/31/20	7.1	70.38	238.8	1,352.6	22.4
	Discount	3/31/20	1.3	81.00	64.7	247.7	24.0

Source: Bankers Trust bond calculator

This third condition — access to low-cost funding — can be problematic for emerging countries. It makes little sense to replace long-term bonds with ones of shorter tenure. So this condition requires sufficient fiscal credibility to issue 15- to 30-year bonds, which can be a tall order unless markets are fairly accommodating, as was the case in 1996 and early 1997. Debt issuance, however, is not necessarily the only source of funding for a buyback. Venezuela, for example, has proposed a Debt Retirement Fund that would be funded solely with proceeds from the sale of state assets. The objective is to align one-time proceeds with canceling long-term government liabilities, rather than allowing the money to be used for current budget expenditures as so often was the case with its excess oil revenue in the past. Brazil is considering a similar arrangement for the sale of its huge mining company, CVRD. These approaches are fundamentally different from, and preferable to, earlier debt-equity swap programs such as that used by Chile to reduce its debt burden.

The early debt-equity swaps were highly inflationary because central banks in effect served as an exchange agent for private sector transactions between foreign buyers who paid in debt instruments and local sellers who received cash. In essence, external debt was converted into local money supply to the detriment of the country's inflation rate. By contrast, debt-equity swaps involving the sale of state assets need not be inflationary, unless the proceeds are used to expand government expenditures to the point of overheating the economy. Legal vehicles that channel sales proceeds into retiring external debt help to preclude government overspending and budget deficits that were the major source of inflation in Latin America during the 1980s. Moreover, asset sales are the cheapest possible source of funding for debt retirement, namely the opportunity cost of international reserves (i.e., short-term world interest rates), which is where the proceeds would reside if not spent in the budget. Clearly, such a low cost of funding approaches those on Bradys, making any freed collateral largely a windfall for the Treasury.

A final consideration is whether the country has a profitable use for the freed collateral. Mexico, for example still had a heavy load of short-term dollar debt at the time of its debt exchange, namely the $10.5 billion in 3- to 5-year loans from the United States that were disbursed in four tranches between March and July of 1995. These loans were expensive — carrying coupons of around 12¼% per annum, which was actually more than the 11½% coupon that Mexico paid on the new 30-year Eurobond in the swap a year later. Mexico subsequently used the freed collateral from the Brady exchange to prepay a part of the U.S. loans in late 1996 and again in early 1997 before their first amortization payment was due. As shown in Exhibit 6, the repayment schedule quickly escalated to almost $1 billion per quarter in 1998, which was no small sum when combined with other government obligations coming due.

In sum, Mexico had every reason to do a Brady exchange: collateral represented almost one-fourth of the face value of the bonds; the government had managed to run a balanced budget even during the deep recession of 1995, boosting its fiscal credibility; markets fortuitously were receptive to issuance of long-term bonds at attractive spreads; and there was a pressing need to refinance expensive short-term debt. One result of the swap was to anchor the long-end of a sovereign yield curve, thereby opening the door to numerous other Eurobond issues with maturities of 5 to 20 years. By extending maturities beyond the year 2000, Mexico managed to level off the small mountain of debt amortization payments due in 1998 and 1999. The shading on the bars in Exhibit 7 represents the U.S. loans that were prepaid with new issues. What was once an ominous external debt structure during the dark years of relying on the infamous short-term tesobonos had become by 1997 a more even and manageable debt service schedule.

Exhibit 6: Amortization Schedule of Exchange Stabilization Fund of Mexico ($ Millions)

| | Medium-term swaps provided on: | | | | |
	3/14/95	4/19/95	5/19/95	7/5/95	Total
Q1 '97	0	0	0	0	0
Q2 '97	0	245	170	0	415
Q3 '97	0	245	170	205	620
Q4 '97	0	245	170	205	620
Q1 '98	0	245	170	205	620
Q2 '98	375	245	170	205	995
Q3 '98	375	245	170	205	995
Q4 '98	375	245	170	205	995
Q1 '99	375	245	170	205	995
Q2 '99	375	245	170	205	995
Q3 '99	375	245	170	205	995
Q4 '99	750	245	170	205	1,370
Q1 '00	0	305	130	205	640
Q2 '00	0	0	0	245	245
Total	3,000	3,000	2,000	2,500	10,500

Source: U.S. Department of the Treasury

Exhibit 7: Mexico's External Debt Amortization Schedule

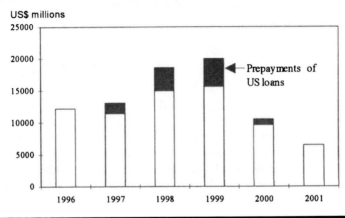

Exhibit 8: Mexican Sovereign and Corporate Eurobond Issues

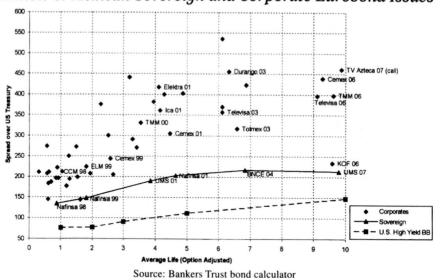

Source: Bankers Trust bond calculator

Another by-product was the development of sovereign benchmarks for corporate issuers. Exhibit 8 shows a scatter diagram of spreads over U.S. Treasuries of selected Mexican corporate bonds. Many of these issues, especially at the long end of the maturity spectrum, became possible in the wake of the Brady swap. Note that the sovereign curve has taken a shape remarkably similar to that of the U.S. high-yield market for companies with credit ratings comparable to Mexico's "BB" from Standard & Poors. Local companies generally cannot receive a rating better than the sovereign "ceiling," so the dots showing corporate yields lie above those for the Mexican government. An observation that is often overlooked is that the private sector usually generates the bulk of foreign exchange earnings, and having access to least-cost financing can be an important ingredient in corporate profitability and hence national competitiveness. A sensible and transparent strategy for public finances usually is a necessary pre-condition for a healthy corporate debt market.

SOME CANDIDATES FOR FUTURE BUYBACKS

Sooner or later, other countries are likely to follow Mexico's lead. Exhibit 9 shows the relevant summary statistics for an analysis of Brady buybacks as of April 1997. Market conditions inevitably will alter the economics of debt retirement as depicted by these numbers, but it is nonetheless interesting to contemplate which other countries might take the next step in the evolution of the Brady market. All the countries listed have a substantial amount of debt outstanding. With the exceptions of Panama and Peru whose Brady plans were finalized in

1996 and 1997 respectively, all the countries also have a large amount of collateral to be unleashed from their Par bonds, ranging from 14% of face value for Poland to 24% for the Philippines.

First, consider the countries with the greatest untapped collateral — the Philippines, Mexico, and Venezuela. Of the three, the Philippines is the least likely to retire debt because with Par bond prices at 85 cents per dollar of face value there is little leverage to reduce indebtedness in a swap transaction. The collateral of $236 million that would be released with a $1 billion exchange would not retire enough additional debt to compensate for the higher interest expense on the new bonds, at least as long as market rates for the Philippines are 8% to 9% compared with the Par bond coupon of 6¼%. Indeed, as a general rule, the prospective yield on the new issue is the overriding factor in the decision to retire Bradys when the Brady price approaches par value or when there is little collateral, as in Panama and Peru. Thus, low global interest rates would foster buybacks, especially in the Philippines and Peru. Otherwise, the Philippines is not a prime candidate in part because the burden of debt service is quite light at 11% of exports, whereas Peru is a possibility because the large amount of debt outstanding is a heavy drain on government revenues. Interest payments alone amount to 28% of tax revenues. The low coupon of 3½% on the Peruvian FLIRB, however, probably removes some of the urgency to pay off debt.

Exhibit 9: Buyback Analysis for Selected Brady Bonds

	Par Bond Price[1] (bid 4/2/97)	Collateral (% of Face Value)	Per $1 Billion of New Debt Issued		Debt Burden	
			Net Debt Retired[2] (millions US$)	Collateral Freed[2] (million US$)	Total Interest Expense[3] (% of Gov't Revenues)	External Debt Service[4] (% of Exports)
Argentina	62.75	18.05	593.63	180.53	10	45.7
Brazil	62.56	16.83	598.85	168.35	23	44.5
Bulgaria	59.63	18.62	677.15	186.21	4	19.5
Ecuador	41.25	16.17	1,424.24	161.74	21	16.5
Mexico	70.69	22.90	414.63	229.04	20	22.9
Panama	69.25	0.30	444.04	3.00	46	11.9
Peru	50.75	0.56	970.44	5.60	28	34.6
Philippines	84.75	23.66	179.94	236.62	20	11.0
Poland	53.13	14.14	882.35	141.42	20	6.4
Venezuela	70.38	22.41	420.96	224.14	19	25.6

Notes:
1. Par bond prices except for Bulgaria, which is a Discount bond, and Peru and Panama, which are Interest Reduction Bonds, per $100 of face value.
2. Net debt retired and collateral freed in US$ million as a result of a buyback of $1 billion market value of the Brady bonds listed.
3. Interest paid on internal and external debt.
4. Balance of payments concept of debt service, including public and private sector payments on external debt only.

Source: IIF and Bankers Trust bond calculator estimates

Venezuela may be a more compelling case. Collateral is high and there still is some potential for net debt reduction at a price of 70 cents per $1 of face value on the Par bond, albeit far less than it was during the early months of the country's IMF-sanctioned stabilization plan during the summer of 1996. Oil prices were climbing and Venezuela's huge budget deficit was disappearing almost overnight, yet the Brady bonds were still trading at deep discounts reflecting the lack of structural reforms. Unfortunately, the government could not capitalize on this extraordinary turn of events because various legal and political issues involving arrears on internal debt were still unresolved. As a practical matter, the Treasury had not cleared its long-standing debt to the central bank, which had advanced the money to pay for the collateral for the Brady plan in 1990. Government pensioners also had not been paid their one-time severances, which represent nearly all their retirement income, since the early 1990s and obligations were becoming explosive under the pension plan's archaic payment formula. Both of these prerequisites to retiring external debt were moving toward resolution in early 1997 and should pave the way for congress to approve a legal entity funded by privatization proceeds to retire debt. If so, Venezuela will have at least three motives for restructuring its debt profile. First, the labor settlements will greatly increase debt service, which could jump to 50% of government revenues unless it could be financed at lower interest rates abroad. Second, a substantial amount of Brady debt, notably the DCBs, begins to amortize in 1997. And third, privatization proceeds if realized would be an inexpensive alternative source of financing a buy-back. In Venezuela's case, the significance of a buyback would pale in comparison with the prospect of stabilizing the government's budget by earmarking excess oil revenues and asset sales into new institutional vehicles designed for this purpose.

Argentina and Brazil are more marginal candidates for buybacks. Both countries could reduce net indebtedness by about $600 million for each $1 billion of a bond swap. The collateral freed in such a deal would only be about $170 to $180 million compared with $224 million for Venezuela. The key motivation for Argentina might be to smooth out the bunching of maturities during the 1997 to 2001 period. Another is simply to pay down the large amount of dollar debt. After all, at more than 300% of exports, the heavy load of dollar debt and the constant need to roll it over leaves Argentina's finances vulnerable to external shocks from world markets. Brazil's story may be less compelling. The debt service schedule for marketable foreign currency securities of the federal government is very manageable from a budget perspective; most of the high debt service ratio (44%) represents private sector borrowing and the low level of exports. Interest on external debt is only 1.2% of GDP, and amortizations of the government's foreign debt amount to a paltry $1 billion during the 1997 to 2000 period. Thus, there is little need for Brazil to pre-finance maturing debt as was the case for Mexico and perhaps Argentina. Brazil's immediate problem is not external debt but the ballooning size and debt service burden of its internal debt. Not surprisingly under these circumstances, there is a lively debate in Brazil about whether privatization proceeds should be used to retire expensive short-term internal debt or the inexpensive foreign debt. The former makes good economic sense but smacks of frittering away assets to pay for current government expenditures when the budget deficit is Brazil's biggest remaining macroeconomic problem. Both countries have thriving corporate Euro-bond markets, perhaps in part because they already have a semblance of a sovereign yield curve composed of some long-dated uncollateralized Brady bonds.

Buybacks may be an intriguing phase for Brady countries and probably signal a new era for sovereign debt management. With some luck, the focus on issuing long-term debt, developing sovereign yield curves, and avoiding the risks of too much short-term foreign financing will continue. In truth, though, even this emphasis on sensible external finance should be a passing phase if emerging countries are to reach their full potential. No country can afford to rely too heavily on external finance. High domestic saving rates of 25% to 30% of GDP coupled with an array of local instruments and saving vehicles such as pension plans, insurance, and mutual funds are critical to financing high domestic investment. The foundations of those institutions are beginning to form in many emerging countries — a development that could mark yet another phase for international finance.

Chapter 14

Infrastructure and Project Financing in Emerging Markets

Paul G. McKeon
Managing Director
BT Securities Corporation

INTRODUCTION

Private sector participation in the provision of emerging market infrastructure services has prompted questions from development economists and investors alike about the forces giving way to such participation and the sources of financing driving the process. This chapter will examine both, as well as draw lessons from two project financing transactions which occurred in 1996.

Since the mid-1980s, when many developing economies began to implement free market policies as part of World Bank structural reform programs, and concurrent ideologies began to shift away from economic nationalism, the developing world (particularly in Asia and in Latin America) witnessed a period of unprecedented economic growth. As economies have grown, so has the requirement for vital economic infrastructure needed to sustain the economic growth.[1] A World Bank study identified a one-to-one correlation between a percentage point increase in national GDP growth and a percentage point increase in a country's stock of infrastructure.[2] Infrastructure has proven to be the pivot point in the cycle of development. As countries grow, increasing demands are put on roads, power lines, and telephone systems. Conversely, countries will not sustain growth if infrastructure is not adequately developed and maintained.

Exhibit 1 below illustrates the levels of private sector activity in infrastructure sectors as indicated by numbers of investment projects and privatizations by sector and region. In regions with the highest levels of activity, East Asia

---

[1] For purposes of this chapter, the term "infrastructure" primarily means economic infrastructure such as public utilities (e.g., power, gas, telephones, and water) and transportation systems (e.g., roads, ports, airports) — the engines of growth in an economy.
[2] *Infrastructure for Development: World Bank Development Report*, 1994.

With collaboration from Kerry A. McKeon, BT Securities Corporation.

and Latin America, strong economic growth has been complemented by a variety of sectoral policy reforms introducing competition and deregulation. In the late 1980s initiatives such as the build-operate-transfer (BOT) law in the Philippines, Mexico's private toll roads program, and Chile and Argentina's move towards a competitive electricity market all attracted high levels of private sector activity.

Exhibit 1: Private-Sector Projects and Privatizations Worldwide (1984-1995)

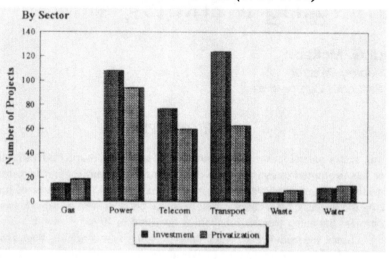

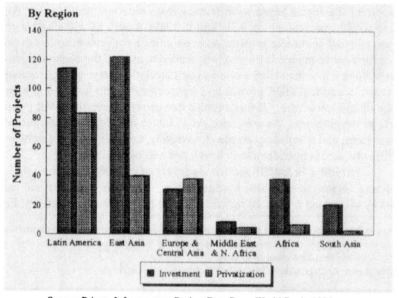

Source: Private Infrastructure Project Data Base, World Bank, 1996.

Exhibit 2: Projected Financing Demand in Asian Infrastructure (1995-2004)

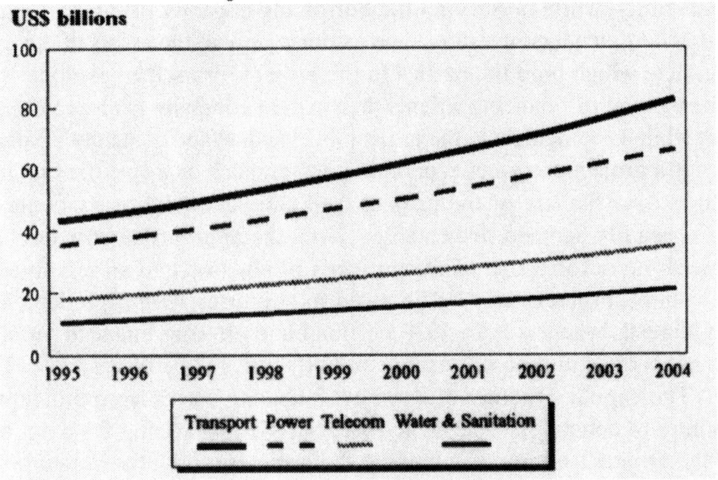

Source: "Infrastructure Development in East Asia and the Pacific: Towards a New Public-Private Partnership," World Bank Group, 1995

In addition to the economic and policy reforms which facilitated infrastructure investment, there have been important fiscal imperatives. Governments simply cannot afford to keep pace with the costs associated with rapidly growing infrastructure demand. As pressure for anti-inflationary policies and fiscal conservatism mounts from G7 lenders and multilateral banks, private financing has increasingly supplanted the role of supranational and national central banks.

The magnitude of the demand for infrastructure can be seen by looking at Exhibit 2: the forecasted financial requirements associated with Asia's burgeoning infrastructure demand. In the coming years, governments will need to look to the private sector to fulfill financing needs, particularly in the transportation and power sectors where infrastructure financing needs between 1997 and 2004 will increase by approximately 65% and 62%, respectively.

Private sector participation in emerging market infrastructure projects has taken the forms of both privatization and new investment (see Exhibit 1). In the case of the former, governments have invited private sector developers/operators into existing infrastructure projects (most often in the form of an acquisition or a management contract) to provide capital and management know-how, as the Government of Kazakhstan did in its power sector. In contrast, new investment in infrastructure has predominantly taken the form of greenfield projects built to add capacity to an existing system.

The financing of greenfield projects has been primarily on a "project finance," or limited recourse basis. This method has proven particularly effective in developing countries because financing is provided based on the strengths of a particular project, rather than of a particular country or sovereign entity. This has enabled the mobilization of significantly greater flows of investment capital, both debt and equity, while preserving the borrowing capacity of the sovereign. In the event of default, lenders/investors have recourse only to the assets of the project and the contracts which bind the parties to the project. From the developer's perspective, this method of financing shields their parent company from project and country risks while keeping debt at the project level and off the company's balance sheet.

If a project can meet economic hurdles, such as a specified return on free cash flows over the life of the project, and can adequately service its debt, the project is usually deemed financeable. Given the appropriate structure, such as a guaranteed buyer (offtaker) of the project's production and an offshore hard currency account, projects may be financed in countries with high degrees of risk, such as Nigeria, where a 1996 $330 million bond offering financed Mobil Producing Nigeria's construction of onshore and offshore gas facilities.

The capital structure of a project financing varies from project to project and country to country. Levels of market risk, the risk arising from not being able to sell the project's output, is a leading factor determining the amount of equity a sponsor may need to put into the project. The level of leverage in any given project should be determined by the conditionality, if contract based, or volatility, if market based, of the cash flow.

The greater the conditionality or volatility for any given project, the lower the absolute leverage level that can be supported as the level of cash flow-based coverage ratios will need to increase to support any given debt level. Toll roads and telecommunication projects have greater degrees of market risk than most power generation projects and therefore may require a greater equity contribution than the 25% typically required for most power projects with contract-based sales agreements. On the other hand, build-lease-transfer structures that provide for unconditional cash flow during the operating period may be able to support 100% leverage as in the case of the Barrancabermeja LPG Storage Project (see the case studies discussed later in this chapter). The sources and mixture of financing are examined in the next section.

PROJECT/INFRASTRUCTURE FINANCING SOURCES

Deregulation in global financial markets, such as the lifting of capital and exchange rate controls, has greatly eased the flow of private financing into developing countries. Infrastructure and project financing in emerging markets encompasses both debt and equity instruments from public, private, and governmental sources (see Exhibit 3). Below are descriptions of these sources and examples of their application in emerging markets project financings. These sources are not mutually exclusive in a project financing and, more often than not, are used in combination with one another. A sponsor's (developer's) decision to use a particular source may depend on several factors including financial cost and rate of return objectives, market timing/investor appetite, ownership, and disclosure issues.

Exhibit 3: Sources of Project Financing

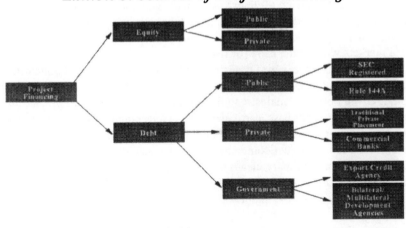

PRIVATE EQUITY

Sponsor Contribution

Sponsors typically invest their own capital to finance project capital expenditures on a leveraged basis. Sponsor participation may vary depending on the amount of equity capital typically required by lenders/investors. The degree of conditionality and volatility of project cash flow will determine the appropriate level of equity investments. Market expectation is to see sponsor equity in projects to demonstrate a greater sense of ownership above and beyond any contractual obligations they may have under construction, operations and maintenance (O&M), or servicing contracts.

Private Placements

Private equity may also be provided via private placements, under Regulation D of the 1933 Securities Act, which are portfolio investments. Typically, participants in these shareholding arrangements include institutions (pension funds, insurance companies, and mutual funds) as well as an increasing pool of dedicated infrastructure equity funds. In most cases, these equity holders do not exercise management/voting control of a project company as a sponsor would. For this reason, a project company may choose a private equity placement to build its equity base (and hence debt capacity) without having to cede control of the company.

Public Equity

Public equity offerings in both international and local markets may provide a source of finance for infrastructure projects. In cases where local stock markets have been relatively strong, such as in Malaysia and in Mexico, public offerings have been used as a finance vehicle as exhibited by Malaysia's Kelang Port Terminal and Mexico's Telefonos de Mexico (Telmex). Alternatively, equity instruments such as the American Depository Receipt (ADR) and Global Depositary Receipt (GDR) have allowed emerging markets companies to raise equity in U.S. markets and international markets without the need for listing on a foreign stock exchange. Examples of these include issuances by Telmex and Indonesia's PT Telkom. Public offerings provide infrastructure companies with a widespread investor base for raising equity capital. Given both the "mainstreaming" of the infrastructure and project finance market with the investor base, particularly in the telecommunications sector, and the increased liquidity in the financial system due to a proliferation of equity funds, some infrastructure/project companies have succeeded in executing initial public offerings (IPOs) as a primary means of financing. In choosing this option, sponsors must consider issues such as their equity return objectives, the widespread financial disclosure required, and the likelihood of ownership dilution.

Private Debt
Bank Loans
The largest source of project financing, bank loans typically provide floating-rate debt with shorter-term maturities and higher costs than the fixed-rate alternative provided by bonds. However, in situations where unfavorable market conditions exist for bond investors and issuers (e.g., such as rising interest rates and/or a glut of issuances), bank loans may provide a more effective means of financial execution. In addition, bank loans offer projects a flexible drawdown schedule during the construction phase. As a result, sponsors do not face "negative cost of carry"–interest payments on the full amount of principal beginning on financial close — which occurs during the construction phase in a bond transaction.

Private Placements
Under the same legal provisions for equity private placements, issuers may undertake a debt private placement, usually in the form of fixed-rate notes. Debt private placements allow issuers to place debt, which may have otherwise been difficult and/or undesirable to distribute in a more public forum, with large institutional investors. The private placement market has witnessed substantial growth in its investor base and is an active source of project financing. Three attributes distinguish the true "privates" market from the more public execution 144A markets covered in the next section: (i) the privates market caters to "buy and hold" institutional investors; (ii) less disclosure is required; and, (iii) due to the complexity of certain projects, they may not lend themselves to being "road-showed" (i.e., marketed to public market, 144A investors) and may be better suited for more sophisticated investors in the private market.

Rule 144A
Named after a provision in the U.S. Securities Act of 1933 which allows issuers flexibility in raising capital from qualified U.S. institutional investors (investors

with $100 million or more invested in securities other than those of the issuing entity), Rule 144A bonds are often thought of as a "half way house" between private placements and publicly registered bonds. Disclosure requirements are not as pressing as for publicly registered bonds and qualified institutional investors may trade between themselves without having a requirement to hold the bonds for one year (a requirement in "Rule 144") before trading them.

Since 1992 when Mexico's Toluca-Mexico City toll road became the first international infrastructure/project financing 144A bond, infrastructure projects have been successful in raising financing in the 144A market. As an indication, the two primary credit rating agencies, Moody's and Standard & Poor's, had each rated more than $16 billion of project finance 144A debt paper as of January 1997.[3] A noted feature of some 144A issues is that they may have "registration rights" allowing bonds to be traded in the publicly registered market, thereby increasing liquidity and reducing investor costs. This provides issuers with an advantage in that they may access the broadest investor base possible.

Investor appetite for 144A issues may largely depend on the rating assigned to the bond by credit rating agencies. Investment-grade issues, those rated at or higher than BBB- and Baa3 by Standard & Poor's and Moody's, respectively, provide issuers with a broader investor base than sub-investment grade, or "high-yield" bonds. Notwithstanding a narrower investor base, high-yield bonds have played an important role in financing projects. Examples of high-yield project financings include more volatile market cash flow-driven deals and instances where sub-investment grade credits provide contractual support to a project. In such a case, the high-yield project investor accepts greater degrees of risk in exchange for higher coupon bonds.

Governmental
Export Credit and Investment Agencies
National export credit and agencies (ECAs), such as the U.S.'s Export-Import Bank (EXIM), Canada's EDC, Italy's SACE, Germany's Hermes, and France's COFACE, provide project financing for those projects in which domestic companies (e.g., construction and/or engineering firms) have exportation roles. Similarly, investment agencies, such as OPIC in the United States, promote foreign investment by domestic firms by providing loans and political risk insurance. ECA financing packages predominantly consist of concessional loans and guarantees. In countries with high degrees of political risk, financial participation by an ECA may provide a "halo" effect on the project by giving investors/lenders the comfort associated with the participation of a quasi-governmental entity.

Multilateral Development Agencies
Since the late 1980s, the growing need for private financing in emerging market infrastructure projects has prompted multilateral agencies to increase their private

---

[3] Deepak Gopinath, "A Second Opinion," *Infrastructure Finance* (February 1997), p.30.

sector involvement. Like ECA participation, multilateral participation may provide a halo effect on projects. The World Bank, the Interamerican Development Bank, the Asian Development Bank, and the European Bank for Reconstruction and Development's (EBRD) have all created units which lend to or provide guarantees for private sector projects.

The World Bank maintains a co-financing program to promote private sector project development. In 1996, the infrastructure sector was the largest beneficiary of the co-financing program, receiving almost half of the $8.3 billion in total funding.[4] The World Bank also facilitates private sector financing through its affiliate the Multilateral Investment Guarantee Agency (MIGA). MIGA's mission is to provide investment insurance which may not otherwise be available in the private insurance market. MIGA covers investments (equity and debt) against risks of currency transfer, expropriation, and war.

The International Finance Corporation (IFC), another World Bank affiliate, lends directly to private sector infrastructure projects. Through its private equity investments, as well as its "A" loan (IFC loan) and "B" loan (syndicated loan) structures, the IFC has facilitated financial flows into countries and projects which may not have otherwise been able to attract private capital. Moreover, IFC has succeeded in leveraging other sources of funding for projects: for every dollar approved by the IFC in 1996, other investors and lenders provided a total of $5.13.[5]

Structuring the Financing

The mix of sources and instruments in a particular project will depend on both the country risk profile and the project's inherent structure and risk. For example, access to public market and/or 144A investment-grade debt will be constrained if the project is in a sub-investment grade country. Similarly, the capital structure of a project financing may also vary depending on the level of market risk for a project.

CASE STUDIES

The two case studies below exemplify the rationale for private sector participation in infrastructure development and the range of private funding sources available in each transaction.

Marmara Ereglisi Power Project

In response to the Government of Turkey's growing need for electrical capacity (nearly 40,000 MW between 1995-2010) on the one hand, and an attempt to curtail public expenditures on the other, the Turkish Ministry of Energy — MENR — authorized the construction of a 478 MW gas-fired private power generation plant

---

[4] "World Bank Annual Report," 1996.
[5] Ibid.

on a build-operate-transfer basis (BOT) in 1993. The project became the first project-financed BOT developed in Turkey.

Given Turkey's status as a sub-investment grade credit and the dearth of project finance precedents in that country, the project required careful structuring to give lenders/investors adequate levels of comfort. Although the project included typical elements of a contract-based project financing (see Exhibit 4) such as a gas supply agreement (with BOTAS) and an energy sales agreement (with TEAS — the state-owned utility), two unique structural attributes emerged to strengthen the project's credit: the Energy Fund and the Government's guarantee of the payment obligations of TEAS, BOTAS, and the Energy Fund. The former acted as a risk mitigant by allowing the fund to make tariff payments to the company in respect of events of *force majeure*, risk events, or buyout. The latter enhanced the credit of the Turkish entities participating in the deal.

In addition to structural attributes such as the government buyout in the event of force majeure, the project made use of the full range of private and quasi-governmental financing sources as shown in Exhibit 5. Each of the tranches of debt, with the exception of the Standby Debt Facility, was reinforced by an ECA or a bilateral agency as follows:

- The Construction Loan Facility included U.S. EXIM political risk insurance and a full U.S. EXIM "take-out", or refinancing, of the loan during commercial operations

Exhibit 4: Marmara Project Structure

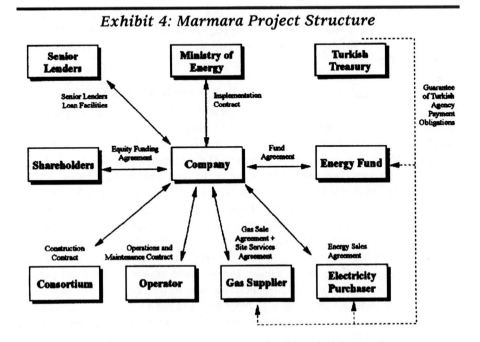

Exhibit 5: Sources and Uses of Financing

Sources of Financing*	U.S.$ in millions	Percent of Total
Construction Loan Facility	$246.21	40.75
Supplier Facility	115.96	19.19
OPIC Loan Facility	91.00	15.06
Shareholder Contributions	151.04	25.00
	$604.21	100.00

* Supplementing the sources of financing outlined above, the Company has arranged a Standby Debt Facility in an amount equal to US$27 million and a Standby Equity Facility in an amount up to US$34 million.

Uses of Financing**	U.S.$ in millions	Percent of Total
Construction Contract Costs (excl. VAT)	$325.03	53.79
Third Party Equipment & Services	59.85	9.90
Develop/Mobil/Construct Mgmt.	75.99	12.58
Bank and ECA Costs/Fees & Other	25.30	4.19
Interest During Construction	118.04	19.54
	$604.21	100.00

** Included in total Project costs is a venture contingency of US$10 million which can be utilized for any cost overruns if verified by the Independent Engineer.

- The OPIC Loan Facility was funded by a bond issuance with an OPIC guarantee during construction and operational phases
- The Commercial/Supplier Facility included a HERMES (German ECA) guarantee or a Siemens supplier credit.

ECA coverage, coupled with the project's structural strengths that minimized *force majeure* risk and government payment default, allowed the Marmara Project to achieve the critical mass necessary to make it the first project-financed BOT project in Turkey.

Barrancabermeja: Liquefied Petroleum Gas (LPG)

In response to the need to expand and increase the safety of its liquified petroleum gas and butane storage facilities, in 1996 the Colombian government, through Ecopetrol, the state-owned oil and gas company, privately financed the construction of a new $55 million storage facility in Barrancabermeja through a "Build-Lease-Transfer" (BLT) structure. This project financing conformed with the Colombian government's objectives of involving the private sector in infrastructure development and expanding the investor base of private financing of public infrastructure projects.

The Barrancabermeja BLT structure involved the building of the new facility by a private construction consortium — Union Temporal, the leasing of the facility through March 2004 by Ecopetrol, and the transfer of the facility from a Trust Company, a subsidiary of Union Temporal, at the end of the lease period. The Trust Company owns the site and its assets during the life of the leasing period. (See Exhibit 6.) In addition to monthly lease payments before the transfer, Ecopetrol will pay advance payments worth $16.1 million. Upon conclusion of the lease, Ecopetrol will purchase the site and facility from the Trust for $55.8 million.

Exhibit 6: Barrancabermeja Project Structure

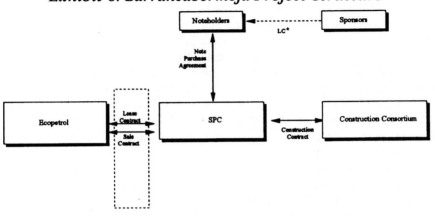

* Letter of credit provided for debt service reserve obligations

---

The project was 100% leveraged, with all the financing coming from the $55.6 million of fixed-rate, privately placed with 144A resale rights debt raised on behalf of the Trust. Because of the absence of equity, investors required project covenants which mitigated both construction and lease default risks.

The project maintained the limited recourse nature of a true project financing in that the notes were secured against the assets of the Trust rather than Union Temporal or the construction consortium members. Despite the atypical financing mix of 100% debt and 0% equity, the sound project structure and Ecopetrol payment obligations allowed the project to achieve financial closing and maintain the Government's objective of a successful public-private partnership.

CONCLUSION

The surge in private sector participation in emerging markets infrastructure over the past decade may be attributed to macroeconomic and structural changes, such as deregulation and market liberalization, which have facilitated economic growth and private investment. Private sector involvement in infrastructure services will continue to grow rapidly in the next decade. In late 1996, the World Bank Group estimated that East Asia would need to spend at least $150 billion a year on infra-structure in order to maintain current growth levels into the next century.[6] Latin America is poised to have similar demands for private financing as Brazil priva-tizes roads, power, and telecommunications in the late 1990s. Eastern Europe and Africa have only scratched the surface for private sector involvement in infra-structure. Hungary, Poland and countries of the former Soviet Union have begun to implement private provision of roads and electricity services, helping to build

---

[6] Jason Booth, "The Emergence of Asia's Debt Markets," *Infrastructure Finance* (May 1997), p.30.

momentum for future participations. Similarly, as demonstrated by the stake taken in South Africa's national telecommunications company by Southwestern Bell and BOT power programs in Morocco, Tunisia, and Egypt, the outlook for growth in the private participation of infrastructure in Africa is positive.

Infrastructure/project finance may also take new forms in the future. As competition in infrastructure services continues to grow in the more advanced emerging markets, governments may be less likely to enter into new long-term project finance contracts (such as BOT power projects, that have been the main-stays in emerging markets, with heavily negotiated contractual structures). Instead, governments may choose to select an increasingly market-based project structure, similar to the electricity systems in Argentina, Chile, Colombia, and Peru and telecommunications in Chile and Colombia. As a result, project sponsors and financiers may be required to structure projects with higher degrees of market volatility and contract conditionality.

In connection with the movement towards market-based structures, global project sponsors with strong balance sheets may choose to finance projects at the corporate rather than the project level. This structure may also provide developers with a cheaper financing alternative, potentially allowing them to refinance by "cross-collateralizing" the cash flows of several different projects in the portfolio.

Finally, local financing institutions will play an increasingly important role. Longer tenors on local bank loans will make local project financing more attainable. In addition, the development of pension and insurance funds, similar to those that have emerged in Chile and in Malaysia, will greatly expand the lender/investor base allowing projects to access capital more easily, and better match the revenue source and payment obligations of individual projects.

Chapter 15

Exchange Rate Mechanisms in Emerging Markets

Daniel Barkan
Managing Director
Bankers Trust Company

Jonathan Silber
Vice President
Bankers Trust Company

→ Pegging

INTRODUCTION

Central banks around the world may employ different and sometimes elaborate means for effective currency management. The long-term goal of any currency regime is to maintain currency stability in an effort to facilitate a prudent monetary policy and encourage both domestic savings and long-term investment. In the early stages of a country's economic development, it is imperative that a central bank establish a solid and credible framework for this continuing mission to succeed. In many instances, however, liberalization of the capital and trade accounts and the relaxation of foreign exchange controls have lead to excessive levels of short-term capital inflows. This so-called "hot money," if left unsterilized, can be inflationary and cause the authorities significant difficulties in achieving their monetary targets. Furthermore, this short-term capital tends to flow out of emerging economies during times of political or economic uncertainty — a process which is destabilizing if left unchecked.

The dynamics by which currencies behave in open emerging economies may result from the balancing act monetary authorities are forced to perform in attempting to maintain a credible exchange rate policy while pursuing responsible monetary and fiscal policies. In this chapter we will list and detail the prominent exchange rate mechanisms used by emerging market authorities in the period following the opening of their trade and capital accounts. We will draw on examples from the Asian and Eastern European countries to demonstrate the role these cur-

The authors wish to thank our colleagues and managers at Bankers Trust Company. Bankers Trust economists Alistair Boyd and Stanislav Rudcenko assisted with valuable reference material. Andrew J. Mitchell was diligent in the collection of facts and figures.

intervention policies by EM auth.

aim: exchange rate stability

rency regimes have played in achieving exchange rate stability as well as the process by which the targeting of a nominal exchange rate can aid a small open economy in conducting its monetary policy. In addition, various central bank responses to international capital flows will be discussed.

Peg - managed appreciation depreciation

Do market forces determine exchange rate?

EXCHANGE RATE MECHANISMS

① BY CENTRAL BANKS

reduce short term volatility

What are some of the key exchange rate mechanisms used by monetary authorities in emerging economies? Some allow market forces to fully determine the exchange rate. Other countries prefer to peg the exchange rate in a more transparent fashion, through a managed policy of appreciation or depreciation against either a single currency or against a basket of currencies. In each framework a central bank might periodically intervene in the open market or even induce short-term volatility in order to insure its long-term goals are met. The following sections detail some key exchange rate mechanisms commonly used by central banks in emerging economies. *— FIXED $ RATE = doesn't reflect home/demand growth which may be volatile ↓ exchange rate*

The Case of Fixed Exchange Rates: *parity may not always be maintained*
Basket Mechanisms and the Crawling Peg

While extensive literature debating the use of fixed versus floating exchange rate regimes in small open economies exists in the academic community, there is much evidence pointing to the successful applications of fixed exchange rate regimes in several developing countries. Economists opposing the use of fixed exchange rates have argued that a fixed regime may be an inconsistent policy measure in economies where the rate of domestic credit growth is volatile.[1] According to this school of thought, a fixed exchange rate regime may break down in cases where domestic credit growth exceeds the rate of growth of the nominal demand for money over an extended period of time. Under such circumstances, and assuming that the central bank would require a percentage of its local money supply to be backed by some of the country's foreign currency reserves (and/or its ability to replenish these reserves via capital inflows or debt), exchange rate parity could not be maintained at a point where the unintended rise in domestic credit exceeded the country's reserve cover.

---

[1] The authors recommend a review of Paul Krugman's ground-breaking work on the subject of balance of payments crises in small open economies. (Paul Krugman, "A Model of Balance of Payments Crises," *Journal of Money, Credit and Banking* 11 (1979), pp. 311-325.) Extensions to the Krugman model which incorporate the actions of speculators, subsequent government incentive to fend off speculation, and the possibilities for self-fulfilling crises can be found in the works of Robert J. Barro and David B. Gordon ("A Positive Theory of Monetary Policy in a Natural Rate Model," *Journal of Political Economy* (August 1983), pp. 589-610), as well as in models presented by Maurice Obstfeld ("Destabilizing Effects of Exchange Rate Escape Clauses," NBER Working Paper No. 3603, 1991 and "The Logic of Currency Crises," NBER Working Paper No. 4640, 1994).

While the authorities in emerging economies have recognized the risks associated with fixing the nominal exchange rate, the benefits of a transparent and credible exchange rate policy coupled with prudent fiscal policies seem to have outweighed these risks. Specific conditions and measures likely to benefit a fixed exchange rate policy and thus improve the probability that parity will be maintained include:

FIXED
FX

1. A competitive local exchange rate at the time of the policy's inception.
2. A prudent fiscal policy and avoiding an over-reliance on monetary policy to achieve price stability. *trying not to care too much.*
3. Effective communication of the terms of the policy to the investment community and the establishment of a credible mechanism whereby the authorities stand ready to back their commitments in the open market.
4. Publication and access to timely and reliable data on the economy to all those who seek it.

BASKET PEG

Specifically, what type of mechanisms are available to central banks in order to target a nominal exchange rate? A currency basket is one such mechanism. Under this form of currency peg, the authorities select a group of major currencies and fix their currency at a rate consistent with the pre-announced weights of the foreign currencies in the basket. The weightings of the foreign currencies should reflect the corresponding distribution of payments and receipts the local country is processing with its major trading partners. The formation of such a trade-weighted currency basket will reduce the fluctuations of the local currency versus the individual currencies in the basket. Furthermore, the policy's transparency will reduce the risk for importers and exporters in the local country (provided these participants believe in the maintenance of the basket, hedges can be established in the foreign currencies versus the local currency) as well as provide the foreign investment community with an observable benchmark through which the country's commitment to the stability of its monetary aggregates can be monitored.

Two examples of a successful implementation of a currency basket mechanism are those managed by the Thai Exchange Equalization Fund (EEF) and The Czech National Bank (CNB). Following successive large scale devaluations of the Thai baht (THB) in 1981 and 1984, the baht was subsequently pegged to a weighted basket of currencies of Thailand's main trading partners. The approximate weights are 86% U.S. dollars (USD), 8% Japanese yen, and 6% German marks.[2] The EEF announces daily buying and selling rates to the local commercial banks with the spread between bid and offer for the USD equivalent to 4 santag (0.04 of 1 baht). The Thai monetary authorities have been setting responsible inflation targets for the economy and targeting fiscal and monetary operations in an effort to achieve a reduction in the country's current account deficit. Despite

---

[2] The weights were never precisely detailed by the Bank of Thailand. The central bank has mentioned approximate weights from time to time. The weights detailed here by the authors are believed to be accurate as of the end of 1996 based on statistical analysis of historical data. Investors should note that the weights may be subject to change by the Bank of Thailand.

occasional market speculation doubting the authorities' ability to maintain the basket peg, the Thai basket has prevailed from 1985 to 1996 as the cornerstone of Thailand's commitment to monetary stability.[3]

The Czech government adopted a policy of nominal exchange rate stabilization following a series of devaluations of the koruna (CZK) in 1990. The exchange rate had been pegged to a series of currencies which included the German mark, the Austrian schilling, the British pound, and the French and Swiss francs. A few months following the end of monetary union with Slovakia (May 1993), the Czech authorities pegged the koruna to a basket of 65% German marks and 35% U.S. dollars. This basket composition, maintained through the end of 1996, has aided the Czech government in achieving progress in structural reform and stabilization of the monetary aggregates.[4]

Exhibit 1 depicts the history of the Thai and Czech currency baskets from 1991 to 1996 expressed as a composite index of the local currency and the foreign currencies. Over a period of almost six years, the THB and CZK baskets have weakened by no more than 4.5% and 7.5%, respectively, when measuring the trade-weighted basket from its strongest point during this period (higher index levels for the baskets depicted in Exhibit 1 indicate a weakening of the local currency versus the foreign currency components in the respective basket). Other emerging countries who have successfully adopted trade-weighted currency regimes include several Eastern European countries such as Poland (1990-1996), Hungary (1990-1996), and Slovakia (1993-1996).[5]

Another method of targeting the nominal exchange rate is via the use of a "crawling peg" regime whereby the local currency gradually depreciates at a pre-announced rate versus a single currency or a group of currencies. From the standpoint of achieving macroeconomic stability, the efficacy of this policy is similar to that of

---

[3] Following a marked decline in the state of the Thai economy throughout 1996 and early 1997, the THB came under attack by the market in both January and May of 1997. The central bank affirmed its commitment to the mantainance of the THB basket regime and speculation against the THB was met with heavy support by the authorities. In addition to conducting open market intervention, Thai authorities implemented a series of measures aimed at curbing the offshore community from accessing the local spot and forward foreign exchange markets. At the time of this writing, Thai authorities are still in the process of implementing new economic measures aimed at strengthening the economy. The authors wish to note the efficacy of the THB currency regime for 1985-1996 but do not rule out a review of the existing currency regime sometime in 1997.

[4] In light of a deteriorating trade account and slowing GDP growth during Q4 1996-Q2 1997, the Czech authorities adjusted their currency basket in May of 1997 to include a full linkage of the Czech currency to the German mark. This measure was taken following 1 to 2 weeks of market speculation against the Czech currency and resulted in a one-off depreciation of the Czech currency by approximately 8% against the German mark on May 27, 1997. The authors wish to note the positive impact of a stable currency basket on Czech monetary policy for the years 1991-1996 and regard the May 1997 adjustment as a necessary step for the Czech authorities to restore trade competitiveness.

[5] At the end of 1996, currency baskets in these three Eastern European countries were comprised of 70% U.S. dollar and 30% German marks for the Hungarian forint, 60% German marks and 40% U.S. dollar for the Slovakian crown and 45% U.S. dollar, 35% German mark, 10% Sterling, 5% French franc, and 5% Swiss franc for the Polish zloty.

the basket regime in that it cannot be relied upon to stabilize monetary aggregates. The policy will only be viewed as credible when coupled with a stable fiscal policy and where the terms of the depreciation are fully transparent. The advantages of reduction in currency volatility also apply to this regime. The crawling peg may be more advantageous for countries in which trade flows are not as diversified and it becomes more suitable to target the local exchange rate versus a single currency. Alternatively, monetary authorities may desire a wider degree of flexibility in targeting the nominal exchange rate or may seek real exchange rate appreciation or depreciation. For example, where the outlook for domestic inflation is volatile, a developing country may seek to adjust the rate of depreciation of the local currency in accordance with the respective annual inflation rate differentials between its own economy and that of the foreign country (or countries) against which the local currency is fixed.

Exhibit 1: Thai Baht Basket (86% USD, 8% JPY, 6% DEM)

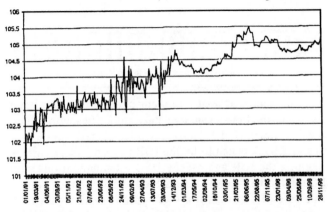

Czech Crown Basket (65% DEM, 35% USD)

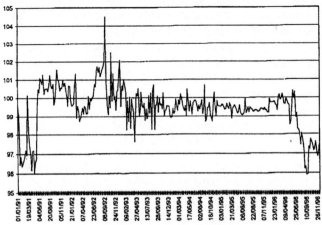

Source: Bankers Trust Global Research

Exhibit 2: U.S. Dollar versus Indonesian Rupah

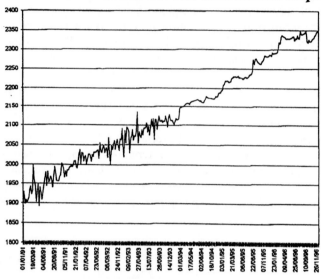

Source: Bankers Trust Global Research

One of the more successful implementations of a crawling peg exchange rate policy is that of the Indonesian monetary authorities with respect to the fixing of the Indonesian rupiah (IDR). Following a large scale devaluation in 1986, the Indonesian central bank began to fix the IDR rate on a daily basis with the intention of weakening the IDR against the USD at an annual rate equivalent to the expected differential between U.S. and Indonesian inflation rates. For the years 1990-94, this rate of depreciation was approximately 4% to 5% per annum. Exhibit 2 charts the rupiah versus the U.S. dollar from 1991 to 1995.

It can be observed from the slope of the line depicting the exchange rate that the authorities managed the depreciation evenly over the course of each year in an effort to avoid market-induced volatility. The crawling peg allowed Indonesia to develop a comprehensive monetary framework, build its image as a stable and attractive country for foreign investment, and ultimately achieve impressive growth rates from the early to the mid 1990s. Countries that have implemented a successful crawling peg regime include Turkey (1994-1996), Greece (1992-1996), and Israel (1992-1996).[6]

---

[6] For the years stated, Turkey, Greece, and Israel implemented crawling peg systems. In all three cases, these currency regimes were meant to serve as "hard currency" policies in an effort to reduce or stabilize the respective country's domestic inflation rates. Annualized depreciation of the Turkish lira was held at 20% to 30% below the annual CPI rate during 1995-1996. The "hard drachma" policy in Greece (1992-1996) has been used as the main policy mechanism to achieve a convergence with average inflation rates in Europe (the drachma was depreciated very slightly despite inflation differentials of 4% to 6% between Greece and the European Community during those four years). The Bank of Israel implemented a managed depreciation of the shekel against a basket of foreign currencies to stabilize inflation in light of the high Israeli growth and consumption rates in the early to mid 1990s.

Flexible Exchange Rate Arrangements

While targeting nominal exchange rates in emerging economies can be advantageous, some small economies have chosen to pursue a more flexible exchange rate arrangement. Under a flexible exchange rate policy, the local central bank maintains some degree of administrative control over the value of its currency but often refrains from announcing a specific target for the currency. The authorities manage the value of the currency via discreet or open market operations. A central bank may choose a flexible regime in extreme cases where:

1. The country lacks sufficient means to defend a fixed rate policy or the authorities expect a protracted transition period for the economy during which such a policy may be expected to break down. A small economy may lack the means to maintain the fixed regime, such as sufficient foreign exchange reserves necessary to defend a speculative attack or proper mechanisms to control local money market liquidity in the event of excessive inflows or outflows. Alternatively, in cases where the economy has experienced a pronounced slowdown, authorities may choose to "grow" their way out of their predicament by adjusting the exchange rate through a periodic weakening of the real exchange rate or by conducting sporadic devaluations in an effort to stimulate exports.

2. The country has a record of strong macroeconomic performance, a relatively high credit rating, and the central bank perceives its position to be strong enough to control the market rate while withstanding speculative shocks. A fixed regime in countries which have established high levels of credibility may exacerbate capital inflows and cause an unwanted appreciation of the real exchange rate.

A successful application of a flexible regime is that of the Singapore dollar during a sample period of 1991-1996. During this period the Monetary Authority of Singapore monitored the external value of the Singapore dollar against an *undisclosed* basket of currencies. The authorities used their currency as a monetary anchor in an effort to maintain a low domestic inflation rate. While this policy was generally known by the market, the absence of a clear and transparent mechanism to fix the currency and the frequent use of discreet market intervention aided the Singapore authorities in introducing an element of uncertainty into the daily and weekly fluctuations of the currency versus the U.S. dollar. This process prevented a quick and steep appreciation of the real exchange rate which could have hurt the export-driven sectors of the economy. Other countries whose periodic success with managing exchange rates under a flexible or non-transparent regime include Taiwan, Malaysia, and Colombia.

INTERNATIONAL CAPITAL FLOWS:
INVESTOR BEHAVIOR AND CENTRAL BANK RESPONSE

While a coordinated fixed or flexible exchange rate regime can bring a developing economy long-term benefits and can serve as a stabilizing factor in preventing capital outflows, the combination of an open capital account, implementation of structural reforms, prudent fiscal policies, and a transparent foreign exchange policy can result in an unintended surge of capital inflows. These flows may present considerable difficulties for a central bank leading to inflationary pressures, an excessive appreciation of the real exchange rate, and a worsening of the current account. It is therefore important to determine the source of the inflows and examine some of the policy options which may be effective in combating this phenomenon.

"Hot Money" Flows

The implementation of a credible fixed exchange rate regime in an emerging economy with healthy macroeconomic performance generally attracts higher levels of direct and local security investment. This can lead to significant capital inflows which the authorities need to monitor and could necessitate the adoption of new laws in an effort to insure that the pace and level of these foreign investments are consistent with the local market's ability to absorb such funds. Most emerging economies are able to deal with these types of inflows and are concerned primarily with pure speculative currency inflows whose proceeds are likely to be invested in short-term money market instruments or off-balance sheet interest rate products. A developing country in which the real effective exchange rate is reasonably competitive, the capital account is open, and investors have good reason to anticipate financial gains as a result of exposure to the local currency, should expect to experience a steady increase of such inflows.

The expectation of positive returns by the currency speculator stems from the existence of relatively wide interest rate differentials between the interest rate of the local currency and that of the foreign currency (or currencies, in case of a basket). In cases where the speculator perceives the rate differentials to be wide enough to compensate for the risks of a potential policy shift with respect to the currency paradigm (or the country's broader monetary policy), an unanticipated sovereign "event risk" (such as an unexpected political change,) or a potential regulatory change (such as a re-imposition of exchange controls due to the sudden deterioration in the country's debt or current account), inflows are likely to ensue. Alternatively, currency speculators may direct their so-called "hot money" towards currency trades where the current yield is low but where there is an expected capital gain resulting from a revaluation of the nominal exchange rate. Clearly, both motivations exist under fixed or flexible currency regimes.

Countries operating under a basket or crawling peg regime, as described in the previous section, are likely to be the ones most susceptible to speculative short-term money inflows. In the cases of the Czech koruna and the Thai baht basket mechanisms, domestic money market rates in both Thailand and Czech exceeded the weighted average rates of the currencies in their respective baskets by 3% to 8% from 1991 to 1996. Given the relatively mild depreciation of the CZK and THB baskets depicted in Exhibit 1, currency speculators have reaped handsome gains by taking advantage of the wide interest rate differentials between the rates of the local currencies and those of the currencies in the respective baskets. Similarly, the crawling peg regime, such as the one enacted in Indonesia, provides speculators with positive returns during years in which the sum of the rate of devaluation and the cost of borrowing U.S. dollars was less than the rate of return achievable in the local Indonesian rupiah money markets. This, in fact, is the case with the IDR since the crawling peg was adopted in 1986.

It is important to note that the supply of foreign exchange entering an emerging currency market is not solely due to traditional overseas institutional investors and multinational financial institutions seeking diversification for their global currency portfolios. In several instances, citizens of the emerging economy have accounted for a significant portion of such flows. Typically, this behavior emerges in an economy which had previously imposed strict exchange controls on its citizens and subsequently moves to a credible and transparent exchange rate regime in which exchange controls have been relaxed. Over time, as credibility is established, locals begin to convert illegally held foreign exchange bank notes or repatriate funds held through friends and relatives abroad. Examples of this phenomenon can be documented in many Eastern European countries during the years following the fall of communism (Poland, Czech, Hungary during 1992-1995, and Russia following the financial reforms and currency deregulation of 1995-1996), as well as in Indonesia (1994-1996) when foreign currency balances held in Singapore by wealthy Indonesians were converted into IDR in an attempt to capture the higher local money market rates. In addition, citizens of the country classified as overseas workers can account for heavy inflows as many will transfer foreign currency earned abroad in an effort to support local kin in their home country. Prominent examples of this include overseas Filipino, Indian, and Turkish workers who over the years have been known as heavy exporters of foreign capital from their counties of domicile.

The example in Exhibit 3 provides details of the cash flows from a THB currency basket trade implemented by a typical currency speculator. All money market and currency rates in this example reflect actual market rates that existed in the market between January-July 1996. Exhibit 4 provides an example of a CZK basket trade. An example of an IDR trade is shown in Exhibit 5. The data in both examples are based on actual market rates which prevailed in 1996.

Intervention and Sterilization

Given the existence of speculative capital in emerging currency markets monetary authorities must choose (assuming the country possesses the proper monetary tools to intervene) the appropriate measures necessary to respond to international capital flows. While not a viable long-term policy option, some central banks may avoid currency intervention altogether if their policy objectives include insulating the local banking system from the inflows or in cases where there may be an attempt to achieve a reduction in the domestic rate of inflation through exchange rate appreciation. The dangers of adopting such a policy include the potential for excessive appreciation of the real exchange rate (which later can be difficult to reverse), and the resulting negative impact on the trade balance. In many respects the decision to intervene is often a result of a government's preference in the conventional trade-off between growth and inflation.

Exhibit 3: Thai Baht Example

	Historical FX and Deposit Rates January 8, 1996	Historical FX Rates July 8, 1996
THB/USD	25.24	25.43
DEM/USD	1.4390	1.5257
JPY/USD	105.20	110.75

6-month THB Deposit   8.5% p.a.
6-month JPY Deposit   1% p.a.
6-month DEM Deposit   3.5% p.a.
6-month USD Deposit   5.6% p.a.

Transactions done on Day 1: January 8, 1996 – THB Index = 100.00

Investor initiates currency basket trade by:

> Selling 100 million USD vs. THB at 25.24 value July 10, 1996 earning 0.36 points.*
> Effective outright rate = 25.24 + 0.36 or 25.60
> Buying 6 million USD vs. DEM at 1.4390 value July 10, 1996 earning 0.0149 points.
> Effective outright rate = 1.4390 – 0.0149 or 1.4241
> Buying 8 million USD vs. JPY at 105.20 value January 10 and roll position forward to July 10 earning 2.38 points. Effective outright rate = 105.20 – 2.38 or 102.82.

* Foreign exchange forward points correspond to money market deposit rates which existed on January 8, 1996 and are noted above.

Day 182: July 8, 1996 – THB Index = 100.01

Investor closes out basket position after six months by executing three spot transactions and:

> Buys 100 million USD vs. THB at 25.43 value July 10
> Sells 6 million USD vs. DEM at 1.5257 value July 10
> Sells 8 million USD vs. JPY at 110.75 value July 10

Cash Flow Summary

Date	THB	DEM	JPY
July 10 (forward trade)	+2,560,000,000	–8,544,600	–822,560,000
July 10 (spot trade)	–2,543,000,000	+9,154,200	+886,000,000
Net Cash Flow	+17,000,000	+609,600	+63,440,000

17,000,000/25.43 =	$668,502
609,600/1.5257 =	$399,554
63,440,000/110.75 =	$572,822
Total Profit on 100 million USD	$1,640,878
THB Basket Position	

Exhibit 4: Czech Koruna Basket Arbitrage Example

	Day 1 August 14, 1996	Day 94 November 14, 1996
USD/CZK	26.64	26.94
USD/DEM	1.4845	1.5090

3-month CZK Depo   12.1% p/a
3-month DEM Depo   3.25%
3-month USD Depo   5.4%

Day 1: August 14, 1996 – CZK Index = 97.60
Investor initiates currency basket trade by:
   Selling 20 million USD vs. CZK Koruna at 26.64 value November 18, 1996 earning 0.459
      points Effective outright rate = 26.64 + 0.459 or 27.099
   Buy 13 million USD vs. DEM at 1.4845 value November 18, 1996 earning 0.0082 points.
      Effective outright rate = 1.4845 – 0.0082 or 1.4763

Day 92: November 14, 1996 – CZK Index = 97.65
Investor closes out basket position after six months by executing three spot transactions and:
   Buys 20 million USD vs. CZK Koruna at 26.94 value November 18 (spot)
   Sells 13 million USD vs. DEM at 1.5090 value November 18

Cash Flow Summary

Date	CZK	DEM
November 18 (forward trade)	+541,980,000	−19,191,900
November 18 (spot trade)	−538,800,000	+19,617,000
Net Cash Flow	+3,180,000	+425,100

Profit: 3 180,000/ 26.94 = $118,040
        425,100/1.5090 =   <u>$281,710</u>
                            $399,750

Exhibit 5: Indonesian Rupah Example

	Day 1 January 8, 1996	Day 182 July 8, 1996
Spot IDR/USD	2,287	2,340
6-month USD Depo	5.6%	
6-month IDR Depo	17%	

Day 1: Midpoint = 2312 (Band fixed at 2,279-2,345)
   Sell 50 million USD Agst IDR at 2,287 value July 10 at 128 points. Effective outright rate
      = 2,415.

Day 182:
   Buy 50 million USD AG IDR at 2,340 value, July 10

Cash Flow Summary

Date	IDR	USD
July 10 (forward trade)	+120,750,000,000	−50,000,000
July 10 (spot trade)	−117,000,000,000	+50,000,000
Net Cash Flow	+3,750,000,000	0
Profit	3,750,000,000/2340 = $1,602,564	

Exhibit 6: U.S. Dollar versus Phillipine Peso

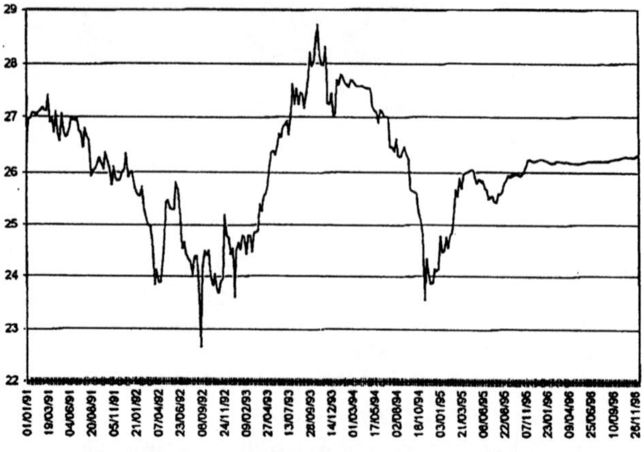

Source: Bankers Trust Global Research

There are also exceptional cases whereby a country may lack the means to intervene, leaving the exchange rate to be determined by market forces. Examples of this include the Philippine peso (PHP) from 1991 to 1995 and the South African rand (ZAR) from February-December 1996. In the Philippines, the authorities lacked both reserves and proper money market instruments to either maintain a fixed regime or manage the PHP in a flexible manner. In the absence of a clear policy and central bank intervention, the market caused the PHP to trade in a range of 23-29 peso to the U.S. dollar from 1991-95. In South Africa following several rounds of speculative attacks by the market against the ZAR in February 1996, the South African Reserve Bank (SARB) was forced to let market forces determine the value of the ZAR given their lack of adequate foreign exchange reserves (approximately two months of imports) and their inability to dramatically raise rates in light of the economy's weakness. The market forced a 28% devaluation of the ZAR vis-a-vis the U.S. dollar (2/96-12/96) despite the SARB's attempt to maintain order and stabilize the ZAR by repeatedly stating their desire to see a stable currency. Exhibits 6 and 7 depict the historical rates for the PHP and the ZAR, respectively.

Once a central bank decides to intervene, further consideration must be given to the impact of such intervention on liquidity and credit in the local money market. If left unchecked, the injection of local currency into the money markets resulting from the central bank's purchase of foreign currency may cause the authorities to exceed their monetary targets and may cause banks to engage in excessive lending in an attempt to deplete their excessive balances of local currency. IMF economists Mosin Khan and Carmen Reinhardt have noted that "when the banking system is unable to intermediate more funds, additional capital inflows through the banking system will exert a strong downward pressure on interest rates, slowing the pace of inflows and lowering the fiscal cost of the outstanding domestic credit."[7]

---

[7] Mosin S. Khan and Carmen M. Reihhart (ed.), "Capital Flows in the APEC Region," Occasional Paper 122, International Monetary Fund Staff Teams (March 1995).

Exhibit 7: U.S. Dollar versus South African Rand

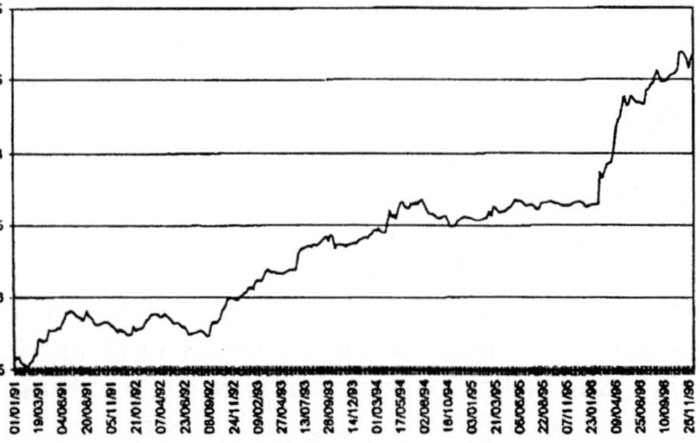

Source: Bankers Trust Global Research

Assuming the authorities are uninterested in the negative side-effects of excess liquidity, the central bank will drain the appropriate amount of liquidity to achieve a proper balance in the local money markets. This process, commonly referred to as "sterilization," requires the central bank to constantly gauge the level of liquidity in the market and stand ready to conduct open market operations. A central bank can sterilize through the issuance of short-term debt, by varying the terms under which banks have access to the rediscount system, or by raising the official reserve requirement. Authorities need to be certain that they have the ability to fine-tune the level of liquidity in the system as excessive drainage can have the self-defeating effect of tightening money market rates which in turn will cause the levels of capital inflows to intensify.

Administrative Responses to Capital Inflows

Sterilized intervention has, by far, been the most common response to capital inflows in the Asian and Latin countries. While the results have been somewhat successful in terms of maintaining exchange rate competitiveness and controlling money market liquidity, the costs of sterilization can be high. Central banks incur the negative funding cost measured as the difference between the rate at which they borrow the local currency and the rate of return they receive when investing the foreign exchange proceeds they accumulate. This "sterilization tax" can be quite significant. In a 1993 study, economists Miguel Kiguel and Leonardo Leiderman estimated these negative funding costs in Latin American countries to range from 0.25% to 0.5% of GDP a year.[8]

When sterilization either begins to lose its effectiveness or the costs become intolerable, central banks may resort to using administrative measures in an effort to contain capital inflows. The use of taxation and exchange controls can

---

[8] Miguel Kiguel and Leonardo Leiderman, "On the Consequences of Sterilized Intervention in Latin America: The Cases of Colombia and Chile," unpublished paper, Washington: World Bank, 1993.

be effective in either promoting currency outflows or restricting inflows. For example, governments can provide incentives for locals to buy foreign assets. In the early 1990s, the Czech authorities began permitting corporates to establish locally held foreign exchange deposit accounts in an effort to reduce the amount of foreign exchange converted by Czech nationals into Czech crown. At the time, Czech authorities suspected that the amount of foreign exchange held abroad by its citizens may be significant enough to erode the local currency's competitiveness should all these proceeds be converted over a short period of time.

In other instances, authorities may seek to tax capital inflows either via the banking system or by imposing zero or negative interest rates on foreign assets held in local money market accounts. The case of Malaysia and the administrative measures enforced in 1994 by Bank Negara, Malaysia's central bank, stands out as an example of such behavior. Following a surge in short-term capital flows into Malaysia in 1992-1993, Bank Negara attempted to sterilize the excess liquidity through a combination of measures which included direct borrowing from the money market, an increase in government deposits to the central bank and the raising of statutory reserve requirements. Controls on non-trade related foreign exchange swaps were also imposed in June of 1992. Despite these measure, currency speculators continued to buy the Malaysian ringgit forcing Bank Negara to impose more strict controls in January-February 1994. The 1994 measures included a limit on local bank's foreign liabilities, full restrictions on the sale of short-term money market instruments to foreigners, an obligation on local banks to deposit ringgit balances of foreign vostro accounts into non-interest bearing accounts at Negara and further restrictions related to swap and outright foreign exchange transactions.

Due to the above measures and a dramatic narrowing of interbank interest rate differentials between the U.S. and Malaysia, ringgit liquidity contracted and capital flows into Malaysia abated in late 1994. The process, however, proved to be extremely damaging to the reputation of the Malaysian monetary authorities due to the high degree of volatility and uncertainty which had been created in the ringgit foreign exchange and money markets. Furthermore, in its 1994 annual report, Bank Negara Malaysia admitted that the administrative measures were never meant to be effective long-term solutions to the problem of capital inflows.[9]

In cases where a fixed or flexible regime determine the local currency and enforce a currency band (such as CZK, THB, IDR), central banks can widen the intervention bands in an effort to introduce more uncertainty and transfer price risk to the speculator. Band widenings have been a key response to capital inflows by the central banks of the Czech Republic (1995), Poland (1995), and Indonesia (gradually from 1994-1996). By widening the intervention bands to 14% in 1995

---

[9] The report stated that "it was recognized that if such measures remained as a permanent feature in the system, possible market distortions could emerge, resulting in an inefficient allocation of resources." See *The Bank Negara Malaysia Annual Report of the Board of Directors, 1994.* For more information on the impact of administrative measures in other emerging economies, the authors recommend reviewing Peter J. Quirk and Owen Evans (ed.), "Capital Account Convertibility," Occasional Paper 131, International Monetary Fund Staff Teams (October 1995).

(from a previous band width of 3%), the Czech authorities were able to reduce their presence as intervention agents in the foreign exchange market. A similar phenomenon occurred in the zloty market when the National Bank of Poland widened its bands from 4% to 14% in April of 1995.

SUMMARY AND CONCLUSIONS

The experiences of several open emerging economies in Asia and Eastern Europe from the late 1980s through the mid 1990s suggest that fixed exchange regimes, while increasing the probability of excessive capital inflows, are a stabilizing factor in the economy and can be an important tool in conducting a prudent monetary policy. A currency basket or a managed depreciation appear to be the most popular methods of implementing fixed exchange rate regimes. Provided these exchange rate policies are clearly communicated, the exchange rate is competitive at the time of the policy's inception, prudent fiscal policies are adopted, and the market is able to easily track the implementation of the central bank's policy, the local currency is unlikely to come under attack by the markets. Flexible exchange rate policies, in which precise currency targets are not specified by the central bank but some degree of administrative control over the value of the local currency is maintained, are less common. Authorities who elect to implement flexible arrangements do so to avoid transparent policies (and thus hope to reduce inflows) or for lack of sufficient tools necessary to implement a fixed exchange rate policy.

Excessive capital inflows are likely to ensue in cases where local currency rates are high relative to the width of a central bank's intervention band. Similarly, this phenomenon can be expected under crawling peg regimes where the expected depreciation of the local currency is less than the interest rate differentials between the local and the foreign currency. In the face of excessive capital inflows, some central banks may chose to temporarily appreciate the real exchange rate and thus completely avoid intervention. In most cases, however, central banks will implement some form of intervention and subsequently engage in the sterilization of excess liquidity. Traditional methods of sterilization include the issuance of short-term debt, altering the terms banks borrow at the rediscount window or raising the official reserve requirements.

In cases where a prolonged process of sterilization becomes too costly and there are low prospects for an abatement of the capital inflows, central banks may resort to administrative measures. Taxation on the importation of foreign capital or the re-imposition of exchange controls have not proven to be effective solutions to the problem of capital inflows. These measures have tended to result in a reduction of investor confidence, high reputational costs for the authorities, and excessive market volatility. Central banks need to be prepared to tolerate some level of "hot money" in their system in order to enjoy the benefits of long-term investment and monetary stability resulting from transparent exchange rate policies.

Chapter 16

Options on Exotic Currencies

Alastair W. Sloan
Managing Director
Bankers Trust Company

INTRODUCTION

As discussed in Chapter 15, it is important to understand the currency regime that exists in emerging markets. The foreign exchange policy, whether it be a crawling fix, a peg, a basket of currencies, a managed float or simply a free and floating currency, has implications for the risks and returns for investing in the market. There will be implications for trade flows, interest rate levels, foreign access to local assets, local access to foreign funds, and for central bank actions. There are extraordinary gains available to be made in trading emerging market currencies. These potential gains reward the investor/hedger that is able to correctly assess the potential risks and the costs associated therein.

There are several ways to minimize the risks associated with positions in emerging markets. The value of information in these markets is far greater than in more developed markets. Those able to decipher this information better and faster than the uninformed speculators are able to reach the aforementioned spoils. The term "event risk" is the term given to mean the risks associated with a departure from the normal course of events. This may be in the form of political change, economic policy shifts, regulatory shifts, or even sentiment changes by market participants. Just as "ten" of the last six recessions have been called by market participants, so too have there been as many calls for currency devaluation or a deviation from the current currency arrangement.

Options on the emerging markets currencies are another form of risk reduction. They are a second generation derivative of the spot and forward foreign exchange markets. An astute investor/hedger is able to reduce their reliance on timely information through the purchase of options on the currencies. The protection that options offer is the non-linear risk that one assumes as opposed to a position in the spot or forward market. Foreign exchange options offer the purchaser the right but not the obligation to enter into a foreign exchange contract with the option seller. In this chapter, we explain these contracts.

LIMITATIONS OF OPTION PRICING MODELS

Option pricing models make assumptions to derive the theoretical value of an option. The underlying assumptions, however, are often not valid for options on emerging market currencies. First, there is an assumed continuous source of hedging. If this were true, then discreet jumps in the price of underlying currencies would not occur. Due to their very nature as a hedging tool among their local neighbors, the emerging market currencies are most liquid during their respective time zones and with adverse news/events, almost illiquid outside that time zone. The need for constant rebalancing of the option is therefore not always available.

Second, the historical volatility of an emerging market currency may show low volatility due to the narrow range in which it is allowed to maneuver due to central bank regulations. Observance of this band relies on an assumption of the continuation of this policy. Once the policy is removed or altered, this currency may exhibit a new range of volatility which may not have been priced into the options market.

Finally, options are priced based on a log-normal distribution of prices. Following this assumption can give disastrous results in these currencies. For some currencies, like the Indonesian Rupiah (IDR) where there is a crawling peg, the currency is depreciated along a path determined daily by the Central Bank at their daily fixing (see Exhibit 1). This means the IDR may be allowed to follow a continuous depreciation path where we may not see these spot levels again until the policy is altered. This alteration might come in the form of a devaluation like we saw in 1986 or in the widening of the intervention band as we have seen several times in the period 1993-1996.

Exhibit 1: Intervention Band of USD/IDR versus Forwards

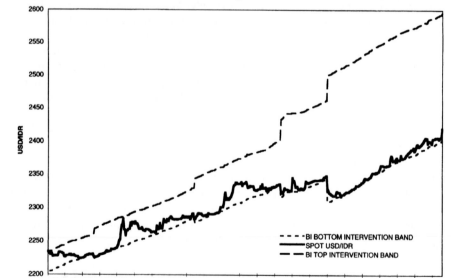

Exhibit 2: Spot USD/IDR and the Central Bank Intervention Band

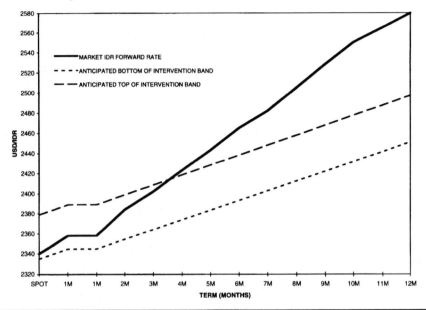

Extraordinary Gains

Currencies with high interest rates are attractive to investors if the causes of those high interest rates are assessible. At the same time they are restrictive to currency hedgers. If a currency is thought to have interest rates that are higher than the perceived rate of depreciation of the currency, then borrowers are reluctant to hedge and investors are keen to invest. Herein lies the benefit of options for the hedger. As Exhibit 2 shows, the rate of depreciation of the IDR intervention band over the year 1996 was expected to average 4% to 5%. With high interest rates that year investors were attracted to the currency. As the exhibit shows, the forward implied IDR spot rate bisects the top of the central bank intervention band between three to four months from spot. If the band policy remains in place over the year, the expected gain from selling USD/IDR outright in the one year is as follows:

IDR 1 yr implied interest rate	15.48%
USD funding rate	5.50%
expected rate of depreciation	5.00%
carry/expected gain	4.98%

Just as there is a potential gain to be made by the investor, there is a cost for those hedging offshore foreign currency obligations. Some of these hedgers are attracted to borrowing in U.S. dollars (USD) and swapping these funds into their local currency. They are then able to purchase puts on their currency to avoid the risk of devaluation and hope that the rate of depreciation will not erode the benefit of having borrowed in USD. At the maturity of the loan they sell their local currency back into the USD and repay their obligations. If the cost of the option and the rate of depreciation is less than the carry, then this has been a beneficial exercise.

We can see from Exhibit 3 that there is a difference between the implied and historical volatility in the emerging markets currencies. The difference we see was in part due to incomplete information. This may come in the form of event risk, policy risk or a skewed expectation of market participants. This could come in the form of market players expecting one result, causing an imbalance in the market. The fact that we have the discontinuous gap risk of prices is enough to command a premium in the market. Together with the fact that a gap can usually change sentiment, liquidity following a move like this can also be unreliable, therefore a premium is likely.

TRADING EXOTIC CURRENCY OPTIONS

In trading these options, there are several nuances that are particular to the emerging markets currencies. We have noted that there is not a continuous distribution of prices and therefore there is not a continuous distribution of outcomes. The risk in the market is more to a decline in the value of a high yielding currency than in its appreciation. Unhedged borrowers of the local currency suffer the risk of devaluation. Unhedged investors looking to reap the extraordinary benefits of the higher interest rates, coupled with the managed currency policy, are also at risk.

Exhibit 3: IDR Implied and Historical Volatility

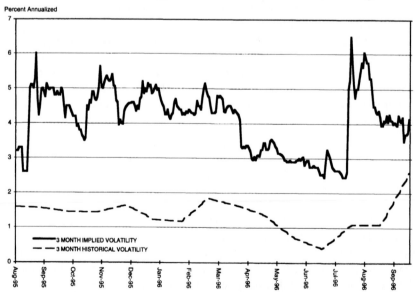

Exhibit 4: Volatility Skew of 3 Month USD/THB

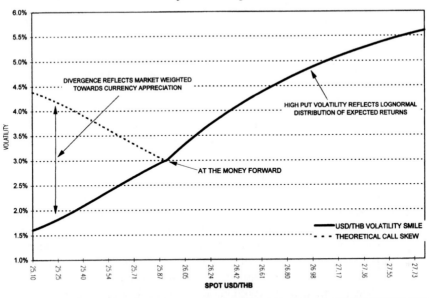

The risk of the appreciation benefits both parties. Due to the skew of these risk profiles, there exists a "differential" in the market for puts versus calls on the local currency. Puts solve the risk of devaluation and therefore they can trade at a premium to calls on the currency. The lower the option's delta, the greater the skew from the at-the-money option volatility. As a seller of options, the maximum expected upside on the transaction is the premium received. Any risks associated with a depreciation of the currency beyond the strike price is borne by them. So, as opposed to some option products where a "smile" exists in the volatility skew, emerging markets reflect a skew against the weaker side of the market. This can be seen in the THB in Exhibit 4.

In order to defray some of the costs associated with the expensive puts in the market, players have taken to selling off some of the benefits of an appreciation of the currency. While this does not fully compensate them for the costs of the puts, it reduces the net cost. This product, a risk reversal, is the simultaneous purchase of a put and sale of a call on the local currency. In some markets like the Thai Baht (THB) and the Indonesian Rupiah (IDR) the skew can be as much as 3-5% for a 25 delta put versus call. This is to say that a put with a delta of 25% may be trading at a premium of 3% over the volatility of a 25% delta call on the local currency.

Trades in the first generation options by investors involve the purchase of calls on the local currency or perhaps the sale of USD against the local currency, and the purchase of puts. An example in the IDR, a currency with a crawling depreciation and bands fixed by the Bank of Indonesia each day, is as follows:

- The IDR intervention band on Day 1 is 2,340 to 2,484
- The spot and forward points for 1 year are 2,345 plus 195
- The volatility for at-the-money-forward options on the IDR are 5.0% giving a cost of 2.02% of USD principal
- USD rates of 5.5% imply an IDR interest rate of 14.58% on the IDR
- The expected payoff for the trade if we are trading at the same level in the band is:

	yield IDR	14.58%
less:	yield USD	5.50%
	depreciation IDR	5.00%
	cost option	2.02%
	net benefit	2.06%

The risk here is that we trade higher in the band and therefore erode any benefit of the carry. If, however, there is a policy shift and the band were to be widened and IDR appreciated, then there would be extraordinary gains for the purchaser.

Therefore for the cost of the option, 2.02%, the buyer has purchased the right but not the obligation to earn the arbitrage benefits of this transaction if the parameters set forth here are fulfilled. An obvious example of where information flows can benefit the investor would be in the approximation of the rate of depreciation of the currency bands to be employed by the Bank of Indonesia.

With volatility of options trading at a premium to their historicals, time has been spent trying to lessen the outlay by the investor/hedger. Here we find the second generation of options trades. Sellers of options are always happy when things are quiet but are wary of the trades when exiting trading ranges. When sellers exit trading ranges set by central banks there is angst. Ways to avoid these ranges but earn money are discussed below.

Range Bets

For a given currency and time period, a benefit described in terms of a rate of return is paid for the time the currency remains within the bounds of the range. In a low volatility currency due to bands that restrict the movement of the spot rates the payoff can be large. Option trading books prefer this form of option as they are not at risk if the currency breaks out of its band strikes. In addition, the buyer of this range bet is actually setting volatility, hoping for the currency to remain subdued.

Quattro Options

A variation on the range bet theme is the *quattro*. In this trade, rather than picking one currency, there is a range of currencies each with their own boundaries and the payoff of the trade is dependent on the sum total of the time spent in their respective ranges.

Bet Options

Similar to the range trade idea, a *bet option* anticipates a high payout if the currency remains within the bounds dictated at the beginning of the period. If at expiry the option has not touched the trigger point then the option pays the previously specified return. Here again, the buyer of the bet is actually taking on the role of selling the volatility, anticipating a low volatility or a skew in the trading range. The payout of a bet option is similar to a digital option where the payout has only a value of 0% or 100% at expiry depending on whether it is in the money or not.

An example where bet options have become popular is the Thai Baht (THB). The nature of this currency is that it is fixed to a basket of currencies, predominantly USD, JPY, and DEM. Historical regression has given expected weights of 86%, 8% and 6% respectively. With local interest rates of 8.5% and lower rates in the basket currencies, gains are available. For the option player the level of the forwards become more important. Since 86% of the currency is fixed to the USD this means the currency does not move in a very large range. This is compounded further by the Central Bank's fixing band having a width of only 0.25%. Therefore, the movement of the THB is predictable by where the future value of USD/DEM and USD/JPY are predicted to be. In periods of high local interest rates, implied move in the G-3 currencies might be outside the investor's range of beliefs and therefore a bet option might be effective.

Barrier Options

Barrier options are those that either fail to exist until or fail to exist after a trigger has been met. This trigger will normally be a level on the spot rate. Barriers describe themselves as either knock-in or knock-out options when the triggers are breached. Up versus down is a term used to describe whether the spot rate needs to go higher or lower for the trigger to be met. As with plain vanilla options, the underlying position here is either a put or a call. One drawback of the barrier options and the bet options is the policing of the triggers. Obviously these are an important criteria for these options and due to the lack of 24 hour liquidity it is difficult at times to determine if a barrier has been reached. Normal options tend to have a delta between 0 and 1. This is the likelihood of the option being exercised. Gamma trading requires the option player to rebalance the delta as the underlying asset moves around. In barrier options the delta can be greater than 1. This requirement of increased gamma trading, especially when in close proximity to the barriers, can cause strains on even the most liquid of markets.

Where barriers are beneficial to hedgers is when the hedger would like to reduce the cost of a normal option or not have to manage the option until the barrier has been breached. A good example for this style of option would be the Czech Koruna. This currency is managed around a basket comprising of USD and DEM. There is currently an intervention band at 7.5% on ether side of parity. Historically the interest rates are high. If a hedger were to purchase a plain vanilla Czech put with a strike at 7.5% away from the forwards for 1 year, the cost might be too prohibitive and the likelihood of exercise is not necessarily good. If, on the other hand, the hedger were to wait until the top of the band has been breached, it is likely the cost of such options would be prohibitive. A reasonable alternative would be to purchase a barrier option with parameters that state the option does not become live until such time as the spot rate has traded through the upper bounds of the fixing band. This style of option can reduce the hedging costs for the purchaser.

Basket Options

Plain vanilla options are used to take away some risk on the underlying security. However, some trades are premised upon the continued existence of a policy direction by the central bank. Under these scenarios it is not always enough to have a series of underlying plain vanilla options to replicate the basket the currency regime follows. In addition to making the trade more expensive by ignoring the cross correlations of the currencies in the basket, it also does not guarantee the expected payoff if the basket is altered. A *basket option* on the Czech Koruna, for example, returns a payoff equal to the interest differential between the Koruna and its basket components of USD and DEM less the cost of the volatility. By purchasing the option in the form of a basket, the buyer is able to cheapen the cost of the option by recognizing there is a correlation between USD/CZK and DEM/CZK.

For example, the CZK Koruna is managed in a band with a width of 7.5% around parity. The basket components are USD/CZK and DEM/CZK. The basket value is given by the formula:

$$USD/CZK \times (0.012305 + 0.036121 \times DEM/CZK) = CZK \text{ basket}$$

An option strategy can be constructed either on the individual components or on the basket policy. A call option on the basket can allow a participant to tackle the complexities of the policy trade with an ease of entry. The payoff can be returned in USD and would be equal to the appreciation of the basket at maturity against the strike at the time of entry. The payoff is described as:

$$Max \text{ [Strike} - \text{Current basket value, 0]}$$

If there is a policy shift such that the component weights for the determination of the value of the CZK basket are altered, then this risk is borne by both parties.

CONCLUSION

Emerging markets are not commodities like their more well-developed brethren. Liquidity is restricted either due to regulation or simply less requirement. The emergence of options markets in emerging markets has allowed more potential players to join the foray. By limiting the downside of hedging or investment strategies through the purchase of plain vanilla options or their derivatives, there has been more interest from risk averse or even less knowledgeable parties. There is, however, no substitute for the research into the nuances of each market. While the frameworks and models may seem to resemble other markets, the policies, economics, and history may not.

INDEX

Lightning Source UK Ltd.
Milton Keynes UK
25 March 2011

169824UK00001B/47/P